Lily A. Long

A Squire of Low Degree

Lily A. Long

A Squire of Low Degree

ISBN/EAN: 9783337311254

Printed in Europe, USA, Canada, Australia, Japan

Cover: Foto ©Andreas Hilbeck / pixelio.de

More available books at **www.hansebooks.com**

A SQUIRE

OF LOW DEGREE

BY

LILY A. LONG

For life, with all it yields of joy and woe
And hope and fear—believe the aged friend—
Is just our chance o' the prize of learning love;
How love might be, hath been, indeed, and is;
And that we hold thenceforth to the uttermost
Such prize despite the envy of the world,
And having gained truth, keep truth ; that is all.

BROWNING.

NEW YORK
D. APPLETON AND COMPANY
1890

A SQUIRE OF LOW DEGREE.

CHAPTER I.

" 'Tis O, for the gay spring weather,
And 'tis O, for the gay heart of youth ! "

A GAY young voice gave a swing to the words that went ringing out on the morning air. It was April weather, all a-dance with mischievous delight that it had escaped the clutch of the winter. The sky was deep and filled to the horizon brim with blue light. In the heart of the woods you might still have found shrunken snow-drifts, slowly dripping their life away among the dead leaves of a summer gone ; but here, in the open, the sun lay warm on meadows that were already delicately green, and the tiny stream that was born of the dying snow-drift found the anemones crowding about it before it reached its journey's end.

" When we roamed through the meadows together,
And the skies were as clear as love's truth."

A plow-boy, turning up the fragrant black soil in even furrows, stopped a moment to listen as the voice came nearer. It was a voice that belonged to the young year and the sunny day—a clear, bold voice, with an elusive hint of mockery in it. You felt that the singer was reveling in life, with a full, nineteenth-century consciousness of the fact. He was laying Nature under tribute, rather than accepting its largess. The plow-boy scowled and drove his share deeper into the soil. Something in the easy freedom of the melody made him feel the invisible fetters that chained his own feet to the field, while others might roam the wide world over.

At the top of a little hill the melodious horseman paused, and, lifting his hat from his brow, looked out over the farm-land before him. An artistic appreciation of the beauty of the scene kindled his eye as his glance swept the undulating horizon-line. It met his approval that the world should be fair. He was a young man, not more than twenty years at most, but even in repose there was a certain air of authority about him that gave a curious charm to his boyish face. He might have been some gracious young prince, forgetting his royal dignity for the moment, but never allowing others to forget it.

"It is a goodly world, after all the abuse the philosophers give it, isn't it, Emir, old fellow?" he said aloud, patting his horse. "Do you suppose the people that live in this favored spot know that they ought to spend their days in writing poetry? I could compose an invocation in the saddle myself."

But he began to whistle instead, as though all the song-birds of spring were circling above his head. The plow-boy, driving a furrow straight toward him, caught his eye, and with a sudden impulse he beckoned him to come nearer. His signal was unheeded. The plow turned up its curling crest of soil, and swung around on its backward path.

"Is he stupid, or only Americanly independent?" wondered the horseman. "Does he take me for a wandering insurance man, born to be snubbed, or is he afraid he will spoil the picture by coming near?— Emir, stand still, sir, till I see if this being on two legs is as unresponsive to my emotions as you are."

He swung himself over the worm-fence and in a minute was by the side of the blue-bloused workman.

"Fine weather for plowing," he said, by way of giving his opponent the choice of weapons.

"Would you like to try it?" was the unexpected reply.

"Americanly impudent," thought the stranger, flushing a little; but, with more self-restraint than his years alone gave him the right to, he answered good-humoredly:

"I'm afraid your furrows wouldn't acknowledge mine as cousins. Do you know this country? Can you tell me where this road leads to?"

"Out into the world, I suppose," answered the plowman. There was scant courtesy in the words, but, as he turned to gaze over the hills where the winding road led, the look in his gray eyes was far from sullen. His companion saw it, and his resentment faded at once into a sympathetic interest.

"I will take a turn across the field with you, if you don't mind. The smell of the fresh earth is exhilarating. Will you tell me your name? Mine is Harry Vanborough."

"I am Alec Macdonald," answered the other, for the first time looking his companion squarely in the face. Their eyes were on a level, and something elec-

tric passed between them as they looked and turned
to look again.

"You won't find much fun in walking the field,"
said Macdonald, steadily guiding the plow, while
Vanborough, with his hands in his pockets, kept even
pace beside him. "Fine weather for plowing, you
said? Too fine to be wasted on plowing, I say."

"I'm not sure I should like it myself, as a steady
job," answered Vanborough, studying his companion
with new interest. Of course he wouldn't like it.
Fancy marching back and forth in the clinging, new-
turned earth all day, instead of skimming the beauty
of the morning on Emir's back! But that a plow-
boy, whose mission in life he had almost supposed it
to be to add a picturesque bit of color to a perfect
landscape, should not be satisfied with that artistic
occupation, was a new thought.

"Do you live here?" he asked.

"Yes, I suppose so. I am working for the man
that runs this farm. I haven't any home of my
own."

"It is a beautiful place to live in; much better
than the close town, you know," said the townsman
with lofty wisdom.

Macdonald glanced at the beautiful green hills
with a frown, and impatiently touched up the off-
horse. Harry felt that his silence was not a sympathetic one, and good-humoredly put his wise aphor-
isms in his pocket.

"What do you do in winter-time when the farm-
work is over? You get your innings then, don't
you?"

"If I can afford to be idle, yes. I will next

winter, now that I can earn a man's wages. And then—"

He did not finish, but his eye went back to where the highway led over the hills. He was making so undisguised and yet so unconscious a revelation of himself that Vanborough felt a moment's hesitation about drawing him out with questions. It might not be altogether fair to put a fellow-being under your microscope as you would a new specimen of beetle. Yet it was a temptation to discover what aspirations belonged to man in the raw state.

"What would you do if you could go out into the world?" he questioned, following up that last unspoken longing in Alec's face.

"I would read." The answer came with a certain doggedness that showed it was a thought which had been fought over. "I would study. I would find out what men have thought and learned. There is so much that might be known. I shall hate to die, when my turn comes, if I don't have a chance at books first."

"Well, why don't you?" cried Harry, his face glowing with ready sympathy. "Why don't you go to work now?"

"That's what I'm doing," he answered, glancing whimsically at the straight furrows. "But it takes money to go to college."

"College? Are you ready for that?" asked Harry in some dismay. His plow-boy was outstripping his neat little formulæ faster than he could make them; but the surprise in his tone had another meaning for Alec.

"I suppose not," he answered gloomily. "I'm

nearly twenty-three. I suppose it is too late, and I might as well give up trying."

Never, so long as he lived, did Harry learn how Alec's earlier years had been handicapped by the care of an old man, no kin, who had taken the unclaimed boy in his desolate childhood, and who had received in return the service of a son in his old age, though at the cost of all the boy's ill-paid labor and, what was more, his scant leisure. Not even in his own thought had Alec for a moment stopped to count the cost.

"Have you read any Latin?" asked Harry cautiously.

"I've read a good deal, so far as mere reading goes; but I've taught myself mostly, and I don't know how well. That's the trouble. I don't know what I do know."

"Have you done much in mathematics?"

"As much as I could without instruments. It is a different matter, puzzling it out for yourself, from where everything is made easy for you."

He smiled, to make his complaint more impersonal. It was not his custom to lament, but a stranger can unlock the secret of our discontents more easily than a friend. He now pushed back his straw hat, and, to lead back to safe subjects, continued: "If you go straight on, your road will take you to a little village a few miles below here, or you can strike off to the east at the next cross-road and reach the river by the ferry."

But Vanborough would not follow his lead. He had made his morning's discovery, and was unwilling to abandon his investigations so soon.

"Did you ever hear of Burns? He was a plowboy and he wrote poetry."

"Yes, and he grumbled as much as I do sometimes," said Macdonald gayly.

"You read poetry, then? Would you mind— May I see that book in your pocket?"

Macdonald handed it to him silently. It was a thin volume of Wordsworth, and a yellow stem of straw opened the pages to his hand:

Like an army defeated
The snow hath retreated,
And now doth fare ill
On the top of the bare hill;
The plow-boy is whooping—anon—anon;
There's joy in the mountains;
There's life in the fountains;
Small clouds are sailing,
Blue sky prevailing;
The rain is over and gone!

"Were you reading this before I came?" asked Vanborough with a new respect in his tone. He was not morbidly self-depreciatory, but he paused to reflect that he probably would have considered the selection of Wordsworth on his own part as rather virtuous.

"Yes, and that's what made me so discontented, I suppose. I don't want to be the plow-boy whooping; I want to stand off and look at him."

Harry reddened guiltily, but a side-glance showed him that no innuendo was intended.

"It isn't that I love farm-work less, but that I love book-work more," Alec went on, trying with a half-laugh to get back from the dangerous brink of confidences to the solid footing of commonplace. "But— talking's no good."

"Don't talk, then. Just do it." Harry's words

were cool, but a sudden glow had leaped into his eyes.

"What do you mean?" Alec asked blankly.

"Let me help you. Leave the plow in the furrow, like the old Roman, you know, and come back into the world with me. You shall learn all that books hold, if you wish."

Prince Hal his friends called him. His handsome, boyish face was kindling now, and as he held out his hand to the youth who stood a step below him he might have been some prince of olden story commanding a faithful squire to accept his royal gift. The squire's face had grown pale. He eyed his companion intently, as though to gather more light than the words had given him.

"I don't understand you," he said, a trifle huskily.

"Nothing is simpler. You want a chance to study. Anybody with so praiseworthy an ambition ought to be allowed his way. I'm sure I would never wish for anything half so virtuous. But I can give you a chance to study in my place. Come home with me, live with me as my friend, and go to the university with me. Then when my conscience says to me, 'Harry Vanborough, why have you wasted your opportunities to study Greek?' I will point to you and answer, 'Alec Macdonald did it for me, and did it better than I could have done.'"

"I can never pay you," said Macdonald, in a low voice.

"Now don't be sordid," cried Harry gayly. "It isn't a business question. I sha'n't be in business till I am twenty-one, and that won't be for nearly a year yet."

Macdonald shook his head and took again the plow-handles which had fallen idly against his side. But his fingers were tense, and there were beads on his brow.

"Don't be obstinate when there is no reason," argued Harry, with growing warmth. "Don't you know that, if we had changed places, you would do for me what I offer to do for you? What good is gained by your refusing? What harm done by your accepting? Don't be proud and uncomfortable. Your turn will come next."

His frank, comradely way lent persuasion to his words. Macdonald, who seemed to have been stricken dumb, lifted his head and looked long and intently in his face. Then, with an almost despairing gesture, he looked out over the hills that touched the sky. Harry put his hand on his arm.

"Come!"

"Wait," said Alec, hoarsely. "Let me go to the end of the field alone. I must see clearer. If you are of the same mind, wait here for me till I come down the furrow again. If you do not hold to it, I will see you ride away."

Harry nodded, and the blue blouse turned down the field. Emir whinnied softly, and his master went up and caressed him, but without speaking. The youth was smiling to himself, and his pulse beat jubilantly. Was it not a deed that he had a right to be satisfied with? He felt a partnership in the joy of Nature. The sun shone down with a friendly warmth, as though it recognized a brother in this princely giver of good gifts. It was very easy to be good, and very pleasant.

Down in the field the steady draught-horses had reached the end. The plow swung about and came back. Of course, this boy would consent to his proposition. He must. Harry felt it had become a personal matter, and he was not in the habit of having his dictates disputed. And yet there was enough firmness in the strong, clean chin of the country lad to give his benefactor a little uncertainty as to the result. It was altogether a strong rather than a handsome face— rather heavy for a boy. He had said he was older than Harry, but the more rapid development of the town and of a life that had its spring in action rather than in thought made Harry naturally assume leadership. Circumstances had always fought on the side of the prince, and he was hardly old enough yet to realize that his victories were not wholly due to the strength of his own right arm. Certainly now he did not intend to allow any absurd scruples to interfere with a project which had the rare quality of commending itself to his conscience as well as to his self-will.

He watched the plow coming nearer, and, true to his promise, he waited till the patient horses reached the end and stopped to breathe deeply. Then he went up to his *protégé*.

"Well?"

Alec met his gaze brightly. The tense look had gone out of his face, though he was still pale. Evidently a light had come to him.

"It's this way," he said slowly. "I want to accept what you have offered if I can, but I can't feel that it is right for me to take it and give nothing. Can you let me earn it? I can't pay you in money, and that, perhaps, you would not want. But can I do something for you? Can you make me worth what you give me?"

"Yes," said Harry, promptly extemporizing a want on the spot. "I need some one to do a hundred things for me that you could do better than any one else. As soon as I go into business I will need part of your time in my office. And this year I want some one to talk to. I always hated to study alone. Then I have a garret full of books that I have always intended to catalogue some day. Oh, no danger but what I will make use of you. I warn you I am awfully lazy. I particularly like to have all my work done for me. I need a companion, Alec, and I need just you."

Alec listened with a solemn gladness.

"Then I will go."

"Hurrah!" cried Harry, whirling his hat into the air. "That is as it should be. If you act as reasonably in everything, you will grow up to be a book of proverbs. Can you come back to town with me at once?"

"No," said Macdonald, with a new ring in his voice. "Not till the end of the month. I will not be free till then."

"Here is my address, then. Come as soon as you can. It will be a thousand years till I see you, as the Italians say."

"It will be only a day," cried Alec smiling. Joy was a stranger guest to him than to his friend.

"Alec, we will be brothers," cried Harry enthusiastically. He held out his brown, slender hand, and the plow-boy took it into his rough palm.

"Till death!"

"Till death," repeated Alec, and the words sounded like an oath of fealty upon his lips.

Emir whinnied impatiently, and with a last smiling nod Harry sprang upon his back and rode away. At the top of the hill he paused to look back and wave his hat. The sun shone down upon his bare head, and his proud young face was lit with the glow of power.

And Alec steadily plowed his straight lines all through the day, though the field was dancing before him in wildest dreams. Had he ever lived before? He seemed to have been waiting all these years for life to begin, and with the quick despair of the young he had thought that it would pass him by. He looked over the fields to the district school-house, for years the only supporter of his aspirations. It had been able to give him just enough to tantalize him with the knowledge of what lay beyond, but he had loved it. And now he was going out into that beyond. He had a kindly feeling for the drudgery he had chafed at. He patted the horses and looked with a cheerful heart over the . weary stretch of plowed land. The beauty of it came upon him suddenly when he no longer looked upon it as a prison. He loved it now that he could leave it.

Many a time, before the night fell, he looked up the road where Harry had gone, recalling every word of his new friend. From that day he began, with all the loyalty of a singularly faithful nature, to idealize the pleasing enough original, until, for him, all the virtues and graces were made manifest to the world in the person of Harry Vanborough.

Alec came of a loyal race. There had been at

least one Macdonald in olden days, who had counted
life itself a light thing to weigh against his fealty.
He was one of those who followed his liege lord to
the Holy Land in those wars of the Cross which awoke
heroism and devotion in many a dull heart that might
otherwise have lived and died without a keener thrill
than that provoked by a fine haunch of venison or a
neighborhood quarrel. When disaster came upon
their banner, he accepted captivity rather than save
himself alone; and when, in the chances of war, he
might have regained his own freedom he passed his
noble master through in his name and himself remained to meet death in his stead.

And the spirit of the old crusader lived again in
the latest of his descendants.

So the two boys made their compact. There was
no questioning on either side, no distrust, no doubt.
It was simply soul to soul, and convention and prudence had no part in it; soul to soul they spoke, and
till death, and beyond, the bond was never broken by
either.

CHAPTER II.

"WHAT new freak is this, Harry?" demanded that
young philanthropist's father with some asperity, when
he was informed in an incidental and by-the-way sort
of fashion of his son's latest departure. "Do you
mean to say you have practically adopted this young
man? How old is he?"

"About two years older than myself, I should
judge, sir," answered Harry imperturbably.

"And you propose to educate him?"

"I propose to give him a chance to educate himself, sir. He has the foundations laid, I fancy. It really amounts to my giving him two or three years of leisure, with the understanding that he is to invest them in a university education."

"And then?"

"Then — why, then he will take care of himself."

"In other words, you take a young man from the working classes, who is respectably earning his own living, make him a pauper for three years, give him a glimpse into a world he is never to live in, and then set him adrift, fit for nothing."

"The educational chances offered at our State University are hardly brilliant enough to unsettle any one," answered Harry coolly. "He will find his companions chiefly men like himself, who look on study as a privilege which they expect to pay for by doing good work for the world afterward. Besides, father, Alec Macdonald is not like the average farmer. He is going to be famous some day."

"Oh, I beg your pardon!"

Harry flushed uncomfortably. His father's accent made him feel that, perhaps, he appeared ridiculous, and that, of all things, he wished to avoid.

"I see I was mistaken in supposing that your acquaintance with the young man was limited to half an hour's chat. I must have misunderstood you."

"I think not. It was more than half an hour, though."

"And in that time you obtained this unusually

clear insight into his character?" Mr. Vanborough's tone was suggestive of nothing but polite interest.

"Not through any special gift of discernment on my part," replied Harry, struggling to emulate the coolness that tormented him. "His character is unusually transparent. I felt that I was dealing with a child in some respects."

Mr. Vanborough permitted himself to smile faintly.

"Of course, I shall verify his story and look him up further," continued Harry, as calmly as though the idea had not that moment occurred to him. "But a fellow who can carry himself on alone as far as he has, has the right sort of stuff in him, father. He wasn't waiting to be helped. And what's the use of being— well, of being a Vanborough, you know, if one isn't going to help out the Macdonalds? What real objection is there to my plan? It wouldn't be like you to disapprove because it isn't what people generally do."

Mr. Vanborough ran his eye carelessly over the columns of the morning paper which he held in his hand, before replying—an indication of disrespect which Harry noted with lowered eyebrows.

"Did it occur to you," he remarked, at last, "that there would be some expense in connection with this scheme? Am I to have the privilege of sharing in the good work by making your *protégé* an allowance?"

"That is a pleasure I must reserve for myself, sir."

"Ah!"

"I have given up the Covert Club. This, with my present allowance, will give all the funds that will be needed until I am twenty-one, when I come into my grandfather's legacy."

2

To save himself, Harry could not keep a little triumph out of his voice. He felt that by this arrangement he had redeemed the fantastic character of his original project, and proved himself not only high-minded, but eminently practical and business-like.

Evidently his father was not prepared for such a display of self-sacrifice. After scrutinizing his heir over the top of his paper for some moments, he remarked, with the habitual nonchalance that had taught Harry his own trick of cool speech :

" Really, it does not seem that my advice or assistance is needed. I hope you will in time allow me to offer my congratulations on your success, and pardon me if I reserve them until that is more assured."

He bowed with punctilious courtesy to his wife, and left the room ; but when he reached the street he allowed his gray mustache to twitch with a not ungratified smile. If you can't carry off the honors of the field yourself, it is something to leave them in the hands of a worthy representative of your name.

Mrs. Vanborough would have been much disturbed if her Harry's father had not yielded to her Harry's wish ; but, now that he had practically done so, she had some dismayed doubt whether that consummation was, after all, so devoutly to be wished.

" But, Harry, you don't propose to bring him here, right into the house ! " she expostulated.

" That is what I would like, *chère maman*," he answered coaxingly. " He would breakfast early with me and go with me up to the university. When he is in the house, he will be studying in his room. You would hardly see him except at dinner."

" A country clown, who probably eats with his

knife!" she said, with a little moue. Bringing it down to details made it more dreadful.

"I will see he does not offend," guaranteed Harry, with, it must be owned, a good deal of boldness. "You see, I will need him at all hours. I am going to have him do ever so many things for me."

"Oh, if he comes as your servant—" began Mrs. Vanborough, smoothing the perplexed pucker out of her forehead.

"But he doesn't. He comes as my friend. If you do not find it pleasant, little mother, I will get a room for him near the university. I'd rig up another for myself, and we could put in most of our time there, and keep out of the way, generally," he concluded, with an innocently unconscious air, knowing well that the suggestion would bring her to his terms.

"Stay away evenings? O Harry, you know I want you here!"

"And you know, my sweetest mother, that it will be more of an education for him to dine at your table than to learn all the Greek that the sirens ever scanned to bewitch Ulysses."

"Flatterer!" said his mother, but smiling, and she let him kiss her fingers, courtier-fashion.

So the day was won, though Harry decorously jubilated in secret. To have his own way, especially when it was a somewhat capricious way, always possessed a charm for the youngest son of the Vanboroughs. The fact that his way in this case was so commendable a one, gave it a unique flavor. He was on familiar terms with the little god of Victory, but he could still be flattered by the smile of the Virtues.

No craft was needed to capture the remaining

member of the family. It was always to be taken for
granted that, however wild the scheme which Harry
might propose, it would receive the devoted support
and sympathy of his sister Dorothy.

She listened to his story with no uncomfortable
questions or doubtings, and was Alec's sworn champion from the moment that she knew Harry had been
obliged to do battle in his defense. Together they
laid plots for the development and nurture of the
young farmer, and Harry the magnanimous would dis-
course at length on the probable fruits of their plant-
ing. Where there was so little actuality to circum-
scribe imagination, the future was susceptible of as-
suming any form that might be pleasing. There were
few careers, from that of poet to that of President,
which were not canvassed in Alec's behalf in those days.
Of course, in the background of each picture there
hovered an unnamed personage who might probably
figure, with certain appreciative epithets, in the great
man's biography, or become an object of interest in
his Life and Letters.

What inquiry Mr. Vanborough deemed it prudent
to institute before admitting a stranger into his household, or what was the information elicited, was not di-
vulged. It was his policy to refrain at least from the
appearance of taking any active part in those entan-
glements of life which he liked to smile at from his
unassailable *laissez-faire* position. If Harry chose to
meddle with ideas about humanity and such things,
the quickest cure would probably be to let him run
his course. This country boy would do very well as
the medium for administering the necessary dose of
experience.

At last Alec came, decidedly shy and awkward, and rather overcome by the glory of carpet and gas-light civilization. Harry fluttered about him like an anxious mother-bird, agonizedly conscious of all his blunders, and with no little heroism maintaining a gay and collected exterior while his *protégé* struggled through his initiation. Why, in the name of all that was trying, should the man blush when asked if he would have soup, or tangle himself up in the rug while trying to hand a lady a chair? Why should the strong, lithe frame, which had been so handsome in the blue blouse, look like a clothier's model in its new suit of tweed?

If it had not been for a wholesome strain of obsti-nacy which was the proper inheritance of a Vanborough, Harry would have set his friend up in apartments near the university at the end of the second day; but the profound courtesy of his father's manner, in which he alone detected the satirical element, had a stimulating effect upon his faltering courage. Was he going to be smiled out of his position? Never!

Harry came to appreciate Dorothy in those days. Somehow the demure little school-girl had a soothing effect on the sensibilities of the young rustic, and while with her he forgot his nervous self-consciousness and showed some of the quiet strength which was his by right of nature. Perhaps it was that she under-stood him, for she herself stood a little in awe of her quizzical father, and knew that she was far from satis-fying her mother's standard. As a girl, and his junior at that, it was to be expected that she would be meek and respectful; but she went beyond what might have been demanded, and was so frankly eager to make

him feel at home, and so ready to go seven eighths of
the way to meet his first shy attempts at conversation,
that it was impossible for him not to feel gratified and
respond with the best wares he could offer.

"Don't you think he is getting on beautifully?"
she would whisper to Harry, after she had lured the
shy youth into an animated exposition of free trade, or
Hegelian philosophy, or some other subject in which
she had individually an equal lack of interest. She
soon knew better than even Harry what leads to follow to bring the hidden ore to the surface, and how to
nullify the unspoken criticism from the other end of
the table.

Harry gave a sigh of relief when he discovered
this condition of affairs, and took care that Dorothy
should have all possible opportunity to assist him in
guarding the chrysalis of the future genius. That innocent maiden never knew why her brother should
have been inspired to delight her girlish soul with a
bracelet she had long coveted when there wasn't a
Christmas or a birthday or even a philopena debt to
give a reason for it.

But Alec soon learned to avoid the plainest shoals
and to keep out of danger's way for the rest. There
were times indeed when Mrs. Vanborough's lifted eyebrows, or the shadow of an amused smile under Mr.
Vanborough's mustache, swept away all sense but a
wild desire to feel his old plow-handles in his fingers
again, with the loose reins about his neck ; but, for the
most part, the human beings about him and their unknown code occupied relatively a small part of his
thoughts. It was an enchanted world that had opened
before him ; and often, when the work of the student

was done, he would wander out to look at the night sky and the quiet city below, unwilling to sleep, because in sleep he lost the keen sense of happiness that pervaded every hour of consciousness.

The scant intellectual fare of his childhood had starved him into a condition that made him fall an easy prey to the reading fever. He grudged every hour spent away from the mines that had suddenly opened their treasures to him. But for his fine physical development he would have ill borne the intemperate zeal with which he sought to make up for lost time, for to the natural heedlessness of youth he added a determined heedlessness of his own. His will would recognize no limitations of flesh, and often the eastern sky dimmed the lamp by which he had read through the night.

Here, again, Harry was his salvation. In the gymnasium at the top of the house, Alec had to forget his books while his friend taught him to fence and swing Indian clubs and even to dance. Harry was a master of universal accomplishments, and lessons of all sorts went on with unabated enthusiasm for week after week, to the secret astonishment of the young instructor's father.

"I suppose that lump of raw material holds the same sort of inspiration for him that a piece of marble does for a sculptor or a blank sheet of paper for a poet," he reflected.

Harry was just finishing his junior year when he took Alec's fate into his hands. For the few remaining weeks of the term he turned the neophyte loose in his own school library and left him to work off his pent-up fire on its natural fuel. Then, when vacation

came, he threw up a proposed plan to explore the
Yellowstone Park with a party of friends, and instead
carried Alec off with him to some unnamed wilderness
without a post-office.   Thence he wrote glowing accounts of their fishing and hunting experiences in vir-
gin solitudes unspoiled by the tin-can of the tourist.
His friends would have stared had they known that
the letters were written on the cover of an atlas, with
a pencil blunted in correcting the exercises of one
Alexander Macdonald   Never did tutor work harder,
nor, it may be added, with better success.

Harry had been a brilliant though desultory student, and had carried off the honors of his class with
an easy superiority that left his competitors wondering
at their own presumption in daring to contest his divine claim.   No one else could have maintained his
popularity as Harry did without permitting a more
equal division of scholarship glories.   In truth, he
gathered them more because they fell into his hand
than because he cared greatly for them.   Harry Vanborough did not need the ratification of the public
to make him command his own approval.   Certainly
none of his own triumphs had given him the profound
satisfaction he felt when Alec was admitted, in the
fall, to the sophomore class, without conditions.
What was the loss of Yellowstone Park to the satisfaction of having your course justified by the result,
especially when you had been just a little uncertain
as to the outcome yourself ?   He announced Alec's
success to his father with military brevity, and then
felt for the first time that he could rest on his oars and
enjoy life in the way Fate intended.

His own affairs were certainly important enough

to justify a certain amount of self-absorption during the months that immediately followed. Soon after Christmas he attained his majority, and his father, as his legal guardian, formally rendered an account of the investments made for his son's benefit, under the provisions of the will of Harry's grandfather. Harry was his own master in the eye of the law, as he had always been in point of fact. When the municipal elections came around, he conferred dignity upon the polls by depositing his first vote. Somehow, the first vote, like the first kiss, hath a charm that appertaineth not to its monotonous train of successors.

In addition to his class interests he began to form relations with the business and professional life of the town. A wider life it seemed, and hours which might profitably have been given to his thesis were spent in eagerly discussing with Alec the new prospects opening up before him.

During all this ferment he more than fulfilled his early promises to Alec. The aspect of patron and client had gradually changed, as the boys came to recognize more fully their natural equality, into a friendship which, while it may have drawn its tenderness from gratitude, found its strength in a community of tastes and a sympathy of nature that was the best guarantee for its permanence.

June came, and the fragrance of commencement roses was in the air. Harry was to be graduated.

"I say, Alec," he exclaimed one day, looking up from his work to glance about the room where they had studied together for a year, "if there is a particle of woe in my valedictory oration, you may thank yourself for it. This has been a jolly good year, hasn't it?"

"Yes," said Alec, rather desolately. The prospective dissolution of their student comradeship meant something of a wrench to his seriously sentimental nature.

"It isn't your turn to be broken up yet," remarked his friend, after a keen look. "Save that until you are called upon to twitch your heart-strings away from the dear faculty."

Alec still looked so melancholy that Harry began to sing, with burlesque tenderness :

> " What will you do, love,
> When waves divide us?"

until Alec sufficiently recovered his spirits to make an offer of personal violence.

"I suppose I must put the expected number of polite fictions into my farewell," resumed Harry cheerfully. "I would like to immortalize my name by telling the bare, unvarnished truth on this occasion, but I suppose it would be setting a bad example to the juniors."

"But aren't you at all sorry to break all this up?"

"Not in the least, shocking as it sounds. Stocks are more intricate than logarithms, and the result is not so tame. I am going to live now, my boy."

But when the handsome valedictorian delivered that oration, he touched so feelingly on the devotion of his teachers that one tender-hearted old professor had to cover his eyes with his hand, and so missed the restrained convulsions of the lower classes in front, who had caught the suggestive quiver of Harry's eyelid.

A year of subjective life, like the last for Alec, leaves

few distinct pictures in the memory; but there was one scene that so long as he lived would come up before him at the sight of the blue corn-flower.

It was the day before Harry's commencement. Dorothy, with elaborate care, had herself arranged the basket of flowers which was to grace his public triumph, and as Alec came into the room she was discussing it critically with her brother.

"Come in, Alec," cried Harry, over Dorothy's head, as he caught sight of his friend at the door. "See how people will vainly try to console a fellow when he has to give up Greek roots and all the other joys of life. This basket will make all the boys jealous. I will tell them it is from the prettiest girl in town."

"Harry!" expostulated Mistress Dorothy, with an abashed glance at Alec.

"It is true, though. Isn't it, Alec?" said Harry teasingly.

Alec looked at her with an air of serious consideration. She had piled up her hair in a young-ladylike fashion, and in some indefinable but unmistakable manner she made him feel that this tall young person, with the pretty color in her face and her frank dismay at her brother's open praises, belonged to a different order of beings from the little school-girl who had been so friendly.

"Yes, I think it is true," he answered soberly.

"Bravo! Give him a flower to reward him, Dot."

And Dorothy, smiling and obedient, chose him a spray of blue corn-flowers. He carried them off to his room, and somehow fell to wondering what if—it might be possible—

"Yes, our only daughter," said Mrs. Vanborough's voice, coming up through the open window from the garden below.

Alec suddenly shook himself free of his dreaming reverie.

"And you are a plow-boy, remember," he told himself, with rather a grim smile.

With a vivid remembrance of his last day's plowing, he hunted up the little volume of Wordsworth and read over the spring verses that he had chafed at that day. Then, with rather a sober face, he shut his corn-flowers in upon the lines and put the book and some idle fancies away.

CHAPTER III.

FOR the next two years the young men lived less in parallel lines. Vanborough had rented an office in the business part of the town, where he industriously spent his leisure in acquiring the art of looking hurried. Macdonald continued at the university, and, now that Harry's active mediatorship was in a measure withdrawn, he fell into a more lonely course of life. He still kept his old room, because Harry would hear of nothing else, and, to support the theory of his service, he spent a few hours every afternoon in clerical work in Harry's office. But their hours were different and their interests no longer identical, and the old familiar talks that had carried them together through all the realms of life and philosophy in the daring fashion of youth were exchanged for greetings that, though friendly, were brief, and to hurried discussions of sub-jects to which Alec, at least, was profoundly indif-ferent.

There were times when the student fancied, with an unreasonable sort of a heartache that his old com-rade was slipping away from him, in this parting of the interests that had heretofore united them. With his own passionate love for books and his exaltation of the scholarly life, he could not fully understand how to a man of a different temperament this distracting whirl of cross-purposes which they called business might seem pre-eminently virile. Neither did he make a suffi-cient allowance for the fascination of novelty. At no other period does the man feel so impressively the dignity of his new estate as during the first six months after the school-room doors have closed behind him.

There was certainly an exuberance about the new life into which Harry had thrown himself that gave some excuse for his intoxication. The coming of a projected railway had scattered the seeds of a boom through the Northwest, and all men's thoughts were throbbing with a fever of speculation. Bubbles were bursting every day, to be sure, but they were so big and so brilliant that they dazzled even the blowers. Even those who at first held out against the demorali-zation soon came to look upon this as the natural way of living, for it is not always easy to distinguish the high pulse of fever from the heart-throbs of fullest life. The leaders, as in most of the newer Western towns, were young men. It was almost startling to find the steady gleam of a trained eye in contrast with a boy-ishly rounded cheek, and to see lips yet unhidden drawn habitually into a compressed line. But under this artificial severity was a natural flow of spirits which gave zest to what, in later years, might become a grind. They seemed secretly to have a frolicsome feeling that they were stealing a march on their elders, and were going to get all the fun out of the situation they could while it lasted.

In all this Vanborough took the place of a chief as a matter of course. His wealth and leading social position, his easy assumption of supremacy, debonair manner and personal charm, made him the pet of the older and the admiration of the younger factions. Events gravitated to him naturally, and without effort he found himself always surrounded by men who talked magnificently

"I'm not doing anything, you know, Alec," he would say with a gay laugh, "but I am tremendously busy. It is great fun, though. Conic sections were nothing to it."

Harry was especially gratified by the subtle flattery of his father's manner. He was no longer teased as a boy, but treated with the respectful consideration due to an equal. Mr. Vanborough was well content with himself and the whole world those days, and not unwilling to share his satisfaction with the community at large. He found frequent occasion to take his daily walk down the street where the new sign swung, and he got into the habit of saying that it was about time for him to drop his hold on active affairs, since the old name would still be represented.

His eldest son, Edward, who had remained in the old Eastern home, had never caused him any very deep thrill either of pleasure or anxiety since the days when he had watched the solemn baby face in its cradle laces. As a child, a youth, a man, he had always been irreproachable. Praise in his case became axiomatic. He had shaped his life upon the maxims which a race of high-minded writing-masters have striven to impress upon their youthful charges, and he probably never put his name to a check without mentally reflecting that "evil communications corrupt good manners" and "vice and vanity are shunned by the virtuous." Yes, Edward was certainly all that a father could wish, and Dorothy was all that a daughter needed to be; but Harry, the brilliant and somewhat erratic son, was the child of his heart. There was a life in the boy that made the old earth spin faster for his being on it.

"He's a rattler, that boy of yours," was the general verdict, and the father played with his watch-chain and smiled calmly. Of course; he was Harry Vanborough.

But he knew very little about the details of that business. The young man carried matters with his customary high-handedness and kept his own counsel. He never talked shop at home.

But when the months had piled up a year and half another, Alec began to question whether there had not come a greater change over his friend than the months alone could explain. Again and again a doubt came to him, an uneasy sense that all was not right under the fair-seeming surface of events. He thought he detected an undercurrent of unrest that had formerly been no part of Harry's frank nature; a fitful moodiness replaced at times the even sunshine of earlier days. He pondered often and somewhat anxiously on the subject, but his fears were too vague and he was still too much under the spell of Vanborough's personal influence for his thought to find its way into words.

One afternoon, while he was busy at his nominal occupation of copying records in the inner office, he overheard a scrap of conversation that disturbed him :

"I say, Van, you don't expect to sell that piece of land, do you? I see you have it listed here," said a man who, with hands deep in his pockets, was tipping himself up on his toes and heels alternately as he scrutinized a large wall-map before him.

"Do you want to buy?"

"Not if the court knows itself. I've seen that land."

"It is sold, all the same," remarked Vanborough coolly.

The man whistled and turned around.

"The party wasn't on the spot, was he?"

"No."

"Who did the—professional explanation?"

"Falkland."

A shout of laughter greeted the name.

"Van, you're a genius. It isn't every one who can pick up the lucre and keep his fingers as clean as you do. I hope you give Falkland something more than board wages."

"Why, what is the matter? The land is all there," cried Vanborough gayly.

"Oh, yes. It is all there." And the man laughed again. "When you are through with Falkland, just let me know, won't you? I think I could use him in my line."

Harry nodded gayly as the man went, and turned to Alec with the laughter still in his eyes.

"Who is he?" asked Alec indignantly.

Harry mentioned a name which had lately become notorious in the little town for its connection with some more than usually "crooked" transactions.

"Why didn't you put a stop to his impertinent insinuations?"

"Because," said Vanborough, dropping suddenly into the steely quiet which was his one sign of anger, "I did not consider him impertinent, and it had not occurred to me to ask the opinion of any one else."

Whereupon Macdonald, of course, became angry in turn, and finished his work in volcanic silence.

Alec generally expected to make the first overtures to restore easy relations when Harry's loftiness strained them; but a few days after this, when he returned from his classes, he found his friend waiting for him in their old study. This had not been a common occurrence of late.

"Jove! Alec, are you always so late? I've been waiting an hour for you. It made me think of old days to look over your books here. What jolly times we had that year when we studied and fenced together! But good things never last."

"I didn't suppose you ever regretted them."

Harry dropped his chin into his palm and watched his old room-mate with amused eyes.

"You are as jealous as a girl, Alec!"

And Alec, who at least had not learned the girl's lesson of concealment, flushed darkly. Of course, he should not have expected that the friendship which had so suddenly illumined his life should withstand

3

the universal law of change, but—the heart does not know the alphabet of the language of reason.

"What are those things on your chair? Books, aren't they? Thought I wasn't mistaken, though it is so long since I have had one in my hand that I wasn't sure. As a business man, the only literature I dare touch is the daily paper, if I am not to lose standing with my class. Just clear those books off, dear boy; sit down, and put away that lofty look. I want to talk to you."

"About business?"

"About business, my discerning friend." He was laughing, but still he did not seem quite at ease. "You have heard of the Panesco Mine, haven't you?"

"The one that smashed?"

"No, no. This is something new."

"Oh, the smash is still in the future tense, then, in this case?"

"Don't be more unpleasant than you feel morally bound to be. The Panesco Mine is the greatest thing out."

"Who is caught this time?"

"Your form of expression might be improved— but let that pass. Here's the prospectus of a new company just organized to operate it. Can't you get up a spark of interest?"

"How can I, having no principal?"

"No one but yourself would think of calling you an unprincipled fellow. But this thing is worth looking into."

"I'm not going to invest. Are you?"

"Falkland thinks it would be more than safe."

"Oh!"

"He is very shrewd about such matters. What are you doing there?"

"Oh, just a little sum. I was trying to estimate the size of the scheme you will probably have on your hands by the end of the year. They are all greatest in turn, you know, and there is on an average about one every five weeks, and 'greatest' raised to the tenth power—"

"You'd better give it up until you have developed the organ of imagination. For that the study of Shakespeare isn't enough. What you need is a few months in a real-estate and land-improvement office. Alec, I wish you would come into business with me."

"Seriously?"

"I never joke on solemn subjects."

"What is there I could do?"

"Much, if you will. Had you decided on a career?"

"Not irrevocably."

Macdonald's face was kindling as he rapidly thought over all that the suggestion held. His dreams had indeed run in another direction, but the actuality of continuing with the friend who had carried his soul captive was worth many dreams to one of Alec's nature.

"I have been hoping for some time that, when you once got your sheepskin, we might work together in the office as we did in the school-room. And, unless you have fully decided on reforming the politics of the country with the editorial pencil, it is a good business opening. It won't be practicing scales on the harp of fame; but, if you take to that, you will leave me behind."

His head had drooped rather wearily, and his handsome, brown face had an unwonted look of appeal that touched Alec.

"All right.   Consider it settled."

They shook hands silently, and, if something made their hearts leap as on that day when they stood in the new-turned earth and made their first compact in the April morning, they deemed it unbecoming their years to give any sign.

"What comes next?   You see I don't know what my duties are going to be," said Alec presently.

"Never mind that, until after commencement.   I only wanted to make sure of you now.   Until then I won't ask anything of you, unless it be some moral support occasionally.   For one thing, you can help me to hold down Falkland."   He laughed as he said it, for Alec's antagonism to Falkland always amused him.   There was a tinge of jealousy in it that was rather flattering.

"I don't like Falkland," said the new partner promptly.   "Why do you have him?"

"My innocent one, you don't need to like a man you do business with.   Falkland is useful."

"What can he do that a man with some character couldn't do better?"

"A great deal, Sir Moralist.   That's where your education is still lacking."

"For instance?—"

"Five years from now you shall tell me.   Never mind Falkland, Alec.   He's away for the present, looking after our Western interests.   Doesn't that sound imposing?   So the atmosphere will be clear for a while."

" That mine affair? You wouldn't let him influence your judgment in a serious matter, would you?"

" Did it ever strike you that I was much beholden to any one for my opinions or actions?"

Alec looked at him with affectionate penetration.

" Ah! it is all very well for you to pretend, Harry, but I know well enough why you keep him. It is simply because you can help him in that way, and no one else would."

Harry rose impatiently.

" Let us talk about something pleasant. I'm not an interesting subject to myself."

The last six months of student-life passed quickly. Alec made his modest commencement bow and stepped down from the enchanted world that had been his for three years.

" You're on my level now, old fellow," said Harry, by way of congratulation.

And, full of fine theories about life as he was, he found himself eager to get at its real work. The feverish desire to know of his earlier years had been stilled. Books had taught him to look beyond themselves into the life out of which they grew.

" You see how it is. Destiny has linked our fates together, and we must work with one another to the end," said Vanborough, half seriously, when Macdonald settled down at the second desk in the handsome office. " I'm glad to have you here. It steadies me. Perhaps appearances flatter you, but you never seem shaken by the rattle."

" I had no suspicion your nerves were affected."

" No, I try to hide the dread secret."

The old familiar personal relations were re-estab-

lished and all went well; but, so far as the business was
concerned, Alec had but little more to do with its
management than before. The legal consummation of the partnership was from time to time post-
poned.

"I must straighten out my crooked accounts before I make a statement of the business for you," Vanborough once said jestingly.

The new partner had no desire to press it, being
well content with matters as they were. There was
something womanly in his nature, shown especially in
his relations with Harry. He had received everything
—he gave in return a love that was at once humble
and protecting. But even he could not help seeing
that his friend's whimsical moodiness increased as the
summer advanced.

"Why don't you take a short vacation from the
office?" he asked one day.

"Why should I?" demanded Harry, looking around
with ungrateful loftiness.

"I think you need it. You haven't been quite
yourself of late, you know," responded Alec, with the
best intentions and the least tact in the world.

"Nonsense! I'm all right."

"In mind as well as in body?"

"What do you mean by that? Don't talk in rid-
dles."

"You are different in some way. I have thought
sometimes—"

"Well?"

"That, perhaps, you were troubled about investments, or something of that sort."

"And that I might want your assistance in getting

out of some scrape that I had run my foolish head
into? That's awfully kind of you, you know."

"And equally uncalled for, you mean?"

"Equally or more so," replied Harry, with unruffled
brow

Alec retired in dudgeon to nurse his hurt dignity,
and left his friend for a while severely alone; but
presently looking up, he saw that his partner had
dropped into one of those moody abstractions which
had become more and more frequent of late, and which
seemed so strangely at variance with his old character.
Harry glanced up and caught the grave look fixed
upon him, and, springing up in a sudden flash of resentment, he flung himself out of the room. When he
came back his natural manner had returned, and, without referring to their unpleasant *quatre d'heure*, he
threw his arm affectionately over his friend's shoulder
while speaking of some trivial office matter. But Alec
understood the meaning of the rare caress.

CHAPTER IV.

"EXTRA edition! All about the Panesco Mine!"
The boys were crying the news in the street as
Alec went down to the office early one afternoon.

"The smash has come, then," he reflected, remembering Harry's unfinished story. He bought the paper
and glanced at the head-lines. As he had anticipated,
they told of the bursting of another bubble; and as he
went on his way he ruminated with an impersonal indignation on the multiplying schemes of the specula-

tors and the ruin that followed them. He wondered
whether by any chance Harry could have been drawn
into the matter.

At the door of the office he encountered Falkland,
bearing upon his person the signs of recent travel.
The return of the agent was unexpected, and struck
him with a momentary surprise, but, with a swift return
of his old dislike, he forbore to ask an explanation and
passed on in. Falkland, with a jauntiness peculiarly
his own, bowed effusively in response to Macdonald's
brief sign of recognition, and twice before he reached
the end of the block he stopped to look back at the
closed office-doors, and to laugh silently to himself.

Harry was standing by the window, looking off to
where a bit of blue sky straggled down between the
chimneys. He turned, when the door opened, with a
thoughtful but composed air that at once dispelled his
friend's half-formulated anxiety.

"Have you heard about the Panesco Mine?"
asked Alec cheerfully.

"Yes, I know."

"Hopeless, isn't it?"

"So Falkland says."

"Oh, by-the-way, when did Falkland come?"

"I don't know. Oh, an hour ago, perhaps," answered Vanborough dreamily. After a few moments
he added in the same manner: "Do you remember
you asked, when we spoke about this once, who was
caught this time? I couldn't answer then, but now—
I am."

Greatly startled, Alec turned to look at him.

"In the Panesco scheme?"

"Yes."

"Badly, old fellow?"

"I haven't examined my books yet."

The evasive answer and unnatural manner struck Alec with foreboding; but he answered quickly, with an assumption of cheerfulness:

"Oh, well, that is one of the chances of war. We will soon make it up, and there is no one who can so well laugh at a little ill-fortune as you, Harry. I have often seen how coolly you have met what would have shaken some men. The money is the least part to you, I know."

Harry listened to the sprightly words with a comprehending smile, but he did not answer. Presently he pulled some papers toward him and made a pretense of being occupied, and Alec said nothing more by way of consolation. But he was more disturbed than he liked to acknowledge, and it was with something akin to dismay that he watched the gathering abstraction and depression on his friend's face.

"Let us take a holiday this afternoon," said Harry at last in answer to his inquiring look. "I want to get out into the open places. We have not had a good tramp for a long time."

"Nothing would suit me better," responded Alec promptly.

In a few moments they had recklessly closed the door against all potential purchasers and struck off at a swinging gait for the country, which nestled closely around the young town. The change of scene, the sparkling air, the quick step, acted like a cordial on Harry's mood. With one of his swift changes he seemed to have thrown off his burden.

"What is the proper form of Wordsworthian invi-

tation to a walk?" he asked lightly. "The leaves are
yellow, the year grows old; come out, dear fellow,
where lots are sold. Doesn't that have the true ring
of the Lakers' Muse? Or don't you read Wordsworth
since you have grown frivolous all along of me?"

"Oh, yes, I read him occasionally, to remind me of
my former estate," said Alec, smiling back. In this
mood the old Harry returned.

"Let us take to the good greenwood, after the
fashion of Robin Hood and his jolly crew. Do you
suppose Robin would have been driven to speculating
in stocks if the greenwood had been forbidden him?"

"If he had, Friar Tuck would have told him that
it was not the unpardonable sin."

"What would the scapegraces do but for the faithful friend who always stands between them and fate?
But I wish I had been one of Robin's men."

"Why?"

"Oh, then things would have been settled by this
time, as far as I am concerned."

Alec shook his head with a friendly frown, and
Harry laughed lightly.

"Come, I know a secret path which should only
be revealed to lovers and poets. Were you ever in love,
Alec?"

"No, no!" protested Macdonald with such startled
vehemence that his friend laughed aloud.

"Your day will come. Sir High-and-Mighty, and
when it does may I be there to see! Look, here is
my fairy path, leading away into the land of enchant-
ment."

They struck off through the trees by an old, grass-
grown road that had become sweet and shy since the

wagons had taken to the dusty new highway. The October winds had already begun to scatter the leaves, and through the thinning branches the cool, fine sunlight fell upon rustling heaps of yellow ghosts. The green seclusion of the exuberant summer growth had given place to open spaces, with vistas of sky and hill and lake.

Harry took off his hat, pushing back the hair that fell heavily over his white brow. So might Apollo have stopped to gaze at the world while the sounds of the chase grew faint in the distance.

"It is a wonderful world," he said quietly, throwing himself down on the brown grass to watch the water gleaming through the trees. "It has a phase to match every mood that flits across the mind of man; or perhaps it makes the moods. I always had a brotherly feeling for the chameleon, and a suspicion that in his place I would do exactly the same thing."

Alec, with his hands under his head, was looking lazily up into the tree-tops.

"Then, in these days of rapid transit, you ought to be able to manage things to suit yourself," he answered idly. "Select the spot that will give you the right environment, go and absorb its influence for a few days, and then come back and work off the effect on society."

"That is what I am doing. I am a hermit, in spirit, at this moment. I wish to know nothing more of your city. Its atmosphere is unhealthy."

Alec gave him a quick look.

"Why do you give yourself up to it?" he asked abruptly. "You can choose."

Harry tossed the leaves into the air, watching them falling about him.

"Because I want to live," he said slowly. "I want
to know the secret that sends the gambler back again
and again to his duel with chance. I want to taste
the hashish, even though it takes me off my feet.
What matter whether I win or lose? The stake I
play for is experience, and the game can not go against
me."

"Oh, well, but there are some experiences one
does not want."

"So you think. So do not I."

"But such a precept would open the door to
license."

"How do you know what is law and what is license? You judge from the circumscribed stand-
point of a man, and a civilized man at that."

"But a man's judgment must be of the size of a
man, not of Omniscience," he answered, rousing himself up to a point of protest against the drift of his
friend's talk.

"Look up there," said Harry, pointing into the
blue above him. "You see nothing but a veil of sunlight, hiding the stars. But you know the stars are
beyond."

"But he would be a fool who ignored the good sunlight and tried to walk by those stars of yours."

"A fool? Yes, I suppose so, poor devil!"

He arose and looked out over the water, while Alec
watched him with troubled heart.

"What does it all matter, after all," he went on,
"all this questioning and troubling about our little
selves? We say sin and sorrow and death, as though
they were facts of tremendous importance, but that is
only because we look from the under side. What is

the worst that can befall a man, or a million of men, when you think of the vastness of the scheme, and the atoms that men are in it? Not worth the fraction of a thought! Yet I dare say the men who are dying now, while this leaf takes time to flutter to the ground, think it of sufficient moment to crowd all the rest of the universe out of mind. Do you ever think about dying, Alec?"

"No, nor about to-morrow's dinner. What's the use?" said Macdonald, trying in his practical way to clear away the unnatural element in the thought of his friend. "What do you say to a plunge in the lake? Our last chance this summer."

"When I am dead," Harry went on unheedingly, "I should like to look up through trees like these, where there are few leaves to keep out the sky. And I should like to know that by dying I had put myself in harmony with the world. It is hard to live on the high planes. To wipe out the smallness of life by a grand death, that would be supreme."

"Harry, if you are troubled, why can't I know it?" cried Alec impetuously, reckless of the anger he had provoked before by his questions.

But Harry gave him a long, kind look, and after a moment's hesitation he answered, very gently:

"Not to-day. This is a holiday, you know. Wait till to-morrow, Alec."

They sauntered on silently through the trees, neither caring to say more at that moment. Macdonald was troubled at heart and gave little heed to the path they followed, but Vanborough walked slowly and looked about him with observant if melancholy eyes. Presently they came to an open glade where some school-boys had gathered. They were practicing in shooting at a mark, and, as Harry glanced from the excited youngster who had his finger on the trigger to the target set up at the other end of the glade, he saw that Alec, with his hat over his eyes, had not understood the situation, and, further, that another step would bring him between the target and the unheeding marksman. There was no time to call. He saw the danger, and leaping forward he threw his arm over his friend's shoulder to drag him down. The next moment Alec was kneeling on the brown October sod, holding Harry in his arms.

The tense lines of pain melted from the white face and in a moment the brown eyes opened wide.

"It is—all right, Alec," he said gently. "Hold me up—higher."

"Can you wait here while I run for help? The boys have scattered," said Alec, trying to keep his voice steady.

"No, stay with me. I need no one but you."

Alec heard him doubtingly.

"Can I help you, then? I must know how seriously you are hurt."

"There is no need."

"You do not think—" He could not finish.

Harry turned to look deep into his eyes.

"That I am killed? Saved, rather. But I shall not use this body again."

"Oh, my one friend!" groaned Alec.

"He did not see you—the boy. I thought you saw him till the last moment. Then I tried—too late—"

"For me, Harry? For me? Oh, I can not bear it!"

For answer Harry lifted his hand as a woman might have done to touch Alec's face.

"It is best—best for me, at least."

His hand fell heavily, and as he lay back with closed eyes a gray pallor crept fast over his face. But he rallied, holding death back with a strong effort. Macdonald bent his head low to catch the faint words.

"Make it—right, Alec," he whispered with so beseeching an earnestness in his eyes that Alec answered as though he were taking a vow—

"I will."

Harry smiled and closed his eyes for a moment in deep content. Alec watched every changing shade on the young face with a breathless awe that held agony down. So calm, so unafraid, might he meet death upon the threshold.

The fine lips moved again.

"Up!—"

Alec held him higher, so that he could see the gleam of the lake between the trees, and the hills beyond that reached up to touch the sky. His eye followed the lines with earnest care, as though he would hold fast the memory of the golden day. Then he raised his hand and waved a mute farewell to the beautiful world. With a faint, half-playful smile he looked at Alec, and then the brown head fell forward against the face bending over it. There were a few deep breaths, then a sudden pause that grew into a silence never to be broken. Alec had hidden his eyes, that he might not see the passing of his friend, but he knew that it was only the body which Harry would use no more that he held in his arms.

Still he did not move, and he held his very thought calm from the distraction of grief. Was his friend, released from the narrow house of flesh, even now preparing for his long journey into the regions of rest? Not by a thought of sorrow would he hold him back on his way. In that moment he knew that death was one with freedom, and the nearness of the mystery brought upon him the peace of a great awe.

He did not know how long he knelt there, with the brown leaves fluttering by and the soft wind stirring the hair that rested on his arm, but presently there came a group of farmers, shocked and curious, led by a boy with a white, scared face The spell of silence was broken, and with a sharp thrill of agony he saw them lift the body of his dead friend and lay it straightly on the grass. They would have carried it to the nearest house, but he checked them.

"Leave him here, under the trees where he died, until we take him home."

"It will be a sad home-coming," said one of the men with honest sympathy. "Perhaps it will be best for you to go on ahead, young man. Give us the address, and we will come on afterward with the body. There will be those that will need some preparing for this, I suppose," he explained, thinking that the dead man's friend seemed too dazed to be trusted to think for himself.

"Yes, that will be best," he assented, though his heart sank suddenly at the thought of the waiting mother. Mechanically he gave the men their directions, and then, after one long look at the calm, dead face, he mounted the horse they brought for him, and went out from the quiet wood into a changed world.

What way he took or how long he rode he never
knew, for his thoughts were not with him on that
rapid, homeward journey. It was not until he turned
into the silent street that he remembered, thinking
anxiously that the sound of galloping feet might startle
the mother. Perhaps they did help to tell the story,
for when he reached the door it was opened from
within, and Mrs. Vanborough met him.

"Where is Harry ? " she asked sharply, as he stood
with faltering foot before her.

He took her hand and led her in silently, but she
faced him again.

"Where is Harry ?" she repeated with trembling
lips. " Can't you speak ? "

" There has been an accident," he began, feeling
suddenly how hopeless it was to try to break such
news or to do anything but tell the unalterable truth.

His words had stricken the color from her face.

"Do you mean—dead ? "

Alec's silence gave the answer.

" Dead ! *Dead?*"   Disbelief struggled with anguish in her drawn face. "It is not true! I tell you
I will not believe it ! Dead? Why, he was here in
this room, this very day ! Do you mean to tell me
that he will never come here again, and expect me to
believe it ? How can he be dead, and *you* here ? "

Alec grew very pale as the question fell like a lash,
but he answered simply :

"He saved my life. It was like him. I can almost forget to be sorry that I must live when I think
how nobly he crowned his generous life by his too
generous death."

"For you? His life for yours? O just God ! "

4

She threw her arms toward heaven with a wild cry and fell backward. Alec sprang to help her, but with a terrible look she repulsed him.

"Don't touch me!" she said hoarsely.

"Shall I call Miss Dorothy?" he asked, with a man's sense of helplessness in dealing with another's sorrow.

She moaned and moaned, but made no answer. But Dorothy had heard the voices, and came gliding in, dusky and slight as a shadow. With a startled look of inquiry at Alec she ran to kneel beside her mother, soothing her in feminine fashion without words, and the bereaved mother, with a bitter cry, hid her face in her daughter's breast.

"He is dead, our darling is dead, and it was to save that man's life!"

Macdonald could bear no more. He stole from the room, and, with a dizzy feeling that he must find rest for a moment, went up to the little study that had been his and Harry's in common. The long shadows of evening fell across the room, and the thin curtains at the window stirred softly with a gentle motion that deepened the calm. All the quiet, hopeful days that they had lived here together, all the brave thoughts that had gone out toward the work that lay in the future, came softly back to comfort him. He went about, picking up the books where his name was written below Harry's, looking at the pictures they had chosen, the scraps of Harry's drawing pinned against the wall. A magazine, with a paper-knife between the half-cut pages lay upon the table. Beside it lay a half-sheet of paper, covered with verses in the hand of his friend. With a sudden rush of tears he read the words Harry had so lately written, "On the Thought of Death" :

As children, fevered with their headlong play,
  Clutch all the flowers the varied meadows hold,
  Nor look beneath the lure of red and gold,
So heedlessly cull we along life's way ;
And whether this be hemlock or sweet bay,
  Heart's-ease, or rue of bitterness untold,
  What poison these pale petals may infold,
What hidden sweetness waits, we can not say.
Then Death bends over us and murmurs, " Peace ! "
  And straight is stilled the restlessness that mars
Soul-perfect calm.   Our clinging hands release
  The sweet snare that our onward pathway bars.
The din of heart's blood, beating loud, must cease,
  That we may listen to the eternal stars.

The calm words echoed the voice he loved; they matched the last far look in Harry's eyes. He buried his face in his arms and ceased to think, lifted up to strange heights of perception. Could he have wished that this friend of his should stay to grow old and at last die when he had forgotten how to live ? So might common souls run their course, but for Harry—Prince Hal—death came most fitly with its fateful call while the bead still sparkled on the goblet of life. And who had lived so keenly, so deeply, as the spirit which now quitted the earth, because in a few brief years it had exhausted the cup it takes duller souls half a century to drain ?

There was a sound of heavy feet below, and, realizing suddenly that he had lingered longer than he should, he sprang to the door. Dorothy met him in the hall, white and wide-eyed.

"Don't go down, Alec ! "

"Yes, I must. The men will not know—"

But she laid a detaining hand on his arm.

"Mamma is there." She looked at him pityingly. "Don't mind, Alec, but she could not bear to see you just now."

He drew back in resentful pain.

"Do you too hate me because Harry loved me?"

"Oh, no," she said simply; "but mamma is too unhappy to think of any one else. You must pity her. Oh!"

The terrible sound of grief came up from below, and for a moment she clung to him, shivering, the big tears falling unheeded from her wide eyes.

"I will go. She shall not see me again," he said brokenly.

"Only for a little while—a few hours," pleaded Dorothy, touched by his face.

But he knew it was forever.

He went back to the room and hastily gathered up a few things that spoke to him of Harry, took a hard though mute farewell of the dumb friends it held, and then went softly down the silent hall. At the door below he lingered for a moment with the same feeling of sorrowful resentment that he should be shut out, but the hush that had fallen on the house awed him with its eloquent demand for sympathy. Without seeing any one he went quietly away in the early twilight.

So he left the house to which Harry had brought him, while Harry lay silent and let him go. And yet Harry went with him, in every thought that throbbed through his brain, in every crushed sob that held his heart still. His friend had become a part of himself, and never, while he lived, could he lose that sense of Harry's share in his life.

CHAPTER V.

MACDONALD went directly to the office. The business part of the town was mostly deserted, and the long shadows of evening, resting quietly in places that ordinarily were strange to all thought of tranquillity, struck keenly on his nerves. It was all so different from what it had been! But everything must be different now.

As he entered the office, a man who had been waiting at his desk arose to meet him.

" Have you been waiting to see me? I am sorry that you were detained," began Alec; but the man smiled so cordially that it at once put all necessity for spoken apologies out of mind.

"Are you Vanborough & Co.?" he asked with a winning geniality.

" I am the Company, Alexander Macdonald."

"And I am William Andrews," said the stranger, putting a bit of cardboard on the table. "Perhaps you may remember we had some correspondence a few months ago."

"About business?" asked Alec tentatively, trying to force his dull thoughts back to the office routine, but finding no recollection of his visitor's name.

"A little investment. I sent on five thousand dollars, you know, but I was not quite satisfied with the security you proposed. I think I have now found what I want, and I believe I will withdraw the money. Of course, this will make no difference in your commissions."

"I think your correspondence must have been with Mr. Vanborough," said Alec, finding himself entirely at sea as regarded the subject. "If you can come in to-morrow, I will have looked the matter up."

"Very well. Will ten o'clock be too early? I am only passing through the town, and shall not make a long stay."

"I will be here at ten."

"Shall I find your partner also? I am a sort of hereditary friend of his, and would like to see him for his father's sake."

"He—he died this afternoon."

The kind face grew quickly sympathetic.

"Died? Oh, I must stay over then, to see my old friend. This must have been a hard blow." Then something in Alec's face made him say, "Poor boy! poor boy!" and put his hand on the young man's shoulder with a frank sympathy that nearly broke down his self-control.

"It was—sudden," Alec began to explain, but he had to stop and set his teeth together.

"Never mind now," said Mr. Andrews, quickly. "It is hard, I know, but it is all right. Take my word for it if you can't see it yet. It is part of the whole, and the whole must be right."

There was something about the man that spoke, more clearly than his words could, of a serene strength born of experience. Alec felt it and yielded suddenly to the sense of rest that comes of dependence, even while he wondered at his own surrender.

"Would you rather postpone the business? Or shall I come at ten, as we said?"

Macdonald nodded silently.

"Very well, then. Good-night, my boy, and try to trust in the great matters as you do in the small ones."

His thin, gray face had the light of a benediction upon it as he beamed a fatherly cheer upon the young man who stood with bent head before him. Then he was gone, and Alec had been looking at the card he had left some minutes before he could see it clearly enough to make out that Mr. Andrews was Professor of Ancient History at the Addison University. He was accustomed to dealing with young men, then. That explained his quick comprehension.

To occupy himself he began to look up the records of the office concerning the loan. He had supposed his memory must be at fault, and that an examination of the books would set him right, but he found nothing. Puzzled and aroused he went over the ground again, and this time he discovered a letter from William Andrews, addressing Harry as his dear young friend, and indicating that he was inclined to throw some business in the way of the young firm for the sake of the name it bore. The letter was dated several months back, and there was nothing to show whether anything had come of it.

Alec had himself made nearly all the recent entries in the books, and he knew well enough that there was no unsettled deposit of five thousand dollars or any other amount in the hands of the firm But Harry had always relied more upon his own knowledge of his affairs than upon his system of book-keeping.

Falkland might possibly know about it, but for personal reasons he would make an appeal to him the last recourse. There was one place still to be examined— Harry's private desk. The papers there might throw some light on the matter.

The chair was pushed back as Harry had left it when he sprang up with his challenge for a walk. Alec rested his hand caressingly on the insensible wood, and for a moment forgot his task in the surging recollections that thronged over him. But it was too soon for him to dare admit thoughts of the too near past. His safety lay in occupation. But, as he fitted a master-key into the desk, it struck him that, though nominally Vanborough's partner, his position was really that of a clerk. The delay in legalizing the partnership must shut him out of all voice in the business, now that Harry was not here to speak. Well, there would be no regrets on that score. It was a more important matter that he should know how to meet Prof. Andrews on the morrow. He shut the desk, and, putting his pride in his pocket, went out to hunt Falkland.

The streets were bright, and busy with passing throngs of people. As Alec pressed in among them he had a curious feeling of strangeness, as though the day that was past had set him apart from the careless crowd. What was the meaning of these hieroglyphic faces, unconscious even that they bore a message? Men passed so near that the garments they wore brushed his hands, yet they were so far that he could not hear a thought. Often Harry and he had wandered thus, questioning, with the far-reaching guesses of youth, where reality might lie. Had his friend found it now, in one step? Instinctively he looked upward to where the stars beamed their serene message down to his troubled eyes. Harry! Harry!

Two men passed close by him, and their voices cut in sharply across his exalted mood.

" It is this spirit of speculation that is ruining some of our finest young men. How can we expect normal and healthy thought when they are in a moral fever?"

It was Prof. Andrews' fine voice, and Alec drew back with an instinctive wish to avoid recognition.

It was late when he reached Falkland's house, and his first summons was unheeded. Necessity made him persistent, and after rapping repeatedly the door was flung suddenly and impatiently open, and a handsome young woman looked out at him with an inhospitable look of inquiry in her unsmiling eyes. Alec knew Falkland's wife by sight, and had thought of her merely as a pretty piece of humanity; but to-night, with her drooping lips and a light like slow fire in her eyes, she was something more.

"Is your husband at home, Mrs. Falkland?"

"No."

"Can you tell me when he will be?"

"No!"

"Do you know where he is? I want to see him on business, and I must see him to-night, if possible," he persisted.

"Why do you come to me? How should I know? I am only his wife."

She flung the words at him with a volcanic bitterness that startled Alec out of his self-absorption.

"I dare say I shall find him down town. He must be busy, of course, the first day of his return. I

am sorry to have brought you out so late," he stammered hastily, after a quick look at her.   One may
wish to comfort all afflicted, but what is there to be
said to a defiant and indignant wife, even if there be
traces of tears on her flushed face?   She would probably resent a sympathy which betrayed that any one
but herself had forgotten that wifehood must stand
before womanhood.   Yet Macdonald lingered.

"What is this little fellow's name?" he asked,
stooping to pull forward a handsome little boy of three
or four years, who was clinging to his mother's skirts.

"Can't you tell your name, Louis?   He knows it
well enough, only he has taken it into his head to be
shy."   She patted the rebellious head, nevertheless,
and her face had softened so encouragingly that Alec
felt relieved.   The childish fingers would be the safest
guide to hold her steady, and it was of no conse-
quence, comparatively, if she ruined the baby's consti-
tution by keeping him up till ten o'clock.

"The sand-man is waiting for you, young man.
—Good-night, madam.   I think I know where to find
Mr. Falkland."

But all the way down the street the woman's face
kept coming before him.   Truly, one need not go far
to hunt for tragedy.   It seemed to be the warp of
every life, and none could think to shrink into obscurity and be safe.   Such a look in a wife's face was an
arraignment of the husband.   Of course, it might be
merely a trick of muscles and coloring.   Actresses
knew a way to get it without breaking their hearts.
But the doubt did not soften his feeling toward Falkland as he hurried back to the rendezvous where he
expected to find him.

This was a sort of club, maintained by Falkland and his fellows, which met in a dingy but jovial room over a saloon. Harry had taken him to it once or twice, and Alec remembered well how his protests had been laughed at.

"Nonsense, my dear Sir Galahad! One must know all sorts of people to be a man of the world. Can't I share their foaming lager, and tell them a story that will make them laugh, without dimming the princely luster you will insist on folding about me? The truth is, Alec, you are of too stern a stuff to do Falkland justice. He isn't your kind, but he is a genius in his way."

When he pushed through the green door of torn baize that opened into the club-room at the top of the dark stairs, Falkland was sitting at the head of a long table, telling a gay story. Several of the members nodded and beckoned through the smoke-laden air, as Macdonald hesitated on the threshold, but Falkland did not pause, or even turn his head. This was his castle. Alec came forward, and, declining the chairs that were silently pushed forward, waited for a pause.

"I want to speak to you about the business, Falkland."

The story-teller stopped at last, having reached his climax. He was a slight, dark man, with a noticeable alertness in face and manner. He was older than Alec by some years, and more than years shrewder, yet there were few lines in his face. It had a smoothness of contour that might have belonged to those fabled beings who knew neither youth nor age, because they had no soul.

"A speech!" he cried, turning to his visitor with charming gayety. "Will you favor the Sworn Brothers with an address?"

"I want to see you alone for a moment."

"Oh, we have no secrets here; not even passwords."

"You haven't heard—there was an accident this afternoon—"

"To our friend Van? Yes, I know. I was just telling one of his famous stories." He looked up with an air of exaggerated *naïveté* into Macdonald's stern face. He expected to shock his loftiness, and excitement in some degree was the breath of life to him. But, in the moment of silence that followed, Alec was only conscious that his old-time jealousy was dead forever.

"It wasn't of that I came to speak," he said briefly. "There was a man at the office this evening—a Professor Andrews. Do you know what business dealings we have had with him?"

Falkland had started with the uncontrollable surprise of a nervous temperament. The dark, sensitive face seemed to have grown suddenly thin.

"The very dickens! What did he want?"

Alec glanced at the others in the room, and Falkland turned to his companions with a laconic—

"That's all, boys. Good-night to you."

"Oh, come, now! We aren't going to be shut off in this way," protested some of the men.

"You'll be shut in, then. I'm going myself," retorted Falkland.

They laughed and grumbled, but did not offer to disobey the hint. For all his lightness, he was the spirit that moved the body of the club. When the room was cleared he closed the door and came back.

"What did he want?"

"Prof. Andrews?"

"Yes."

"He spoke of some money he sent us to invest. He wants to withdraw it."

"Ah, really?"

"What do you know about the matter?"

Falkland sat down on the arm of a chair and swung one foot meditatively.

"Why do you come to me? You ought to know more than I do about it," he said, innocently.

"Before you went away, and before I had a share in the business, you were really Vanborough's confidential clerk. For that reason I thought you might know something about an old matter like this. If you don't, all right."

"Well, perhaps I do. I'm not saying I don't. But, I say, did it ever strike you that Van had a great knack for getting out of the disagreeables? Dying to-day instead of to-morrow, for instance."

"If you wouldn't mind being intelligible," said Alec, with ferocious politeness.

"This fellow from the East—from some college, isn't he?"

"Yes."

"Well, he knows as much about business as I do about the people in Saturn. It is against nature not to follow up such a chance."

"Well?" said Alec, impatiently.

"He sent the money all right enough. I remember making the deposit at the bank that day. And I remember that by a mistake the bank put the amount —five thousand dollars, wasn't it?—to Van's personal credit, instead of to Vanborough & Co. I had both books with me. But it made no difference, for the Co. didn't mean anything, you know."

"Well?"

"You refuse to imagine? Very well, then. Suppose—I'm not saying it was so, of course—suppose Van needed five thousand dollars. And suppose— just a guess, you know—that that wise fool from the East insisted on having his money lie idle because he wasn't satisfied with investments offered. I wasn't in Van's secrets. I wasn't going to be a partner. But I happen to know that as a heavy stockholder in the Panesco Mine he *was* called on for five thousand dollars a week ago. The last assessment. He said at first that the witch of Endor couldn't raise another red on his property. By-the-way, I suppose you know he was in the Panesco pretty deep?"

Alec nodded. He had no words.

"Nothing that went down that shaft was ever heard of again, and I guess he had put in pretty much everything. Then the last call for money came. Things were blue, but it seemed that luck must turn if the money could be found. He said at first he couldn't send another cent, but—he did. Five thousand dollars. You understand?"

"No, I don't understand," said Alec, slowly. "You say, or seem to say, that Vanborough used for himself the money intrusted to him for investment. That is what you say. Now, what do you mean?"

"I mean just that."

There was silence for a moment, while the words

made their way to Alec's brain.   The next moment a
hand was on Falkland's throat, shaking him as a dog
shakes a rat, and Alec's face glared down on him in
black rage.

"Liar!   How dare you?"

"I say, Macdonald!   Hang it all!" gasped the
smaller man, in angry astonishment, wrenching himself free.

Macdonald let him go, and stood back, breathing
hard.

"What do you mean by such a lie?"

"You've a pleasant way of questioning!"

"See here, Falkland, I apologize.   I was out of my
head—anything you like."

"You might at least take a fellow of your own
size," muttered Falkland, still eyeing him with surprised distrust and something of personal fear in his
look.

"Tell me all you know about this matter."

Falkland hesitated between anger and trepidation,
but he answered sullenly :

"I have.   At least I've told you enough.   You can
find out the rest by examining the books.   You will
find that he was ruined, or I am much mistaken."

Alec sat down by the table.   In truth, he could
hardly stand for the strange trembling of his limbs.

"Strange he didn't tell you about it, such cronies
as you were.   But I suppose you kept him up to such
a strain with your virtuous ideas that it was a relief to
him to come down to another level occasionally."

Alec looked up with fierce impatience.

"Never mind your theories.   Will you be at the
office to-morrow?"

Falkland laughed shortly.

"What for? The business is closed, I suppose. Neither you nor I have any place there now. Besides, I leave town to-night."

Macdonald seemed not to have heard him, but after a moment he aroused himself and repeated:

"To-night? But you may be wanted—"

"I'll be wanted, then. I have some matters of my own to attend to and some people to—keep clear of. I can't leave my address, even with you."

"Prof. Andrews is to come to-morrow."

"You can refer him to the executors. Lucky for you that you weren't quite a partner, eh?"

Alec buried his face in his hands and groaned. His companion watched him from under his eyelids, and then winked at the kerosene lamp swinging dingily overhead. That's what came of being so precious virtuous.

"When do you go?" asked Alec at last.

"As soon as you will permit me to lock the door."

He rose heavily and walked out.

"Better take your hat," suggested Falkland.

He went back for it mechanically, and then stumbled slowly down the dark stairs.

Falkland stood in the street watching him for a moment with a look of elfish enjoyment. Then he scowled and felt of his neck. Then he struck off toward the railroad station, whistling one of Harry's tunes.

———

CHAPTER VI.

Lied is a rough phrase ; say he fell from truth
In climbing toward it.
                                        BROWNING.

MACDONALD walked steadily back to the office and
without hesitation opened the locked desk. His face
had the set look of a man who has nerved himself to
meet an expected blow, but unconsciously to himself
he tried to evade the moment of fatal certainty. Now
that the papers were open to his hand he dallied with
his task. He noted, and immediately forgot, the arrangement of the various objects on the desk, he han-
dled the æsthetic trifles Harry had loved to collect, he
read with elaborate care long letters and memoranda
which he knew had no bearing on his search. When
finally he took up the memorandum book, which he
had known from the first would tell the story, he tried
to make himself believe it was nothing of moment,
and as he read the entries he was watching, not for
the truth, but for any loop-hole by which he might
escape the conviction forced upon him. He fought
the idea of dishonor as he would have fought a man
who stood with lying tongue over Harry's grave.

But it was not a long search. There had been no
attempt at concealment. The memoranda were simply Harry's private notes, made with no thought that
they would ever come to any eye but his own. It was
clear that he had speculated almost from the beginning. At first he had been successful. The little in-
terjections between the business records were boyishly
jubilant. Then there had been failures. With the

5

gambler's fatal faith, he had doubled the next ventures, and sometimes he had lost and sometimes he had gained. Then came the Panesco Mine scheme. He had invested heavily at first, and upon additional calls for money he had withdrawn what he had out in other directions, until practically everything he possessed was in it. Then had come a call for five thousand dollars more. Things were beginning to look unpleasant, and ready money was imperatively demanded to save what had already been invested. He didn't have the five thousand dollars, but that amount, intrusted to his care by Prof. Andrews, was lying subject to his call in the bank. The sum was comparatively a small one—merely a drop in the bucket. The need was desperate, but of course only temporary. The money had been withdrawn, and Harry's assessment paid. Alec noted the date, and wondered whether it was on that day Harry had asked him speculatively whether he thought Portia could have saved the merchant if he had mortgaged his soul to Shylock instead of a pound of his flesh.

There were few more entries. The last one, made in pencil that morning, was simply:

" Fool ! "

Alec left the desk, and, throwing open a window, leaned out into the night. That Harry could have done this thing—that was the agony of his thought. If he himself had fallen before temptation, it would have surprised him less cruelly. But that he should lose the friend who had been the ideal of honor, that he must tear his image from his heart and walk evermore desolate and bereft even of the memory of the past, crushed him. For the sake of the Harry he had loved he was hard on the Harry who had sinned. He could have struck Falkland to the ground for calling his friend false. What could he do but strike that friend from his heart for being false? His misery made him hard. In the bitterness of his soul he smiled to himself that he should have mourned when kneeling by the dead under the trees.

Yet Harry had never meant to wrong any one. He had dared to take the money because to his warm imagination failure had been out of the question. Success was certain, and success meant honesty. Failure—did that mean dishonesty, when failure or success did not depend on him? For his part, he would have much preferred to be successful. Alec heard the bantering logic as plainly as though the handsome, willful fellow had stood beside him in the old nonchalant fashion.

At last, for very weariness, he turned from the present and let his thought dwell upon those years which lay safe beyond the touch of desecration in the past. Then, while judgment was silent, memory brought back one after another the familiar traits of his friend, and pleaded for the love that had been. Forgotten incidents came back uncalled—a look, a tone, a motion of the hand. When had he ever been cold to judge or slow to help? When, since the day he had taken the unfriended farmer boy to his home, had he ever stopped to weigh and measure the claims of friendship? In all things he was a royal giver, and he trebled the value of his gift by the grace of his giving.

Ay, Harry was dead, and could say no word in his own defense, but as his friend, with bent head, listened to the pleading of his own heart every fiber of his soul stirred with eager desire to side with the dead against himself. The bonds the past had woven were woven forever, and fainter than threads of gossamer though they were, all else was weak if tried against them. After a last, faint struggle he bent his head low, and as his eyes grew dim with tears he saw clearly, as never before, all that his friend had been and what he had lacked.　.

He had been blinded by dreams. His pulses had beat too high with the fever of the times. Should a man be held responsible for the delirium of his sick fancies? Never, while in his right mind, could Harry Vanborough have done a dishonorable thing. Who could know that better than the man who had shared his high thoughts, his true ambitions? His very failure was but from excess of what in another direction would have been strength. The young eagle, who could fly into the heart of the sun undazzled, had always grandly disdained the limits of weaker wings. He had been too daring, and had fallen from the thin, cold heights, but let no buzzard dare peck at him.

So he made battle for his love in the gray hour, and in the dim dawn the real Harry came back to take the place of the idealized dead, and Alec's heart received him with a tenderness that had never been possible before. And it was now for all time. Doubt, once slain, never reawoke in his mind, for it was one of his characteristics to trust his decisions. From the moment he rested on the theory that Harry had been mentally and morally sick when he forgot his high principles, he felt that he could still love, still honor his friend. And he would still protect him. That thought was a necessary corollary of the first. The only question was how to do it.

He went back to the desk and carefully examined certain papers he had laid aside, among them a package of canceled checks just sent up by the bank. One of the latest of these was for five thousand dollars and payable to his own order. Harry had made the check to him as a matter of convenience, he remembered. He had gone to the bank for the money, but it was the senior partner who had afterward dispatched it to his Western correspondent. As he held the slip of paper in his fingers a sudden thought came to him. What if— Their writing was not dissimilar. He wrote Vanborough's name on a scrap of paper again and again until he produced a signature that might pass, if not closely scrutinized, for an autograph. Then he filled out and put Harry's name to a check, payable, like the model before him, to Alexander Macdonald. The cancellation stamp of the bank was easily imitated, and when he had finished the two torn checks were identical—except that one was a forgery. This he replaced with the others, and the original, with the memorandum book, he quietly burned. Falkland knew the truth, but he was away, and he would have no object in telling. In a few days at the most the business would be investigated and the fact disclosed that everything was gone. But those who had known Harry had always known him reckless. There should be no hint of dishonor—if he could help it.

Then he stretched himself out on the steamer chair which had been his extravagant partner's latest indulgence, folded Harry's office coat under his head, and

slept as quietly as did the friend who lay calm and
still in the hushed house of death.

It was late when he awoke to stare helplessly for a
few moments at his strange surroundings and to
wonder vaguely what the forgotten thing was that op-
pressed him with a consciousness of heavy pain. Then
in a flash all came back. He was to see Prof. Andrews, and when that was over he would have cut
free from all the past. Already he felt half a stranger
in the place, and the room which had been almost a
home held nothing but furniture, which looked mourn-
ful and forsaken.

Some hours were still before him, and drawn by an
irresistible longing he went to walk past the house
where Harry lay. It stood apart from its neighbors,
surrounded by a wide sweep of lawn, and in its darkened silence it seemed to have drawn itself aloof to
hide its sorrow from common sympathy. He looked
up at the windows of the room where he knew they
had laid him, and a quick resentment stirred within
him that they should be darkened too. Why was the
clear sunlight to be shut out from him who had lived in
it as in his own element ? Even as the thought crossed
his mind, the blind was softly opened and Dorothy
stood within, revealed in the pure, cool light of the
morning. Alec, watching unseen from under the elms,
bared his head, and the peace he had been struggling
for came unsought upon him.

As he turned away with a mute farewell an old
man, with feeble step and down-bent eyes, came slowly
toward him. The yellow leaves on the walk rustled
dismally about his feet, and he leaned heavily on his
stick. It was not until close beside him that Alec

recognized Mr. Vanborough. He had always stood somewhat in awe of the keen, polished, invulnerable old gentleman who had seemed to treat the world as a fair pageant spread for his indifferent heed, but now in the wan face and broken gait he saw only the common, stricken humanity, and a yearning to give and ask comfort leaped to his face. But with unseeing eyes the father passed slowly by, and the melancholy leaves settled down upon the walk.

At the appointed time Prof. Andrews appeared at the office. Alec had been waiting for his step for half an hour and had thought himself fully prepared, but as the fatal moment came a strange tremor shook him in spite of his steady will.

The professor gave him a friendly nod and a keen look.

"A pleasant morning," he said cheerfully, as if well content with what he had discovered.

Alec assented rather absently, while he pulled a chair forward.

"This is my first visit to your part of the country, and it keeps me busy looking about. You are very much alive out here."

"It is a necessary stage to be lived through, I suppose," said Alec abstractedly.

Prof. Andrews looked at him curiously. This grave-faced young man hardly seemed to fit into the sectional type. Alec, on the other hand, was studying his visitor with even greater interest. If one might judge from the index of his delicate features, he was a kindly man, sincere, guileless, better versed in the ways of truth than of what is called the world. Not a business man; that was well.

"Prof. Andrews, may I take a few minutes of your time before we speak of your business?" The sound of his own voice gave him steadiness, and he added, "I have a story to tell—and a confession to make."

"Ah?"

There was a note of disappointment as well as surprise in the word that hurt Alec. He would have liked this man's good opinion. A letter-knife which he had seen in Harry's hands the day before lay on the mantel by which he stood. His fingers closed over it, and in a moment the first shiver of dread had passed. He thought no more of himself, but only how he might make the man whose questioning eyes were regarding him believe the story he was going to tell and ask nothing he wished to keep back.

"A few months ago there was a boom in mining stocks. Men were making their fortunes by a turn of the hand. There was a fever in the air that made it hard to see things in their true relations. I am not trying to excuse—myself. I only want you to understand the situation."

"I understand." He was still watching Alec with that puzzled, disappointed look.

"To speculate one needs ready money. Can you understand how a young man might be tempted to use money not his own because he felt absolutely sure the speculation would succeed? But it failed."

"Didn't he think of that possibility?"

"A speculator never sees but one side in his dreams. The other comes afterward."

"You are speaking of yourself?" the professor asked gravely.

In the inappreciable moment that passed before he

bent his head in assent, Alec had time to recall how Harry had once asked ruefully : " Isn't there some mild, pale-colored fib you could tell, Alec, just to put you on a fellow's level, you know?"

" You left your money here without security," he went on. " It was so easy to think it could soon be replaced."

" I was to blame," murmured the professor uneasily. " I was to blame. But I did not know."

" Neither did I know," said Alec in a low tone.

" But the money—how did you get it? It was sent to Harry Vanborough, and surely — though I don't know much about business ways—it was not in your hands?"

Alec had hoped this question would not come, though he had foreseen its inevitableness. He pulled out the check he had prepared the night before and laid it on the table.

" That is a forgery."

Prof. Andrews looked aghast.

" A pity—a pity," he murmured under his breath, and his eyes were fixed on the young man, not on the scrap of paper.

" Vanborough had not seen that package. It came up from the bank after he had left the office for the last time."

" And he never knew ? You went right on—"

" If words could help what is done," interrupted Alec hastily, feeling that questions were dangerous, "things would not be as they are. But the past is fixed. I can't change it. My hope was that you would let me redeem it."

" To be sure," said the professor quickly, a light

breaking over his face. "That you can do, my
boy."

"Will you consider this a debt and let me pay it
in installments? I can secure you by a policy of life
insurance, so that you will be paid if I die, and if I
live I will pay you before I feel that I have any right
to my own future. Do you think you can trust to my
good faith?"

"That sounds fair," said the professor with an air
o great relief. "We all make mistakes, some in one
direction and some in another. But the best any of
us can do is to try to make them right, and that I believe you will."

"Make it right, Alec," Harry had said with his
latest breath.

"May I draw up the papers, then, to put it in
proper form?"

"Yes, do so."

There was a short silence, as Alec filled out the notes
to cover the debt. Prof. Andrews watched him closely, with eyes trained in such study, and with every moment he felt better content with his action. It would
all have been different if Macdonald had been dealing
with a man who would have thought more of the financial side of the question and less of the development
for good or evil of the human being whose fate was in
his hands. He had never seen this man before, was
never to meet him but once again, but this half-hour's
interview set the current of his whole life.

At last the papers were signed and delivered.

"That settles matters between you and me. Now,
for the rest, will you let me help you if I can? Let
me tell the story to Mr. Vanborough, who is an old

friend of mine, and get you as clear as possible of any entanglement on this account with the estate."

Alec looked up with unspeakable relief.

" I would thank you if I could."

The professor cleared his throat apologetically as he added, while gathering up his hat and gloves :

" I am not going to lecture or ask a pledge ; but you won't mind if I say I hope you will let that sort of business alone hereafter. I am an older man than you, and I can perhaps see more clearly than you, who are in the thick of the fight. Keep clear of chance."

" Do you think I can ever forget your trust, your generous kindness ? " replied Alec as earnestly as ever rescued sinner might have spoken.

" Oh, that's all right. We understand each other." He held out his hand, and Alec pressed it with a most real and sincere gratitude. Then he went away with a glad feeling in his heart that it was his money the reckless young fellow had meddled with.

" If it had been some one else's I am afraid he might have been goaded to get deeper and deeper into the wrong, for he has a strong face. Not a man easily driven, nor easily led. He must have the reins in his own hands, I suspect."

Which was truer than the good professor knew, for it never occurred to him, wise as he was, that the young man's stronger personality had so guided the conversation that he had carried away just the ideas Alec wished him to have and no others.

And Alec put Harry's letter-knife in his pocket, turned the key in the door, and set his face steadily to find a new place in the world.

Was it a mad thing to do? He did not think of playing the heroic. His friend had saved his life for him; could he not spread the poor mantle of his name to hide the one fault of the generous nature he had known as the world never could? What was it to him that men might call him a hard name and shrink from him? He was alone in the world; no heart would be saddened, no brow shamed by his disgrace. He had no other possession in the world than his truth. Might he not deal with it as he would? If this cloak would serve to keep out the wind that pierced his friend's doublet, must he still keep it to muffle his own hands, while he who had shared his heart with him went shivering out of the world?

Oh, it was all very fine and very extravagant, and there are many enough who could prove beyond a debatable point that the hot-headed fool who plays with such unusual tools as generosity and self-sacrifice will get hurt and be sorry for it in the end. Fortunate that there are cool logicians to keep the giddy earth straight on its path in a good, conservative fashion, instead of letting it run off among the planets; yet fortunate too that there are souls who do not live by syllogism and rule, but sometimes make grand mistakes that are worth more than a lifetime of the narrow precision which never blunders into a fine heroism. When they learn that the mistake is not a necessary part of the heroism it is all the better for them and for the world. But in the mean time let us not blame them too severely for failing to be wise in self-preservation. There are plenty of us, more's the pity, to keep the balance. When we see the universe in danger of going to pieces because of negative gravity or negative selfishness, then let us preach that no one shall do himself a wrong in order that he may do his friend a service.

CHAPTER VII.

MACDONALD'S plot was entirely successful. People are not so much given to inviting shame that the plea " Guilty, your honor," is often disregarded by the twelve good men and true who weigh the evidence. Who, save indeed the dead friend he was shielding, would have any reason to distrust his story? Certainly not that friend's father, especially since, in this case, judgment was biased by sentiment.

The story of Harry's generous self-sacrifice was of the kind that delights the public, and the jaded reporters, grateful for an incident that needed no making-up behind the scenes, did their prettiest for it in the way of refurbished adjectives. Eulogy and personal descriptions and reminiscences crowded the local press, and his friends, which meant practically the whole town, came forward publicly to add their tribute to the hero of the hour. Mrs. Vanborough read and wept over the paragraphs, and felt that she could never forgive the man who was living in Harry's stead, and though her husband protested faintly against this as feminine injustice, he himself had little love for the young man who had come so unnecessarily into their home and brought desolation with him. He meant to be just, rather because he owed that to himself as a Vanborough than because he owed it to

Macdonald as a man ; but it required an effort at the
best, and all the doors that had been so slightly barred
against dislike gave away once for all when he finally
heard the story which Professor Andrews had hoped
to soften in the telling.

"What is the matter, Wilfred ? " asked his wife,
when he came into the room, white and tremulous,
after shutting the door behind the departing peacemaker.

He stopped in the middle of the room and looked
at her in silence for a moment, as though his tightly
drawn lips would not relax into words.   Then—

" Damn the fellow ! "

It was an anathema rather than an oath, but Mrs.
Vanborough looked reproachful and Dorothy dismayed.

" Do you know what Andrews has been telling
me ? " he went on, his gray face more terrible in its
passion because of its habitual calm.   " Why, that he
is a scoundrel, that Macdonald, and that our boy's
life was given for a villain ! "

" What has he done, papa ? " asked Dorothy, clasp-
ing her fingers hard under her black needlework.

" Forged Harry's name for five thousand dollars.
Speculated with the stolen money and lost it."

" They will send him to prison, won't they ? " asked
Mrs. Vanborough sharply.

" If it had been any one but Andrews he would,
and there would have been a disgraceful scandal, with
Harry not yet—" He choked for a moment.   " It
was Andrews's money.   Harry only held it in trust.
For our sake he will keep it quiet, and he has made
some arrangement with Macdonald to let him pay it

off. But even as it is, look here." And he spread out a crumpled sheet whereon some imaginative mind, working on a few indiscreet remarks of the professor, had made a sensational paragraph in which names were indicated by initials and mysterious hints given of what the all-knowing reporter for the present withheld.

"But will he get off? Will nothing be done to him?" asked Mrs. Vanborough with tearful anger.

"What can we do? Everybody knows how Harry trusted him. Do we want them to know that he was tricked and befooled by a common thief? Our hands are tied. But may God deal with him as he has dealt with us!"

And Dorothy, carrying the paper to her room, read every word of the cruel paragraph, and blotted the false print with her true tears for the friend she had lost. On her dressing-table stood a photograph of the two boys, taken on one card some years before. Now she carefully cut the traitor's face away and dropped the poor little bit of pasteboard into the fire. And Harry's face she hid away because the blank made her remember that other.

Macdonald saw that paragraph, too, but he was in too strained a state of mind to feel the prick. He read it carefully and calmly, as a physician might take note of his own symptoms during an experiment on himself with some new poison. It worked well, and he threw the paper aside as serenely as though he had never, by his evil deeds, helped a newsboy to earn an extra nickle from a crime-loving populace.

But his new stoicism was tried when he presently heard that the Vanboroughs were about to leave the

place.   He had not reckoned upon that.   In his
thought he had unconsciously dwelt upon that time in
the future when he could know that his old friends
had been rewon.   Not at once, of course.   Not while
the bitterness of their condemnation was fresh.   But
surely in time character must have its weight.   He had
not thought of their leaving him and making this the
end.   Without giving himself time for second thoughts
he went to bid his former friends farewell.

It was with a curious feeling of isolation that he
rang—as any stranger might—at the house which, for
three years, had been his home.   A new servant asked
his name, and gave him in return for it a look of astonishment that made him tingle.   As he stood waiting in the familiar room, he began to wonder what he
could say now that he was here, and the impulse that
had carried him beyond his judgment looked childish
and inconsequent.   The stand he had taken admitted
of no half-measures.

A step on the stair made him start.   It was only
the servant with a message that Mrs. Vanborough
begged to be excused.

" And Miss Dorothy ? " asked Macdonald, promptly
forgetting his wise reflections a minute old.

" She begs to be excused," repeated the stiff official.

As he walked across the lawn, feeling a little dazed,
he met Mr. Vanborough, leaning on a stouter stick
than the one he had swung in Harry's time and with
his proud, white head a little lower.   The old gentleman calmly met his eager gaze, and then passed slowly
by without sign of recognition.   So, he no longer existed for those who had treated him as one of themselves.   He sternly told himself that was well and fit-

ting, and that henceforth and forever he had no share in the common joys of existence. The blood of youth beats too fiercely to be tuned to the placid rhythm of common sense, and Macdonald had spent too many years in a dreamland to be much more than a boy yet in the world of men and women.

The next day he chanced to see Dorothy Vanborough on the street. The undisguised sadness of a face that he had never known anything but contented struck him with a sudden shock of pain and made him forget everything but the necessity of speaking to her. He crossed the street to follow her into the public library, but at the door he faltered, and then walked slowly by. What was the use of trying to hold fast what was gone? What was there that he could say? Better let things rest as they were and as Fate had thrown them. He put these arguments to himself so convincingly that when he reached the end of the block he turned, with an obstinate look about the mouth, and walked straight back to the library.

Dorothy was sitting by a table in a deserted corner of the reading-room, and there was no one near enough to hear if he stopped, in passing, to say a word of greeting.

"I hear you are going away, Dorothy," he said at once.

"Yes," she answered. Her natural manner told him that she at least had no quarrel with him.

"Soon?"

"Very soon. In a day or two."

"Do you wish to go?"

"Oh, I don't wish for anything now," she said with wistful dreariness.

6

"Are you ever coming back?"

"No, I think not. Mamma could not bear to live here and see every thing the same, as though it made no difference whether Harry lived or not."

The quiver in her voice made him tremble.

"I would like—" Then he stopped. Was he mad enough to forget that he of all the world might not dare to offer her sympathy? "I wanted—I could not see you—I wanted to at least say—good-by," he finished incoherently, and turned to go.

"Alec!"

He turned back quickly.

"Is it true?" she whispered.

He met her appealing look steadily for a moment, neither assent nor denial in his face. Then his eyes fell before hers and a crimson flush swept over his cheek.

"Good-by," he murmured, and turned swiftly away.

A few days later he heard that the family was gone.

Then a new phase of life began for him. The debt he had assumed gave him something tangible to work for, which was fortunate. That must be paid before he could spend any thought on himself, and he bent his energies to the task so fiercely that if the sky had fallen about him at that time he would hardly have stopped to brush the blue fragments out of his way before he pushed on.

An old journalistic ambition opened a practical way, and he found a place among the purveyors of news to the public. There was plenty of hard work in it, and, what was even better, a chance to study

one of the classics with which he had as yet but a superficial acquaintance—humanity. He was in no im-
mediate danger of the Midas touch, but as time went
on he began to see a way out of his financial perplexi-
ties. He was no genius, but he was clear-headed, industrious, and terribly persistent, and before many
years the working qualities of these prosaic virtues
began to tell. He conquered a place for himself
among his fellows, and in the struggle the boy, with
his nebulous dreams and crude capabilities, was
changed, unconsciously to himself, into a self-reliant
man with trained powers.

For a time he caught anxiously at any news of the
Vanboroughs, but people ceased to speak of them before long, and amid the new interests demanding his
attention the old gradually faded into the softened
shades that pressed memories take on. Then, one
day, he saw a notice of Mrs. Vanborough's death.
" Heart-failure," the paper said, but Alec knew well
that it was the bullet aimed at him that far October
day that had carried off the life of the mother with
that of the son. It made him a little graver and sad-
der, but then he had never been anything but grave of
late. Then some years went by, and he heard nothing.
The shifting population of a Western town brought in
new faces and carried away the old, and people would
laugh at any attempt to recall matters buried under
the dust of half a dozen years. There were few of
Macdonald's associates who knew anything of his
early life, and those who remembered vaguely some
rumor of a youthful indiscretion felt that he had lived
it down and earned a new right to confidence.

He paid off the last of the debt, and then, for the

first time since that fatal October day, he walked out to the glade by the lake where Harry in dying had charged him to right his wrong. The leaves rustled softly about him and the same blue sky bent over, and in some mysterious fashion he came to know one of the world's secrets, which is that he who presses on to the inmost heart of sorrow will find there naught but peace.

Then he felt free, and began to consider what use the world could make of this - instrument which the years had been grinding. His newspaper work had led him to form some defined ideas on the right and wrong kinds of journalism, and so eventually he decided to start a paper himself on rather lofty standards. For a time he had some difficulty in striking a balance between the standards and the monthly bills, but his name was beginning to have a certain weight in local matters, and the town was rather proud of the *Dial*, even if it did listen more zealously to the *Key-Hole*.

One day one of those new friends who had no memory for the past, asked him casually if he had happened to know a Harry Vanborough, who had lived in the town in such a year.

Yes, he had known him. The name had for so long been spoken only in the silence of his own thoughts that to hear it now on the lips of another made his pulse beat strangely.

"He died here, perhaps you know," his friend went on. "Broke the family up completely. The mother really died of the shock, and now the father has gone too."

"Mr. Vanborough? He too?"

" Oh, not from that exactly. That must have been some ten years ago. But it shows how a family breaks up when it once begins."

"And the sister?" asked Macdonald, as memory came flooding in.

"Oh, I suppose she is married, or living with the older brother. A stiff old cove; cool and polished and hard as a glacier. I hope it is a husband."

Yes, it probably was a husband, Alec thought, as he remembered the shy girl who had always seemed so fair to him.

" There is a cousin of the family newly come to town—Richard Ellis. Come around and be presented. The wife is worth knowing."

Alec went, and found the cousin to be a quiet man of business, without a trace of the brilliance which he had somehow associated with all of the Vanborough blood. He greeted Alec cordially, but the warmth was more due to the last editorial in the *Dial* than to any family reminiscences. After Macdonald forgot to think of him as Harry's cousin, he came to like the man for his own unpretentious qualities, and an undemonstrative good feeling was established between them. The wife was gay and pretty and friendly, and Alec had so long been a stranger to the home-world that he found the welcome they gave him to their fireside very pleasant.

" Richard, was Mr. Macdonald ever in love?" asked Mrs. Ellis, after a meditative silence, one evening.

" I'm sure I don't know."

"Ask him to-morrow, won't you?" suggested Ralph Wendel, a young man who had the honor of being Mrs. Ellis's brother.

"Oh, I don't see exactly how I could," demurred Mr. Ellis, looking up in some perplexity from his paper.

"It is fortunate for your family's bread and butter that you never tried the newspaper business yourself, for you haven't an atom of imagination, Richard, my dear," calmly remarked his wife. "You needn't mind Ralph's suggestion. I will find out for myself, and Mr. Macdonald will never even suspect it."

"And then?" queried Ralph, with a look of indolent amusement.

"Then I shall try to find the proper sort of a heroine for him. And what is more, I shall probably succeed."

"And do you count on my standing by and giving no sign of warning?"

"Oh, it is all very well for you to make fun, but I consider that I am engaged in a benevolent and educational work. That is what he needs next."

"Benevolence and education?"

"Happiness. Don't you see it? Of course Richard doesn't notice such things—he doesn't even hear what I am saying now—but I supposed that you, by virtue of your relationship to me, would have more discernment."

"I have sinned!"

"But you can redeem yourself." She looked at him, hesitating. Then she added, with a great show of frankness: "For instance, by not falling in love yourself with Blanche Horsford, if she should happen to come to Hawthorne."

"Upon my word, Nellie, if I hadn't been your

younger brother so long, that would be just about
enough to give you a sister-in-law."

" But having been my younger brother so long—"

" I know when it is prudent to obey. Yes,
madam."

" Then you will be rewarded by sharing with me
the satisfaction of knowing that you have helped on
the soul development of a human being. What is it
your Browning says ? "

" That match-makers are responsible for all the
misery that haunts the human race."

" He doesn't ! "

" Eh ? Have you read Sordello ? "

" N-no."

" Then how do you know he doesn't ? "

" Don't look so absurdly triumphant or I will talk
to Richard. Are you going to help me ? "

Ralph stopped to arrange the sofa cushions more
comfortably under his lazy head, and then he looked
at her with a queer smile.

" Would it at all interfere with your little object
lesson to know that Macdonald is already engaged ? "

" And you never told me ! "

" Well, you see it is only just arranged and of
course I felt a little conscious about it," he simpered.

" What do you mean ? Who is it ? "

" Madam, 'tis I. Remember we are both young,
and temper your severity with mercy. I mean, of
course," he went on rapidly, to stem her wrath, " that
he has engaged me as co-publisher and I have engaged him as co-editor of the *Dial*. We are going to
make it the standard timepiece of our country's journalism. My money will be put to some use, and you

will have to find something besides my aimlessness for a subject, when you are trying to be more than a mother to me."

Mrs. Ellis had received, assorted, catalogued, and filed away the information before the last word left his lips.

" That is very satifactory," she said promptly. " I wouldn't flatter you if I could help it, my beloved Ralph, but the truth is that being in business with you will give him the guinea's stamp, so to speak, that unadorned merit does not always possess in Blanche's eyes."

The business prospered under the new alliance as prosaically as though there were no ulterior object just out of sight, and before long the old feud between idealistic leaders and realistic settlements had practically ceased.

So Alec Macdonald wove a long stretch of gray-colored duty into the web of his life, and pretty dull weaving he found it at times when he forgot, in the monotonous tossing of the shuttle, the pattern he had drawn for himself. But it was firm and strong, and the time came when he learned that but for that patient work he would never have earned the right to throw in the threads of gold that trace the fantastic design of happiness. And no other background so fitly sets off the gleam of the delicate tissue.

CHAPTER VIII.

"But you can't travel alone!"

"Oh, I think I can, Edward." There was a quiver of repressed eagerness in her soft voice. "I—I'm thirty-two years old, you know."

"That has nothing to do with it. You never have traveled alone, and I never wish you to. It is all very well for some, but not for you or Gertrude."

She leaned back in her chair and looked out of the car window with a restrained protest in her face.

"It isn't a long journey—less than three days," she said at last. "Richard or Ralph will meet me at Hawthorne. And what else can we do?"

Her brother frowned irresolutely and glanced from the inflowing stream of passengers to the watch he held in his hand.

"I can't imagine what keeps Mr. McConnell. If it were not simply impossible I would go on with you myself."

"Oh, no, no," she protested. Not that he would have paid any attention to her protest, or that she expected it. If Edward took it into that masterful head of his that it would be best for her to do or not to do a certain thing, it would not have occurred to either of them that her own opinion could have any bearing on the question.

"It is just possible that he is on the train and has not found us yet, though I gave him the name of the car. In that case he will find you after the car starts."

"But I should not know him."

"Why, yes, you will. You met him last summer."

"I don't remember him at all."

"Oh, you must. Have you your ticket safe?"

"Yes. Edward, was he that little man who talked so much about Egyptian monuments?"

"No, no. How absurd! I wish you would try to remember people, Dorothy. It is one of the delicate forms of flattery that are a woman's peculiar business. There is nothing more lacking in tact than for you to show that you have forgotten a man's very existence."

Dorothy looked uncomfortable.

"You'd better see if you can find him, then, for I am morally certain I shall not recognize him," she said desperately.

"Yes, you will, when you see him. He will find you, so it will be all easy for you. Still, I'm not sure but what it would be best for you to wait over a day, and perhaps I can arrange to go on with you."

"Oh, no, Edward. That would really be too child-ish," she urged with unusual self-assertion.

A warning whistle from the engine told them that there was no time for discussion.

"Well—if it must be; but I don't like it. Good-by, Dollie. Take care of yourself. Don't go out on the platform. Here's your bag and book. Do you feel a draught? Don't let anybody talk to you. Good-by."

He pulled a shawl, which she didn't want, about her shoulders, gave her a fraternal kiss which made her glance with nervous deprecation at her fellow-passengers, and hurried away. She saw an inter-change of ideas and coin pass between him and the porter, and then he swung himself off. The train be-

gan to move slowly, and she held her breath, almost
afraid for a moment to let herself realize that she was
going to be alone and free, lest the strange fact should
wither under too scrutinizing a thought. There was
something dazzling about the idea of independence.
Edward always seemed to think that she would not
know how—

"Dollie!"

He was on the platform under her window.

"It is all right. Mr. McConnell is on board and
will find you. Telegraph me when you get to Hawthorne. Here's the message. Be careful—"

She lost the rest as the train pulled away, but he
had thrust in a yellow telegraphic blank with a message addressed to himself and signed with her name
already written out. How like his thoughtful self!
She felt a little remorseful that she should be so glad
to escape from his care, but at the same time she resolved that before the operator at Hawthorne trans-
formed that message into electricity, it should be
copied in her own hand. She would use his form of
words, so that his suspicions might not be aroused,
but she felt that the consistency of her new departure
demanded that she should write her dispatches herself.

Then she gave herself up to the enjoyment of the
moment. She was vividly conscious of every tree that
slipped past her, measuring the distance she had come
on her way to freedom. She felt the throbs of the
engine in sympathetic unison with the beating of her
own pulses. Why had Edward insisted on finding Mr.
McConnell? He would come prepared to take care
of her in the officious way people always assumed with

her, and which she found so tiresome. It was a thousand pities he had not missed the train. As this benevolent wish crossed her mind her eye was caught by a man who had just entered the car. His face struck her directly as one that she had seen before, and some instinct told her that this must be the mythical Mr. McConnell, but she was in a rebellious mood.

"I don't believe he knows me, and I certainly won't help him. Besides, I am not sure that it is he."

But this weak subterfuge was swept away, for some one said : " Hello, McConnell," and she saw the stranger stop to answer the greeting.

She improved the moment to give her prospective escort a swift scrutiny. She had certainly seen him before and talked with him, but where? Memory was silent. Yet Edward would require that she should at least pretend to some recollection of their past acquaintance. Had he been one of the railroad magnates Edward had given a dinner to, or was he one of the scientific delegation that had followed? People were always coming and going, but of course Gertrude was the hostess. Dorothy did not readily remember faces, and had rather shirked her responsibility, but now Nemesis faced her, for certainly perfection in the art of delicate flattery would require that she should know whether to turn the conversation upon stocks or stones.

Before she could decide he was coming on toward her. With a perverse impulse, she turned to the window and tilted the paper she held so as to hide her face until she heard him pass by and the door close. Then she laughed softly to herself. He must eventually give up the search, and she would be left to herself in spite of Edward.

Then with a sigh of content she settled down to think matters out in detail. Next summer Gertrude would be back from Florence, and Edward would arrange so that they could all go off somewhere together, as usual. It was the greatest good luck—that is—of course Gertrude and Edward were as nice as possible, but—yes, it *was* the greatest good luck that gave her this winter all to herself. It had never happened before ; it would probably never happen again. And while of course it was very sad that Nellie's mother should be so feeble, and very trying for Nellie to have to leave her home in order to be with her, yet the situation could be regarded with tempered distress since it enabled Dorothy to take care of Nellie's children and superintend her household and incidentally to be her own mistress and look out on the world as a free woman.

First and foremost, no one should call her Dollie. What had Richard called her in the old days ? Dot, Pet, Ditto, Mousie—it was to be hoped he had forgotten those names by this time, or made them over to Nellie and the children. They were as bad as Dollie for a woman grown, and never, for one instant, during all this winter, was she going to forget that she was thirty-two years old. She would take her cousins unaware and make a stand. She would assert herself. There would be no one to guess how Edward and Gertrude would have stared at that idea. She repeated her full name to herself—Dorothy. Dorothy Vanborough. It gave her a sense of dignity. So would she be known in Hawthorne. She was not going to be a nonentity. She would make herself felt. Mentally she practiced saying, with varying degrees of firmness; " I don't agree with you at all." " No, my dear Dick, I must say that I think you are mistaken." This assumption of a new personality gave her much the same sense of freedom that one finds at a fancy ball in a mask and domino.

Presently the train boy came by with his arms full of books, and marked Miss Dorothy for his own.

" Like to look at some books, ma'am ? "

" No, thank you. I have a book," she answered so gently that he at once deposited his burden on the vacant seat opposite and began to display his wares.

" Here's a new book by Haggard. Ever read any of his ? Awfully excitin'. He's one of them Anglomaniacs, you know."

" I don't care for it, thank you," she said, wondering what there could be about her that should make this infant pick her out as a devourer of " shilling shockers."

" Here's something you'll like, I know. It is just like you, pretty and sweet," ventured the handsome little fellow with a wheedling flattery that his experience had taught him would be laughed at and forgiven. He dived into the depths of his collection for " Rosebuds of Rhyme and Pansies of Poetry," and fairly thrust it into her hands. Dorothy really didn't know how people managed a refusal, and she had begun feeling helplessly in her bag for her purse, when she caught the eye of one of her fellow-passengers gravely regarding her over the edge of his paper. The inspiration of having an audience nerved her for an effort as it does a timid actor. Thrusting back her purse, she said with stern emphasis:

"I don't want them—please. Not any of them— thank you. Will you kindly take them all away?"

The youthful student of human nature gathered up his merchandise with an air of perplexed grief. It was only chagrin at his total misapprehension of the character of his victim, but Miss Dorothy's tender heart read a disappointment in it which made her patronize him when he brought around the salted almonds and sweet oranges to an extent that still further disturbed his preconceived notions of her mental bent and drove him, in sheer desperation, to bullying a meek old man in the next car who was innocently reading a religious weekly into buying a full set of Robert Ingersoll's tracts.

The landscape flashing past had begun to grow dim in the twilight before Dorothy gave another thought to her presumable escort. Perhaps it was because other trains of thought were exhausted that she began to have some remorseful twinges for the conscienceless way in which she had thrown him astray in his search. If he had as misty a recollection of her as she had of him, he must have had frequent occasion during the past few hours to wish himself a citizen of some land where friends with sisters were unknown. How many times had he brought down an indignant "Sir!" upon his devoted head in his futile attempts to discover the particularly lone damsel that Edward had committed to his care? She laughed to herself at the thought, but resolved that if he eventually appeared she would try to expiate her wickedness. As if to take her at her word the object of her thought at that moment re-entered the car.

There are faces that tell the story of the souls that live behind them to all the world, and there are faces one must study a lifetime if one would know the secret message of blessing or banning they bear. Dorothy was not a physiognomist, but with the sure instinct of a child she knew that the face before her was one she could trust absolutely and without question. One more learned might have noted the lines that tell of honest fighting and wondered that the square chin should be matched with so serene an eye. Dorothy only knew "past all doubting, truly," that the strength meant helpfulness and the quiet meant restfulness and that here was one who would never misunderstand. She turned toward him, and the remembrance of her Machiavelism of the afternoon brought the shadow of a penitent smile to her demure lips.

He stopped with a look of uncontrollable surprise.

"Miss Vanborough!"

"Were you looking for me, Mr. McConnell?" she asked, inviting him by a gesture to take the vacant seat before her.

"No," he answered after a moment's pause, during which he had still been regarding her with that look of unnecessary astonishment. "But I am very glad to have found you," he added, with a sudden flash of warmth over his face that amply confirmed his words.

"I hope my brother did not give you the idea that I am in the habit of falling off the platform or putting my head out of the window. I really am a well-behaved person as the world goes."

He smiled in answer, but looked so mystified that even Dorothy could not help noticing it.

"Didn't you see my brother just before we started ? "

" No."

She colored swiftly.

"I thought he had told you that I was on the train. He meant to ask you—to take care of me, I think," she said, with an embarrassed laugh.

"That was most certainly unnecessary," he answered promptly. "You must know how glad I am to be of the slightest service to you."

She smiled gratefully, with a quick return of her first confidence. Not all Edward's friends were so mindful of Edward's shy sister.

"It is one of his theories that a woman can't travel alone, and the only thing to be done with a theory like that is to keep it safe out of danger's way, you know. So he couldn't make up his mind to give me a fair chance to disprove it."

"You must allow me to be grateful that you will postpone its overthrowal till the next time," he answered lightly. Then with a certain hesitancy he added : "You have been living with your brother of late, then ? "

"Since my father's death," she answered. But the question seemed odd, since it must have been there that he had seen her.

"It is so long since I have heard. I have often wondered, but you had gone into another world, and I did not hope to ever find you."

It was Dorothy's turn to be mystified. Who was Mr. McConnell that he should take the tone of an old

7

friend when she had counted on a traveling companion only? Her treacherous memory must have involved her more deeply than she had suspected. It was clear her companion was taking a certain past intimacy for granted. When she spoke he seemed rather to watch her lips than to listen. He was undisguisedly absorbed in renewing some past of which she had no knowledge. With a dizzy feeling that she had gone beyond her depth, she tried to steer the conversation clear of personalities.

"Do you see that we are driving right into a snow-storm?"

"Yes." But he had hardly glanced at the window. His eyes were fixed on her face with an intentness that was almost embarrassing.

"Doesn't it seem reckless to tempt the anger of the king of this region?"

He smiled responsively.

"You are not afraid, I know."

"Do you think we will be snow-bound?"

"Oh, no. Delayed a few hours at the worst."

"Were you ever snow-bound?" she asked, astutely reflecting that if she could get him started on the track of personal reminiscences the conversation would take care of itself for at least half an hour, and in the mean time she might have a chance to recall her scattered memories. But he answered with disappointing brevity:

"Never."

She debated with herself for a brief moment as to the safest general topic. If she had dared she would have tried to shape some leading questions which might draw out what she wanted to know, but it was too dangerous to be risked. If she were to ask concerning the health of his family, the chances would be that he had none. If she inquired as to his wanderings since they last conversed, it would undoubtedly prove that his common life was matter of national information. Yet his next remark showed that it was equally unsafe to leave the conversation to him.

"You have changed very little. I could almost believe that all these years have been a dream."

He was regarding her with a frank directness that took her consent for granted. Dorothy smiled confusedly. How long had "all these years" been?

"Are you as much the Dorothy of old in everything else as in face and smile?"

"I don't know," she answered faintly. His use of her given name had made her catch her breath, yet she dared not resent it. Into what maze had Edward's counsel drawn her? The consequences of her innocent deceit were beginning to appall her.

"What have you been doing all this time?" he persisted, bending forward smilingly to look into her eyes.

"Since when?" she asked bravely.

"Since the day we said good-by."

"Oh, just living, I suppose," she answered helplessly.

' That is enough, beyond question. But I want to know all about it in detail. There is so much I would ask, so much I must tell! Not here or now, but soon. I thought you had gone out of my life, but when you look at me in the old way I am ready to think everything else has gone instead. Do you believe in fate?"

He was speaking in a low, rapid tone, and though
there was no smile on his lip, it glowed just out of
sight, lighting a countenance that was naturally serious
with a radiance that betrayed a profound and tremulous happiness.   Dorothy had listened with an amazement that deepened every moment.   This was not the
tone of a man she might have met at a dinner party.
To add to her dismay, a growing sense of familiarity
was creeping over her, though without giving her any
clew to her companion's identity.   The poise of the
head bent toward her, the direct gaze, the curve of the
lip trembling on the edge of a smile, were coming back
to her from some dim-grown memory as the tints and
lines of an old painting wake into renewed life under
the restorer's sponge.   Her playful assumption of recognition had seemed at most a joke, while Mr. McConnell was still an imaginary being.   Now that the color-
less figure was replaced by this distinct personality,
she felt that she was simply drifting at the mercy of
the waves upon which she had rashly ventured.

"Do you believe in Fate?" he was asking.

"Yes," she said, glad to keep the talk off of personal snags if only for a moment.   "Being on this
train I believe that Fate will carry me to Hawthorne."

"In that Fate is kinder to me than her custom
has been.   How long do you stay?"

"It is uncertain," she answered, wondering if his
words could mean that by any chance he too was
bound for Hawthorne.   "I am going to a cousin
there."

"You will find the place much changed."

"Do you know Hawthorne?" she asked, forgetting
her *rôle* in her curiosity.

" I am still living there," he replied with an answering look of surprise.

Dorothy promptly acquitted her memory of any treachery here. She might have forgotten Mr. McConnell as an individual, but she certainly would not have forgotten any association with Hawthorne.

" It is thirteen years since you left the town. Do you think to find many of your old friends there now ? "

" No," she answered after a moment's calculation. How did he know so accurately what she had almost forgotten herself?

" There is no one but my cousin and his family that I shall know. I do not know whether you may have heard, but I had a brother once who died there, and that, and—and the loss of a friend at the same time have made my memories of the place rather sad ones. Have you lived there long, Mr. McConnell ? "

Her eyes had grown misty as she spoke of her brother, and to hide them she had talked on with lowered lids. She therefore missed the look of blank wonder that grew and deepened on her companion's face at her words, or the flash of comprehension that crossed it when she spoke his name. But she did wonder at his unresponsiveness, for it was not until she lifted her still dewy eyes that he spoke, and then evidently by an effort.

" I beg your pardon. Yes, I have lived there— longer than I knew."

The gladness had gone from his face as when a light is quenched in a window, and in its place had come the steady look of one trained to habitual self-restraint. Strangely enough, it seemed even more familiar to her in this phase than before, and she was struggling with her disorganized recollections when he arose and stood beside her.

"Pardon my thoughtlessness in talking so long. You must be tired. I will see you to-morrow, if you will permit me. Good-night."

"Good-night," she responded with gentle acquiescence.

The lamplight fell upon her uplifted face as she turned it smilingly toward him. In its simple confidence it was like the face of a child.

CHAPTER IX.

THE snowfall that had begun in the evening was still veiling the country when Miss Vanborough made an ineffectual attempt to look out on the world the next morning. The engine pushed steadily on into the white cloud, but it began to be a question whether the forces of Nature or machinery would triumph in their struggle for the time-table. The train men and a passenger in the corner who was absorbed in a pocket edition of Plato persisted in wearing an air of serenity that seemed like a challenge to Fate, but as the morning went by and they fell farther and farther behind the schedule, the majority of the passengers gave away to a frank impatience. Must they disarrange the programme of existence by dropping an entire morning on these prairies? Would not life stop, for all good purposes, until their desks knew them again? They might have been kings' messengers, each bearing a royal pardon to save his beloved from the scaffold at sundown, but they weren't. They were only Western business men.

As for Dorothy, the question of whether she would reach Hawthorne in time to see Nellie was entirely lost sight of in the nearer problem of what she should do with Mr. McConnell. She was almost inclined to throw herself upon his mercy and confess that she had not the faintest idea in the world who he was. It would be better to have it over with at once than to prolong the agony and increase the chances of blun-dering. Yet her courage failed her before that heroic course. He might be the most humble man alive, though he didn't look it, but even then he could hard-ly help feeling mortified by her avowal, more especially after her first tacit acceptance of his claims to remem-brance.

But the hours went by and Mr. McConnell did not appear. Certainly his guardian duties did not weigh heavily upon him. Dorothy was at first relieved, then surprised, then mildly resentful, and ended by assum-ing an attitude of lofty unconcern which would have crushed the offender if he had not been happily un-conscious of it. To emphasize her indifference she gave her attention to the tangled chatter of her fellow-passengers.

"Is there any chance of our making up the time we have lost, conductor?" some one was asking.

"I am afraid not," responded the suave official, with a look of soul-felt sympathy.

"There isn't any danger, is there?"

"Oh, no," drawled a tall Westerner, taking up the conversation. "Leastways, not unless a train should run up behind before we could signal her. And then there is a chance that she will bank up the snow ahead of her like a cushion and just push us in. That reminds me," he continued, posing his picturesque angularity on the edge of a seat, "I was in a train once that was blocked out West, when another train came tearing up after us. There was one man with us who had his wits about him pretty constant. Cool? There wasn't a refrigerator in use in his block. He saw that train coming and he knew that it would have to go over us or through us. What did he do but set all hands to shoveling snow on to the track at the rear end of our last car, and when the other train came along it just ran up the embankment and along the tops of our cars as neatly as you please."

"And what then?" queried a logical passenger.

"Well, you see he hadn't had time to make a slide at the other end, so when the top train came to the end of our train it naturally tumbled all in a heap. But you can't expect perfection the first time."

The small train boy was leaning against Miss Dorothy's chair listening to this veracious narration with chuckles of enjoyment.

"It isn't true, you know. He's only funning," he remarked *sotto voce*, fearful that the innocent lady's topographical ideas might be warped.

Whereupon Dorothy organized an impromptu Sunday-school class of one and tried to instill some moral precepts into the mind of her youthful friend. He listened with attentive gravity, and when the session was ended he sat down at a little distance where he could gaze upon her and ruminate. She thought he was laying the lesson to heart.

And still Mr. McConnell did not come.

Early in the afternoon they stopped at a little way-station to wait till an east-bound train should pass them. The railroad buildings on one side of the track were the only sign of man's presence in this white wilderness. On the other side there stretched an undulating region that might reach to the edge of the world for all visible boundary. Some twenty rods away on a little knoll was a grove of low trees, which in summer must have been a jubilant home of harmony, though one would scarce believe that there could now be any life in its black and white depths. An ambition to explore its secrets sprang up suddenly in Dorothy's mind. It was so wonderful, that wide, white space, so full of the freedom that she too was beginning to share. Self-repression had so long been an instinct that the possibility of putting her wish into action did not at first occur to her. But why not? Edward was not here to say her nay. Her new independence was not very steady on its feet, but it had wings, and with a dizzy sense of yielding to a delightful dissipation she hurriedly drew on her wraps.

Several of the passengers had already left the cars and were gathered on the waiting platform or in the station room. Dorothy did not care to encounter them and stepped off on the other side. As she did so some one called sharply :

" Miss Vanborough ! "

She stopped, and the next moment Mr. McConnell had swung her back to the steps and was holding her there while a train thundered by upon the side track on which she had stood.

" All safe now, I think," he said coolly the next moment, and leaping down he held out his hand. "Were you tempted to a wrestle with the elements?"

"It was so stupid in there, just waiting," she began, in a half-frightened sort of self-justification. "I thought I would try to reach those trees and see what the world is like outside. But—"

"That will be easy, if you don't mind a windy path. We can follow that ridge, which seems to be swept pretty clear of the loose snow." He came and walked beside her in a matter-of-fact way that made it the most natural proceeding in the world for ladies to be wandering alone into the deeps of snow-storms.

After a moment she looked up, still a little tremulous.

"I suppose that you really saved my life then."

"I would like to think so."

"It is strange that death and life may be so near together—only a few seconds between them. To think that instead of walking here I might have—"

"But you are walking here, you know," he interposed quietly.

"How am I to thank you?"

"By forgetting your danger. See, here is the trodden road. We get the force of the wind, but there is more snow in the air than under foot, and that is pleasanter on the whole. You don't want to give up your explorations?"

"No, no. I am glad I came. I feel as though I had never seen the winter before, this is so different."

"Are you thinking of the poor, bedraggled thing that loses its way in the streets of the town? It isn't half-cousin to the real winter."

Dorothy never forgot that entry into the north-land. It was a whirl of whiteness that enveloped her, and at times she could see nothing else. Then the bewildering maze resolved itself into a transparent mystery that hid the secrets of the winter's heart. The white veil swept about her in eddying folds, sometimes hiding, sometimes revealing the placid stretch of field and meadow taking their rest. The spirits of the air had come out of their invisible dwellings to frolic with the children of the earth. If a human eye caught sight of them straight they vanished, and nothing was to be seen save a wreath of wind-blown snow-flakes, and nothing might be heard but the delicate tinkle of snow-crystals, which sounded like the echo of an airy laugh. Through the trees ran white pathways, winding in and out and tempting one to follow, follow, till he should reach the land of marvel, to which they must surely lead. There was a soft murmur in the air, and the little branches shook down their burden with gentle rustlings. It was a place to wonder and delight in, and when something white, with long ears, hopped suddenly from under their very feet, Dorothy laughed like a child.

" Did you see it ? Do you suppose it came out to offer us the freedom of its city ? "

Looking up, she found her companion regarding her with the intent gaze she had seen in his eyes the night before. It was gone in a moment, and, with a return of his impersonal manner, he answered :

" It should have been more persevering, then, in its hospitality. I am afraid it was moved by no loftier motive than curiosity."

" It certainly can't be half as curious about me as

I am about it.   How do you suppose it lives among
the snow-drifts ? "

"Oh, I suppose one may grow to have a fond-
ness even for snow-drifts if one lives in them long
enough."

Something in his voice made her turn toward him
with a surprised look of questioning.

" Do you mean rabbits or people ? "

"Both."   But his smile was not tragic.   "Here
you get what view there is.   I am sorry there isn't
something picturesque to reward you for coming, but
this is the sort of country that the farmer appreciates
more than the tourist."

"Oh, I like it," she cried with unworn enthusiasm.
" It is so still.   I like the hush over everything.   There
isn't a trace of the busy summer life about now, is
there ? "

"It hides itself pretty well," he answered.   But he
was scrutinizing the low bushes back of them with a
practiced eye, and presently he pushed his way in
among them, knife in hand.

Dorothy watched him shaking the light snow off
the branches and trampling the powdery masses under
his feet, and she took time to congratulate herself surreptitiously on the placid relations that the morning
had established.   This was better than yesterday.
Then he had seemed to expect the welcome of a long-
lost brother—or cousin at least—and here he was dispassionately looking out for her and talking about
commonplaces in a manner that Edward might have
taken for a model.

Very soon he returned, bearing a winter trophy of
berries and fruit husks and lichen-covered bark that

had a gayer look, coming from the frozen woods, than ever roses wore in June.

"How did you know where to find them? I didn't see them. I never would have dreamed of suspecting them," she cried delightedly, examining the bunch with light touches.

> "I, country born and bred, know where to find
> Some blooms that make the season suit the mind,"

he quoted gayly. He was beginning to catch the infection of her mood.

"Country-born? That's valuable information as far as it goes," thought Dorothy.

"People, as a rule, don't know much about Nature in her rarer moods," he went on, making a screen of himself against the wind. "Nor of each other, for that matter. That sounds like sophomore philosophy, doesn't it? You know life is always useful to balance a simile in an undergraduate's essay. But did it ever occur to you how little we really know about each other?"

Dorothy might truthfully have replied that that reflection had indeed occupied some portion of her attention recently, but she was too much discomposed to answer except by an assenting glance. She felt herself hopelessly drifting to destruction. Perhaps he suspected her secret tribulation, for he looked down with a quiet laugh in his eyes.

"To use another sophomore simile, people are like the icebergs, of which our geographies tell us only one ninth is visible. We think we know a man, we can tell all his history and define his character and judge his actions, but after all it is only a fraction of the

man that we have seen. To estimate his true weight
we must remember the eight ninths below the surface."

"Of course," assented Dorothy cheerfully. Abstractions were eminently safe.

"I wonder if you will?"

"I am not sure that I would," she answered honestly. "I suppose I am as apt to judge by appearances as most people, if that is what you mean. What
else is there to judge by, in most cases?"

"But women should be charitable."

"Why more so than men?"

"I don't know. Because they have occasion to
exercise charity oftener, I suppose."

"Oh, if you stop my mouth with a compliment, of
course I will agree to anything you say. I generally
do," she added with a frank laugh.

"Do you? I used to think you usually had an
opinion of your own, though you kept it in reserve till
other people had worn theirs out by common use."

Dorothy cast a startled look at him.

"Don't you think it is time to go back?" she asked
irrelevantly.

"You are not cold?"

She shook her head with a smile and held out both
hands to catch the wary snow-sprites. Every look betrayed how keenly, how childishly happy she was. She
had reminded her brother of her thirty-two years, but
they had only given her the capacity for happiness,
without satisfying it. She had not worn out her emotions. They awoke and stirred their soft wings in her
breast at the call of this new liberty of hers, and lent
the glow of their joy to the new life that was beginning to seem real, and to this snow-storm into which

she had wandered, and to the friendly stranger who cared for her.

"Just as Edward might," she said to herself, and then, lest candor should force her to unsay it, she hurriedly thought of something else.

As they turned back the storm was practically over. The flurries of loose snow that the wind tossed in their faces came from the trees rather than from the sky. Before they had reached their waiting train the wind had dropped and there was a saucy composure over everything, as though Nature, having taken her position, were waiting to see what man's countermove would be.

"There comes the train we have been waiting for," said Dorothy's guide, as a distant whistle echoed clearly through the sharp air. "We shall soon be far enough from your little grove."

"I shall forget a thousand places before this," she answered, stopping for a last backward look. The wind caught a stray end of her scarf to flutter, and as she stood there with her tall, slender figure outlined against the white background she looked very girlish and eager, and very unmindful of eyes that might be watching. But when the east-bound train flashed by she shivered a little.

"I am glad it did not come in that way," she said in a low tone.

He did not answer except by a tightening lip.

As they entered the car they were greeted by the jaunty notes of a violin. A self-appointed committee on entertainment had discovered, their placard announced, a distinguished virtuoso who had consented to "weave a spell to fetter *ennui.*" Miss Dorothy's companion raised his eyebrows when he caught sight of the musician, and, instead of taking the vacant seat beside her when he had established her in her old place, he went back to the door and waited, listening.

The violinist was a small man, with a singularly delicate and mobile face. For the time being, at least, it might have been the face of some elemental spirit whose life was sound. As he drew the ransomed melody free from the violin which had held it captive his whole being seemed a part of the instrument he wielded. It was a mad, rushing, rollicking tune that he played, and his slender figure swayed in rhythmical harmony as he passed his bow with marvelous lightness over the strings. It had nothing to do with notes and keys It was a voice—the voice of some imprisoned thing that had more than human joy and merriment to express. His long hands seemed to hold a wand. The music came because a magician willed it, not from any mechanical vibration of wood and chord.

He finished with a flourish and dropped his violin to his side with a gay bow to the applauding audience. Dorothy, watching his face with something akin to awe, was conscious of a sudden chill. The rapt artist vanished and the thin face that had seemed to feed on diviner food turned from one to another in the crowd with a sharp expectancy that made her think irresistibly of an organ grinder's outstretched hat. It was applause, not coin, he wanted, but he wanted it with the same hungry eyes. His roving gaze fell upon her new friend, and Dorothy, still watching him, saw his sensitive features flush and shrink. Then with something of braggadocio in his air he made his way down the aisle.

"Well, Macdonald, how did you come to allow yourself to be snowed in like us short-sighted mortals? I supposed you had the elements under better control."

At the mention of his name Macdonald had glanced uneasily at Miss Vanborough, but she was too far away to catch the low-spoken words.

"It was an oversight," he answered. "Where do you come from ?"

"Last? Oh, really I don't remember. It is such a bore to keep a record of one's comings and goings that I gave it up long ago. Besides, it is safer."

"At least you are going to Hawthorne ?"

"Not that I know of. Why should I ?"

Macdonald did not answer except by a questioning look.

"Why should I ?" he repeated with smiling insistence.

"A wife and child might make a reason."

"Don't preach."

"I don't intend to, but I wish you would preach to yourself, old man."

"From your text, of course."

"From every man's text—home."

"What if it is only the ghost of a home? That's what mine is."

"Because you have killed it yourself, then."

The musician laughed.

"I shouldn't have given you that chance, should I ? At any rate, I have the good taste to prefer ghosts at a distance." Then, with a sudden irritability and an angry flash in his changing eyes, he went on. "If she wants me to stay home, why doesn't she make it

8

pleasanter when I am home, confound it? If a fellow hasn't a right to expect things easy there, where has he? You may be a saint, Mac, but I am not, and I don't even pretend to like a sermon once a week, let alone once a day." He laughed, and added with another change of manner, "I know what you are thinking—that it is all for my good and I will be grateful for it when I grow up. But that isn't the way I am made. I never did like what was good for me."

His exaggerated air of recklessness seemed a challenge to conscious virtue, but it was not taken up. He began to snap the strings of his violin softly, and after a moment he said, with his head bent low over the instrument.

"You spoke of the boy. What of him?"

"He is too old, Falkland, not to wonder where his father is and why he knows no more about him."

"Never mind that. What of himself?"

"He is a fine boy; all alive and as quick as a flash. You will be proud of him one of these days."

"He is still with you?"

"He is in my office."

"That is good of you, Macdonald," he said with a new softness in his voice.

Taking up his violin again, he drew out from its cell low, plaintive murmurs that stole through the car, hushing all other sounds. Sweet as a vanishing dream, tender and searching as the cry of one human soul to its mate, the thrilling strains trembled through the silence. It was a voice of calling, longing, yearning, and faces were startled into unconscious self-betrayal as the spell fell on every heart   Only Macdonald,

after one look at the rapt face of the musician, turned
his own away with a hard line about the mouth.

" He is thinking of Louis. He will work off all the
parental tenderness of his nature in a passionate
traumlied, and then his conscience will be clear as re-
gards the boy for twelve months more."

Dorothy, startled and thrilled, had turned toward
them and was responding with every pulse to the
magic of the charm. Falkland's eyes, still radiant
with poetical rhapsody, fell upon her face and lingered.
The last chords were a maze, breaking the tense spell
of the music. Then he turned to Macdonald curiously.

" Isn't that Miss Vanborough over there? Smooth
hair and fur cloak. Agatha—Dorothy—what was her
name? Prince Hal's sister, you know."

Macdonald's face had darkened with a sudden
wrathful flash.

" Well ? "

" You knew her, of course ? "

" Yes."

" And she you ? "

" No."

" I say, sha'n't I present you ? "

Alec's look was like cold steel.

" Have you her authority ? "

" Not I. But I'd present myself first. She would
be glad to know me, as an old crony of Van's."

" Better not."

" Why not? She's that kind. And she's alone."

" Better not, I say.'

" I say, Mac, I have a tender feeling for you, but
when you look like that I am ready to throw you and

your dollars, past, present, and future, overboard.
What makes you so confoundedly dictatorial?"

Macdonald answered in rapid undertone:

"You must not talk with her because you know
well enough that you can not trust your tongue. You
will begin to drop hints of what she must not know
and what you are bound by your word, and what is
more to the point, by your interest, not to tell any one,
her least of all."

"Whew! Doesn't she know either?"

Alec pulled himself up.

"She doesn't know that you do."

"Oh, I see. You want to save her feelings. All
right. She hasn't saved yours very much, but that is
none of my affair. Is she going on to Hawthorne?"

"What is that to you—or me?"

Falkland laughed.

"Nothing, of course. That is why we are so ready
to flare up at a simple question. I suppose you will
find some chance to make yourself known to her in
time."

"It is quite possible."

Falkland smiled again and began to strum lightly,
with his amused, scrutinizing eyes still on his companion's disturbed face.

"Do you know," he said, after a moment, "I believe I am going to Hawthorne, after all. Your arguments have converted me to the true faith, St. Alexander   By the same token, my exchequer is low."

He laughed softly under his breath and put his
violin against his chin. The sun broke through the
parting clouds and threw a cold gleam over the fields
of snow. At that moment the train started, and while

Dorothy, looking backward, watched the little wooded knoll grow dim in the distant sunset light, the flying train left a trail of weird and mocking music floating over the white fields.

CHAPTER X.

"How long now before we reach Hawthorne?"

"Half an hour."

"And back to the common world again! This has been so different."

"Is the difference plus or minus?" asked Macdonald curiously,

"Oh, plus, by reason of the adventure in it and by the near view of winter, and plus by the fun, too, since it is for so short a time. If there were more of it I suppose it would be less."

"No other factors?"

"What else?"

"You are determined not to feed my masculine vanity. Of course I wanted you to say—or to imply, in your subtle feminine fashion—that I was an addition."

"An addition is not always an acquisition," said Dorothy demurely.

"Well, I would rather be counted on the minus side of the equation than to be ignored entirely."

"I was counting the difference. You belong to the common world as well as this."

"I am afraid that is a quibble, though I suppose I must let it pass. At any rate, it gives me leave to reappear in the play after the conductor puts an end to this prologue."

"I am glad to know you don't anticipate annihilation," she answered lightly. But the suggestion sent her back to her old and still unsatisfied puzzlement over her companion's identity. The elusive hint of familiarity of which she had been conscious at the first had been partly overlaid by the new impressions which three days' intercourse had woven into something like friendship. One can not carry on a thousand-mile conversation with one person without getting below the surface, especially if one is too uncertain of one's ground to dare resist an unobtrusive determination on the part of the party of the second part to lay deep the foundations of a fuller acquaintance. He had said nothing that could give an answer to the unspoken questions in her mind, but, whether intentionally or not, he had said much that revealed himself, and though she knew no more than at first who he was, she had lost all feeling of strangeness.

"Here we are at last. I supposed it would come to this in time," he said with a melancholy air, as the outskirts of the town of Hawthorne gathered them in.

"This? Surely it can't be!" She stood up to get a better view. "But it is not the same place at all! It might as well be called something else, for all its likeness to the Hawthorne I remember."

"Then why not take it as though it were new?" he suggested. "Don't you think it would be fairer to the Hawthorne of to-day to drop your memories of the other one out of your estimate of the new?"

"But I can't. And I don't think it would be fair, either."

"Are all your memories so tenacious?"

"Not all," she confessed consciously. "But I remember places better than people."

"There are some people it is well to forget—for their sakes. What can I do with this thing?" He picked up a shawl-strap and looked around for something to which it might be applied.

"That shawl and book—thanks," murmured Dorothy composedly, but with some secret exultation. So her turn to command had come at last! It wasn't unpleasant on the whole.

There was a rush when the train stopped. Cabmen, porters, and other adjuncts of civilization fell upon it, and special letter carriers caught the sorted packages of mail-matter and rushed away to feed the failing fires of business.

"What important and valuable letters they must be," thought Miss Dorothy innocently. Then she caught sight of Ralph hurrying through the crowd with the slight limp she remembered of old, and she called to him eagerly.

"Ralph! Ralph! There is my cousin," she added, turning to the spot where Mr. McConnell had been standing a moment before. He had disappeared.

But Ralph heard her.

"Dorothy at last," he cried, reaching up gayly to shake hands through the window. "Is it your custom to announce your coming with all the trumpets of the air? Not that the event doesn't justify such a prologue. Wait till I can come in by way of the door."

Dorothy nodded and smiled at him, but the smile faded when she turned from the window to look again for her unaccountable "friend, counselor, and guide."

She was not exacting, but she was a woman, and though she was ready to set aside for the higher claims of baggage she did feel that at least the empty ceremony of an apology was her due.

Ralph reappeared to scatter her thoughts.

"Nellie was broken-hearted in half a dozen different languages not to see you, but she dared not wait over another day, so you have just missed each other. She left messages for you with every member of the family, so you may expect to receive them in installments for the next few days, as we happen to think of them. She also left you a lengthy epistle. Nita has that in sacred trust. Nita is waiting for us just outside. I made her stay in the sleigh as a piece of premonitory discipline. She is growing to be a self-willed young woman, and you will have to begin early to make her recognize your authority."

Dorothy was regarding him with so dismayed a countenance that he stopped in his occupation of loading himself down with her belongings to laugh at her.

"You can call on me if you want any help. She always defers to my wisdom."

"Oh, here you are, Cousin Dorothy," said a girlish voice just behind her, and a saucy face thrust itself between them. "I wasn't going to let Uncle Ralph have the cream of everything, so I came out too."

"My dear Nita, I particularly wanted you to come," blandly responded the gentleman referred to. "You see, Dorothy, as I was saying, she can always be depended on to do what I wish. It doesn't matter by what devious ways that result is attained."

"Are you really Nellie's baby?" asked Dorothy in an awed tone.

"Why, no, Philip is the baby. You never saw him though, did you? He is six years old. I am sixteen, you know."

"Yes, and she knows exactly what she thinks on woman's suffrage and dress reform and the single tax and capital punishment, and all the rest of the test questions," said Ralph in a pretended aside.

They were making their way through the waiting-room by this time, and Dorothy glanced about her with more persistent scrutiny than seemed demanded by the regulation assortment of humanity there to be seen. If by any chance she was thinking that a certain gray overcoat might come up for a tardy farewell, her faith in the native courtesy of man must have been further shaken.

"Cousin Dorothy, what wonderful secret have you with mamma?" demanded Nita abruptly, as they were flashing through the white streets.

"I didn't know of any."

"Not any at all? In a letter?"

"No."

"Oh, dear, I wonder if it is just about clothes and housekeepings and things. I thought it might be something exciting, mamma was so particular about it. I just love secrets—when I am in them."

"I didn't mean to tell," said Ralph slowly, "but—"

Nita put both her hands upon his lips.

"You mustn't, Uncle Ralph. I am dying to hear, but don't let me tempt you. You really mustn't."

Ralph patted her shoulder and nodded at Dorothy.

"See? All my work. Nothing like maintaining a high moral standard in the house."

"It is well you maintain it somewhere," retorted Nita, with dark obscurity.

"That is just her little way," explained Ralph. "She really likes me, you know."

At the door they were met by Richard Ellis, who had astonished the solar system by taking an hour away from the office in the busiest part of the day. But Dorothy had always been his favorite cousin.

"You are very welcome," he said simply, drawing her into the house. "Nellie was very sorry to miss you, and charged me to say that you must not let us impose on you."

"Message No. 1," checked Ralph.

"I am sure I shall be very happy here. Is this Philip?" she asked, bending shyly to kiss a grave-faced baby who was regarding her with calm eyes.

"My name is Philip Rodman Ellis," responded the small man with elaborate distinctness.

"That is the boy. What do you think of him? You will know him better before you go. Ah, Dorothy, it took you a long time to make us your promised visit."

"Edward thought it couldn't be conveniently managed," murmured Dorothy.

"Well, now that we have you here, let Edward look to his rights," cried Ralph. It had occurred to him before that the family rather set Dorothy aside. Now for the first time he thought that she might possibly like something else better.

"Yes, let's keep her. Here, Uncle Ralph, Philip, papa, join hands and we will draw a magic circle around her so that she will be bound fast forever," cried Nita, dancing around Dorothy's chair and dragging Ralph and Philip with her. "Papa, why will you be so provokingly dignified? You spoil the charm by holding back. If we ever lose her now it will be your fault."

"Nita, don't be childish. Your cousin is too tired for such nonsense."

"Do you think it is nonsense? But you like it, I can see you do by the little smile in your eyes."

"I think Nellie said you should be taken to your room at once for a nap," persisted Mr. Ellis with studious solicitude.

"Oh, I am not tired."

"But, my dear Dorothy," cried Ralph, "if Nellie said you should take a nap, what can you possibly know about it? It is settled for all time."

"You came through alone, didn't you?" asked Mr. Ellis.

"No, a friend of Edward's, a Mr. McConnell, was on the train and was very kind. Do you know him? I think he said he lived here."

"McConnell? No, I don't know him. Hawthorne is a larger place than it used to be. Nita, take your cousin to her room, and don't tire her with your chatter."

"I like that!" flashed Nita indignantly, but Dorothy restored her equilibrium by gently drawing her with her and asking about Nellie's letter.

"I'll get it. I want to see if you like your room first. Here it is."

She opened the door and then stood back to watch the effect. Dorothy recognized the touches of her girl-hostess in the overabundance of cushions and rugs, which must have robbed the rest of the house, the juvenile novels, and the dish of chocolates on the table.

"What a nest! It is so restful that it persuades me to believe that I am tired. You arranged it for me, I know. Ah, you have a taste for chocolates, too!"

"Do you think you will like me?" asked Nita, dropping down on the floor beside Dorothy's chair and looking up seriously into her face.

"I am sure I shall," she answered with a quick comprehension that made the girl press her cheek swiftly against her cousin's open palm.

"I won't chatter now, but just wait," she said, springing up. "Now I will get mamma's letter." She was back with it in a moment, and then vanished with a nod and a smile.

Dorothy sat alone with the letter in her lap, and in a moment her thoughts went back, as thoughts will, to the hours she had just left behind. She leaned back with closed eyes and felt again the motion of the cars and smiled to herself as some of Mr. McConnell's words came back to her. She had hoped her cousins might know him. Perhaps he might call. Simple courtesy would require that, and he had been more than simply courteous. He had looked as though he liked to talk to her. Yes, she said, as she sat up very wide awake, undoubtedly he would call. Then—

Then she opened her letter.

"My dearest Dorothy, I wish I were a heathen. Then I could make propitiatory offerings to the gods for fair weather, while now even that forlorn hope is denied me, and I can do nothing but pack my trunk and make my moan and go away without seeing you. Of course I wanted to see you for your own sake, for you are an angel to come and take care of everything for me, but there is one thing I wanted to tell you that I simply can't write about. It isn't the household. You may do just what you please with that, my dear. You may give them my best preserves three times a day and I will not give my anguish voice. But dear cousin, sweet cousin, pretty cousin, an you have a woman's heart in you, lend me your help in a matter which is more to me than even my parlor furniture.

"The truth is, I have turned match-maker in my old age. (Behold one of the disadvantages of Cadmus's invention! If you were here I could tell now by the expression of your eyebrows whether to go on with my confession or to pass this off as a joke. Well, I must e'en trust to you as a woman to be interested in any match, and as a cousin not to betray me if you are not.) Surely there is nothing reprehensible in match-making, except that it is generally done in a haphazard manner because the parties chiefly concerned can't, in the nature of things, be in love and in the full possession of their senses at the same time. It is only a fair division of labor for some one to take the burden of thinking off lovers' minds.

"Blanche Horsford (yes, she is the prospective heroine) is spending the winter in Hawthorne with her father. I don't say that I may not be partly responsible for her visit. Of course I told her how delighted I would be to have her come, and I may have dwelt somewhat strongly upon the charming experience which a winter in the North would be to one who has lived mostly in the South. Did I ever say a word about the contemplated hero? No, my dear, strange as it may seem, his existence was not so much as mentioned. Are you beginning to be wrought up? Are you feverishly asking yourself who the hero may be? I have saved that to the last, because now you must be excited, seeing as 'ow you used to know him. His name it is Alexander Macdonald, and Richard tells me he used to be quite a chum of Harry's. He is Ralph's partner, and the whole family have rather adopted him. So you see everything is ready to make your *rôle* of *dea ex machina* an easy one.

"My dear, are you the least bit shocked? But why? You would have no scruples of conscience about putting your rose bush into a south window, and that is, figuratively, all that I ask you to do. It is for their good. Blanche is an admirable girl, but she will be all the more admirable when she has known the softening influences of love, and Macdonald needs to learn that a home is a better place than an office from which to look out on the universe.

"Do write nice, long letters, and tell me all the steps of the plot, like the dear, good cousin that you are, or were six years ago.

"Nellie."

Dorothy had read on with a smile of gentle amusement. It was like Nellie's wild ways. But when she turned the last page and read the name of Alexander Macdonald, she dropped the letter and sat for a minute looking into space with a startled face. He? He in Hawthorne? She had not thought to see him again. There was no smile in her eyes as she folded the letter away. She wondered if Nellie could know how Harry had died, thirteen years ago. Best beloved of brothers! All the devotion of her childhood, all the romantic idealization of her girlhood, had been centered in him. In her tender thought of him there was no room for a shadow. She had purposely striven to forget that false friend who had proved himself so unworthy of Harry's trust and Harry's sacrifice. And now it was expected that she should not only meet him as her cousins' friend, but Nellie wished—what?

All during the rest of the day, while she was interviewing the cook and examining stores and getting the reins of government into her hands generally, she was conscious of that unpleasant and unexpected background to the picture which had been all bright in her anticipations. She was still perplexedly revolving it in her mind when Philip came to her down-stairs in the early twilight. He was so sedate a child, so serious and wise-looking, that she was secretly half afraid of him. In her own mind she held to the conviction that boys in general were cynical young iconoclasts, born with a lofty scorn of all that was feminine. But while she was wondering how to couch her friendly advances, the wistful mite, sitting stiffly on the edge of a chair, remarked with lingering plaintiveness:

"I wisht you would tell me a story."

"Do you, really?" cried Dorothy in grateful surprise.

"Yes, I do *wisht* you would," he repeated, wagging his head earnestly.

"Would you like to hear about the little princess who wandered into the beautiful country?"

"Yes'm, I guess I would like that pretty well," he answered politely but with reserved enthusiasm.

Dorothy's fairy tales were a generation old, and plain fare compared with the elaborate confections prepared by modern artists and poets to tempt the sated palate of childhood, but perhaps "the music of her voice" may have been as effective as colored inks in making them attractive. At any rate Philip soon drew his chair close beside her and folded his arms upon her knees. Nita, too, had come in, and though that progressive young woman was rather inclined to regard the twilight hour as an extravagance on the part of Nature, which might more profitably have been invested in solid daylight or good lamplight, she also lingered and listened.

It was upon this home-like scene that Wendel and Macdonald, entering the unlit hall, stopped a moment to look.

"And so," the soft voice was saying, "she went on into the beautiful land, and the farther she went the more wonderful it became. She had seen flowers before, you know—they grew all around her father's palace at home—but she had never seen flowers like those that grew in that country. And she had heard birds before, but never birds that sang so sweetly as these. And she had had playmates, but never any so kind as the children who came around to invite her to join their games. 'What is the name of this country?' she asked one of her playmates one day. 'You will know when you come to live here,' he answered. 'Will you tell me?' 'Oh, you will know without telling. It is a puzzle.' And then they all joined hands and danced around, singing 'It is a puzzle! It is a puzzle!' until the little princess joined with them, though she didn't know what the game meant."

Ralph turned an appreciative eye to his companion to see if he caught the effect of the twilight picture. To his surprise he saw something in Alec's face that was more than appreciation. It was so unconscious a revelation that he felt that he had no right to speculate as to its meaning, and with a hasty movement he pushed back the *portières* that had held them in shadow.

"Oh, here's Uncle Ralph!" cried Philip, adding with the proprietary air of a discoverer. "She can tell stories too. Shall she tell you one?"

"When she wants an appreciative audience she will. Miss Vanborough, I scarcely need to introduce Mr. Macdonald, since you are an older friend of his than I am, but I can not deny myself the pleasure, even if the ceremony be superfluous."

Dorothy, with the glow of the fairy tale still upon her face, had turned at the sound of his voice. Now she rose, drawing Philip against her with one arm. She had grown suddenly pale, and she looked very tall and severe as she faintly inclined her head to Ralph's companion, but without a trace of a smile on her even lips. Ralph felt the chill, but without comprehending it.

"Macdonald was on your train," he said cheerily. "Why didn't you discover each other?"

"I recognized Miss Vanborough," said Macdonald quietly, "but I saw she did not know me. It would have been surprising if she had."

There was a crimson spot on Dorothy's cheek, but she added no word of explanation. To be so cold, so far, so uncomfortable, no one would have supposed possible for the gentlest of women.

9

"What in the name of feminine incomprehensibility is the matter?" thought Ralph resentfully.

"I hope your journey did not fatigue you." Macdonald uttered the commonplace with curious hesitancy.

"Not at all, thank you."

"But we were tired of waiting," said Ralph with a winning smile.

Unresponsive silence.

"What is the effect on one's mind of being blockaded, Alec? Does it induce resignation and piety, or the reverse?" went on the peacemaker laboriously.

"It was an experience for which I was most grateful," he answered, with a quick glance at Dorothy.

There was no relaxation in her cold face.

"Oh, I say, Nita, how did you come out with De Senectute to-day?" asked Ralph desperately.

"I've saved the knots for you, thank you kindly. Now just look at this one moment," and she pulled out her books on a distant table.

He followed her with devout relief. Alec and Dorothy must be friends, and the sooner the first plunge was made the sooner it would be over. But while helping Nita hunt down an irregular verb his mind was busy with other matters. Wasn't there some old story which he had heard and forgotten about Macdonald's early connection with the family in Prince Hal's day that would explain Dorothy's coldness? He must ask Richard about it. But it was absurd to let a quarrel, or whatever it had been, last thirteen years.

"Do you blame me for not making myself known

to you?" Macdonald had asked immediately upon Ralph's retreat.

"Oh, certainly not. Why should I! It was entirely my own fault," answered Dorothy loftily.

"There was no fault, at least on your part. I thought at first you recognized me, as I did you. Then I saw it was a mistake, and—"

"And you let me go on in the mistake!"

" I meant not to, but the next time I saw you you were standing on the track, you remember, and there was no time then to hesitate."

Yes, she remembered. But was he to be forgiven because he had happened to save her life?

"I had tried to find Mr. McConnell, but unsuccessfully. You were alone, and I thought I might have the good fortune to render you some assistance—"

"Which I would have accepted from Mr. McConnell."

"And not from Alec Macdonald. I knew it, and for that reason I was glad you did not know my name. Under my *incognito* I hoped that we might begin a new—if I may not say friendship, at least—acquaintance without drawing on what is past."

There was little encouragement in her impassive profile as she busied herself arranging Philip's collar. He came and stood before her, filled with a great desire to break down this intangible barrier which was pushing him so far away from her real self.

"Do I ask too much?" he persisted. "Can't you forget that you ever knew Alec Macdonald before, and let me come now as any stranger might to win your—your regard or not by what you find me now."

Miss Vanborough rose, and though she was still pale her soft gray eyes met his steadily.

"We will meet as Richard's friends and Nellie's. Nothing more is necessary."

"Nor possible?"

"No. I can not forget. Come, Philip." She caught the child's hand in her own and hurried away, leaving Macdonald quivering as under a blow.

"*Adeo*, to draw near, to approach," said Ralph, with his eyes on the book but his mind anywhere else.

"Why, what are you thinking of? It is the adverb," cried Nita with delighted superiority.

"Oh, all right. I guess you'll manage the rest." He pushed the books away and limped across the room to his friend. "You'll come again, Alec?"

"Yes, again and again." He smiled, though the red stain had not yet faded from his cheek.

Ralph affectionately threw his arm over his friend's shoulder as they walked to the door, to convey the sympathy which as a man he could not put into words.

"The cold-wave flag was up this evening," he remarked inconsequently.

"Yes, we are in for the winter, I suspect."

Ralph lost no time in consulting Richard about the forgotten family history.

"Why, I don't exactly know the details myself," said Mr. Ellis uncomfortably. "There was some discovery after Harry's death—some crookedness in the accounts that Macdonald had kept. Something not quite honorable. Hard to believe it, isn't it? But he made some sort of an arrangement to repay the money, and of course has done so long ago. I don't want to hear anything more about it, I'm sure."

"Do you suppose that is a reason why Dorothy might not care to know him?"

"Nonsense. The sooner that story is forgotten the better, and Dorothy will have to forget it in my house. My cousins are an intolerable set, Wendel. I can just understand how they would consider themselves personally aggrieved, because Harry had taken a lordly sort of interest in him. Harry would never have made the man Macdonald is. But Dorothy can't wish to bring that old matter up. She is too soft-hearted."

Ralph was beginning to have his doubts about the soft-heartedness. That was the family tradition, to be sure, but—

A few days later there occurred what he considered a most favorable opportunity for a reasonable discussion of the subject, and believing as he did that frankness was as necessary as sunshine to a healthy state of mind, he determined that Dorothy's secret antagonism should be dragged out to the light of acknowledgment. Nita, over her books in a far corner, was out of the range of conversation, and Mr. Ellis, after a heroic struggle between politeness and weariness, had at last gone undisguisedly to sleep in his arm-chair. Dorothy had tucked Philip into bed with an elaborate care that defeated its own object, for he lay awake to speculate whether this era would continue or not. She had come down-stairs at last, and had taken up some sewing in a housewifely fashion, which Ralph mentally characterized as the unconscious feminine instinct for suitable stage-setting.

"What a home look you have, cousin. Does Hawthorne seem at all like the old town you knew how many years ago?"

She smiled brightly.

"I have been thinking so much about this important household that I haven't noticed the city in general. But of course there must have been changes."

"Shades of departed real-estate agents, hear her," murmured Ralph.

"Do you think I ought to?" she asked, with a little pucker in her forehead. "Perhaps for Philip's sake—"

"My dear Dorothy, I have a profound regard for my nephew—they say he looks like me—but you are not to sacrifice yourself on his altar. Not to mention the higher claims of—well, say his uncle for sake of an illustration—you really are entitled to some consideration yourself."

She laughed softly at his half-teasing protection.

"I think I must put you on your honor to do only what you really like while you are out here, or you will get us into the family conspiracy to make a saint of you before your time, in spite of ourselves. Come, confess, what is it you particularly dislike to do?"

"To read newspapers, Mr. Editor."

"Then you are to read none except the Hawthorne *Dial*," he responded blandly. "Have you examined it yet?"

She looked up penitently.

"I was just going to. Of course I will like it, Ralph. Oh, that is serious. I know it is worth liking."

"That is what we are trying to make the public believe."

"Of course it must be different from other papers, since it is your work."

"That is so flattering a delusion on your part, cousin mine, that I am tempted to let you cherish it, but it is a delusion. Macdonald had made the *Dial* what it is before I knew the paper or its founder."

All the gayety faded out of her face at his words.

"What an unconscionable little bigot it is, after all," he thought to himself. Then aloud: "You know there has always been a good deal of talk about the need of reform in journalism. The critical public disapproves of the sensational public and its tastes, but the publishers of newspapers haven't had enough faith in the critical public to trust it to support the kind of a paper it pretends to want."

There was neither assent nor dissent in the grave face just opposite; only a look of predetermination, quietly resolved not to be moved.

"Macdonald had the daring to try, though his daring is of that quiet sort that hardly knows its own audacity. I remember one evening he picked up a sheet I had been reading, and asked in his quizzical way if I thought it was a fair index of the point reached by our Western civilization. And, come to think, there wasn't much civilization in it. You know when we set up to pity our poor forefathers of a few hundred years ago, we always point to our art, our literature, our sciences, as a proof of our advancement. Well, it is seldom enough that any of these matters get a word in your morning paper. You will have three pages of the misdeeds of people you would never have heard of but for their crimes, and three lines of the latest discoveries or philanthropies."

She was looking interested in spite of herself, and he went on more easily.

"Of course it is a newspaper, and the riot and the prize fight have their line with the other news items. But they are kept down to the narrowest limits possible, instead of being padded with imaginary conversations with the pugilist's wife. The events of real importance are the ones that are discussed at length. This is Macdonald's work, and this, and this," he went on, pointing out one article after another in some papers he had gathered up from the table. " And his theory governs everything that is printed."

"You are a very true friend," she said, with a little wonder in her face.

"Because he is the truest man I know."

"What has he done to make you his champion?"

"Done? Why, I hardly know. It isn't what he does alone, but what he is. Isn't it enough that out of a rough piece of soul material he should have carved a real man? What else is all our doing for, after all?"

"Oh, if you are going to get into metaphysics—" she protested, with a tremulous smile.

"It isn't necessary. I could count off and ticket a sufficient number of reasons to justify my adherence and to compel yours, but it doesn't seem fair to him."

She was beginning to quiver under the pressure of his persistence, and, because she trembled, she rushed on to meet the issue.

"I am glad if you have reason to believe in him," she said in a low tone, "but you know why I must think differently."

"Because the boy once made a mistake? Well, committed a crime, if you will. The man has most scrupulously retrieved it. Must you follow him forever with that blunder? Do you think the man by any possibility could repeat it?"

"I don't know."

"No, you don't know, because you don't know him, and you never will know him until you let yourself be generous enough to forget. Have you made up your mind not to like him?"

"He repaid Harry's trust with treachery, though Harry died for him. No, I do not like him, nor shall I."

"Oh, cousin-in-law," groaned Ralph, "you soft women are like the palmetto forts of the old war time. You receive all the shells of argument than can be rained upon you, and at the end you smile back as serenely unmoved as before the storming."

"What does it matter what I think?" she asked. Her temples were throbbing.

"Why, everything," he answered, bending forward to look into her lowered eyes. "It matters to you whether you hold a right opinion or a wrong one. It matters to Macdonald whether he is wronged or not, even in another's thought. And it matters to me whether my friends will like each other or not. I want you to know him as I do. If I had a Raphael in my room, do you think I would leave you in peace until you saw its beauty? I would take you through all the drudgery of line and perspective and harmony until you reached a point where your awakened artistic sense forced you to your knees before my Madonna."

"But what if I knew that your Raphael was only a Perugino at best?"

"What would I care how the catalogues named it if it held a message for me?"

"Uncle Ralph, how do you construe this ? "

Nita was holding a book before his eyes, but it wasn't Cicero. So far as one could tell at a glance, it looked very much like The Courtship of Miles Standish, and a saucy finger was directing particular attention to the line :

"Why don't you speak for yourself, John ?"

Ralph's blue eyes looked rather bewildered for a moment, and then with a flash of comprehension he sprang after the retreating damsel and made a laudable but vain attempt to box the oversharp ears.

But Dorothy's hands were trembling so from the contest of wills that she had to fold her work away.

When she went up-stairs Ralph held the door open.

"You are going to make me let you believe what you please, Cousin Dorothy, just as Alec makes me let him do what he pleases. I must believe in you in spite of all."

She met his reassuring smile rather tremulously.

"Good-night." He still held her fingers in his.

"Good-night."

"You forgive me ? "

"What for ? " she asked, with wide eyes.

"Oh, I don't know, only I feel condemned. For obstinacy, perhaps." She was the only one who had been obstinate if he had stopped to think.

But Dorothy laughed at last, and he let her go, though he watched her to the top of the stairs.

CHAPTER XI.

A BUSINESS counting-room would not be classified ordinarily as one of the chosen haunts of day-dreams. To be sure, they are daring little rogues, these sprites, and have even been known on occasion to risk a tumble into an ink-well in their venturesome excursions, but they certainly had not been habitual visitors at the publication office of the Hawthorne *Dial*. They might perhaps have peeped in through the keyhole, or fluttered out at times from the pages of some old book on the shelves, but they had not stayed long. Perhaps they found the atmosphere too cold, for they dearly love the drowsy sunshine; or perhaps too busy, for they much dislike a bustle. At any rate, they only lingered long enough to shake a little sparkle of silver dust from their wings before they fluttered away to rock themselves to sleep in some bough of apple blossoms from which a hammock might be swinging, or to nestle down, all a-dance with mischief, in some dim folio of olden verse, whence they might spring gayly upon the idle student who had thought to find nothing but printed words.

But it happened, a few days after the events related in the last chapter, that one of these airy spirites, chancing to lose its way, lit upon a file of bills on Macdonald's desk, and before that hapless mortal had time to think he had been whisked so far away from the region of the multiplication table that he would not have been able to say, on oath, whether six times seven made two and carry four or four and carry two. Probably he could have told more readily how many letters went to compose the name of Dorothy, and he might even have gone so far as to deduce therefrom a new theory explaining the veneration of the ancients for the number seven.

How little she had changed, he thought first. The same shy, friendly eyes, the same gentleness of manner that had made her fifteen years ago an angel of light to the country boy he was then. No wonder she had not known him. Fifteen years of hard living make a difference in the face of a man, while she had been perfect from the beginning, so there had been nothing that time could do for her.

Too sudden a surrender? But life does not always work on the surface. Its streams flow underground at times, and when they break out with sudden strength we hardly trace them to the tiny rill that sparkled far up on the hillside and then vanished from sight to wander its hidden way. He had not called it love in the old time, or even friendship. The gentle creature whose look had drawn a magic circle about him wherein he was kept safe from the stings of unkindness until he should need no shield, was so different from the rough boy she protected that no one, least of all the boy himself, fancied there could ever grow from it anything more than bounty on one side and grateful homage on the other. Perhaps he might in time have come to dare teach the family that the game of gracious lady and faithful swain is a dangerous one for young people to play at, but before the stage was ready for the masque of Cupid, he was called upon to play a part in another drama, which for years left him no time to study love scenes. During the busy years that followed he forgot the tender dream on whose borders he had stood. If the whole truth must be told, Dorothy herself faded out of his conscious memory. But the seeds that had fallen from her girlish fingers bore magic flowers that kept the garden of his heart free from all other blooms, and, though he knew it not, waiting for her She had made herself his boyish ideal ; when the man might have loved he had waited for that ideal, and did not find it until he looked into her face again.

Something of all this the day-dream sprite told to his inner sense, and just to what lengths it might have led a sober man's fancy can not be known, for there came a knock at the door that startled it away and set the multiplication table straight in Macdonald's head in an instant.

"Shall I say particularly engaged?" asked a youthful clerk, springing up from the desk where he had been scratching away with ostentatious industry. "Shall I ask them to call again?"

"Quite unnecessary," put in a cheerful voice at the door. "You see I am in already."

"Hello, Falkland, how are you?" exclaimed Macdonald, though with no more cordiality in his voice than the law demands.

"Well, of course. Nothing like an untroubled conscience to give one a light heart, you know."

"I thought you practically reversed that saying. Nothing like a light heart to keep a conscience from being troublesome."

"It is the same thing practically. Ah, Louis, my boy," continued Mr. Falkland, turning with paternal emotion to the industrious scrivener, "it makes my bosom swell with pride to see you with your foot on the ladder, even if it be the lowest rung, that leads to glory and that sort of thing. It reconciles me to everything."

Louis, divided between a desire to be companionable and an ambition to preserve the ceremonious discipline of the office, in which he delighted, hid a grin under a frown and scratched away at a rate that would soon raise the price of pens.

"Have you seen our fair friend yet?" queried Falkland, looking around for the match-box. "How does the land lie—"

"Wait a minute. Louis!"

The boy stood before him in the attitude of attention before the word was fairly out of his mouth.

"When did you go around with the city collections?"

"Yesterday, sir."

"I think you'd better go around again to-day."

"Yes, sir," responded Louis in a tone that plainly said it was not his to question why, not his to make reply, his but to go and collect. He flung himself into his coat and caught up his cap and bills, indulging himself only in a glance at his father signifying, "that's the way we do things here." There was a look of his father about the boy, but he had the saving grace of youth upon him as yet.

"That was considerate of you, Macdonald," said the visitor, blowing tiny rings of smoke into the air and watching them float upward. "It is just as well to have the boy out of the way."

"Don't thank me," said Macdonald dryly. "It wasn't for your sake that I did it."

"Frank as ever," cried the other with great good-humor. "I love frankness."

"Then, to be frank, what is your business with me?"

"Money," was the airy answer. "Money, my dear fellow. That's what we all work for. The mechanic gets up at five o'clock in the morning, not for the sake of the sunrise, but for money. The tradesman learns to be polite for money. The real estate man tells fairy tales for money. The poet—well, the poet may see his rhymes in print for money." He delicately flicked the ash from his cigar and smiled serenely.

"And where do you list yourself in the category?"

"I? Oh, I keep my own counsel—for money."

"It is an article of barter, then?" Indignation was beginning to come to the surface.

"My dear sir, say that I am a dealer in the commodity called information. I happen to have a piece of information which you wish me to keep to myself. Why shouldn't you pay for it? You wouldn't expect to control anything else I may happen to possess without first paying for it."

"The demand fixes the price of an article, I suppose. Have I any rival bidders for this piece of information of yours?"

"My dear Macdonald, of course I would come to you first," he protested.

"Because your secret is valueless except so far as I may choose to value it. The most sensational newspaper of the town couldn't afford to give more than three lines to so insignificant a ghost, brought back to tell a thirteen-year old story."

"I know the market is not very active," conceded
Falkland. "My price is correspondingly moderate."

Macdonald had justified himself in his own mind
for yielding to Falkland's claims before by classing it as
one of his charities. He knew very well that the man
would turn up at intervals with his show of airy im-
pertinence and dusty threats. To buy him off was
perhaps not the noblest way of dealing with the beg-
gar, but it was the easiest, and, if he did not wish to
give up now what he had spent some years to protect,
Harry's fair fame, it was the wisest way. There was
no doubt but that Falkland, if disappointed in what
he had come to consider a legitimate source of income,
would publish the old story from mere waspish revenge. And if the money did him no good, that was
surely his own lookout. So at least it had always
seemed before. To-day for some reason he felt an
unusual repugnance to paying the blackmail. His
mind had been working in a different direction and
things wore a new color.

He sat silent a moment before he answered the
last remark. Then he said slowly :

"The secret is not one that would discredit me, as
you know well. What have I to fear from its publication, if I refuse your demand ? "

"Why you should care to keep it of course I
can't guess," responded Falkland with ingenuous
frankness. "I shouldn't, in your place. But since
you have already thought it worth while to pay something, not only in money but in reputation, for the
sake of keeping the true history of the old business
quiet, it doesn't require much divination to see that

you will probably be willing to pony up again." He smiled with captivating sweetness.

"How many times have you been here before with this argument?"

"My dear Macdonald, I have no head for statistics!"

"How would you like to find a post where you could earn a living for a change?" suggested Macdonald tentatively.

"I asked you for a biscuit not a cobble-stone," murmured the other reproachfully.

Macdonald mused, making idle marks with his pencil on the back of an old envelope the while, and Falkland watched him furtively. He did not care the ash of a cigar what circuitous routes the man of money and a conscience might find it necessary to take to reach a conclusion, so that the conclusion was the one he wanted. But he chafed at silence and began to wonder whether it were possible that since his last application his friend might have had his eyes opened. Could he have made the sensible but highly undesirable decision that it was hardly worth while paying longer to keep another man's secret? To precipitate matters he said casually:

"Others may care to keep it quiet if you don't. There's the sister—" Then he got upon his feet suddenly, with his hand on the back of the chair. For a moment he had thought Macdonald was going to spring upon him as he had once before in the old club room.

"Of course, I don't really mean that," he concluded, with a weak laugh.

"If there were anything you held sacred, I'd make

10

you swear it," said Macdonald slowly. His lips were white with the sudden passion that had swept over him and the restraint that had curbed it.

"My pocket-book might do, if it were not so flat," suggested Falkland, quickly recovering himself. The storm was going to blow over, then. After all, there was some advantage in growing old, or, rather, in having other people grow old.

Alec took a turn in the room, and then stopped and put his hand on his visitor's shoulder.

"Sit down and listen to me. We must understand each other. Vanborough was my friend, and for that reason I have for years shielded his name with my own, as you know. It was a purely selfish reason, however. I did it because it pleased me to do it." He was choosing his words as a painter chooses his colors, to produce a certain effect.

"Yes, I suppose some people are made that way."

"And if my interest in the matter is drawn on too heavily the funds may not hold out. The man may not feel bound to honor all the foolish promises of the boy."

Falkland's barometer-like face fell.

"You are getting as mercenary and calculating as the rest of the world," he exclaimed with unconcealed disappointment.

"I don't pretend to be particularly proud of myself, but, as for being calculating, I fancy I'm not much ahead of you there, old man!"

"Well, it is a deal easier to be high-minded with a bank account to back up your conscience than when you have to stuff your pocket-book with bits of paper to keep the boot-black from knowing that he has exhausted your resources with a single shine ! "

Macdonald laughed perplexedly, but ended by drawing up a check, which would cut off the demand for old newspapers for many a day, and pushing it across the table.

"What a trump you are, Mac ! " said the recipient, easily, rising as though his business were done.

"Sit down again. I haven't said all I want to yet. You spoke of Miss Vanborough a few minutes ago."

"That was all salt, you know."

"Did you know Miss Vanborough when she was here before ? "

"I ? Bless you, no. Van was free enough in the office, but, as for introducing me to his sister—oh, that's quite another matter, dear boy."

"This sister was hardly more than a child then. She grew up to believe in her brother as she believed in her prayers. His death has made him a sort of a saint, and all these years she has kept this ideal in her heart until it has become more to her than any reality."

"I say, you've been getting pretty confidential."

"If you tell her, with your interpretations, the story of her brother's mistake, are you prepared to take the consequences ? You might possibly get her to buy off publicity with her pitiful bits of gold, but could you ever make up for the pain she would suffer ? It would be a heavy memory to carry, Falkland."

"I won't—if I can help it," he said soberly. "But don't run me too close, Mac. How the mischief am I to get along without money ? I simply can't earn it, you know, and I must have it."

"What are you doing now?"

"Do you think I'd better be confidential? You would only feel bound to labor in prayer with me, you know, and that doesn't pay a cent's worth."

"How long are you going to stay in Hawthorne?"

"Just long enough to get this check of yours cashed."

"Then where to?"

"I don't know. Somewhere."

"Are you determined to throw off everybody? Confound it, Falkland, you make me preach in spite of myself! That is no way to live."

"Well, I haven't thrown you off. You will always know where I am, if any one does. You are hard on me, of course, but— Oh, well, that's all right. I know what you have wanted to do for me if I had let you, but we can't help the way we are made." He stopped to light a fresh cigar with fastidious exactness. "Good-by. Can't say when I may see you again. But "—he stopped at the door—"I won't go to Miss Vanborough."

"I trust you," said Macdonald, "since I needs must," he added to himself.

But Falkland meant it at the time. There are some natures like the "water-hammers" used in laboratory experiment. The heat of a hand will make them boil with all the busy bubbles of honest work, but, as for cooking an egg—oh, that they could not do in an eternity.

CHAPTER XII.

"Don't be afraid. This strong right arm shall be your ward," said Ralph cheerfully.

It was Nellie's evening "at home," and he had come down to find Dorothy surveying the big, empty parlors with a look that was a clear betrayal of her secret trepidation. She turned to meet him with a conscious laugh.

"Do you suppose many people will come?"

"Everybody we know, probably. They will all want to make their bow to Nellie's vicegerent."

"Truly? I don't mind filling a corner or being one in a crowd, but to become a hostess by a sudden jump is a good deal of a trial, though you don't look very sympathetic. What does Nellie do with them?"

"Oh, Nellie talks. Just plain talk, too. The ideal hostess of course would use such an opportunity as this to raise the tone of society, you know. See that you talk about elevating and improving matters, coz. If any one goes out of that door to-night without realizing that he is a better man than when he came in, it will rest on your shoulders."

"Ralph! Ralph!"

"Why, such a little thing as that doesn't frighten you, does it? Oh, moral influence is easy; that will come natural to you. Statistics may be more difficult, without some preliminary coaching, and Mr. Worden will depend on you for his evening supply of general information. You are a new field, you see, and he will want to gather your opinions while the dew is on them. He will probably ask you what you think of the West, and how it differs from the East. Difference in the human nature produced or the ruling market-price of eggs—all will be equally acceptable. All is grist that comes to his mill. But you must have your facts and figures ready, or woe unto you, you cumberer of the earth."

"Can't you stay here and give the statistics," suggested Dorothy anxiously. "I really can't, but I will indorse anything you may say."

"Will you? Let's make up a code of signals," said he, pulling up a chair and looking very well content.

It often happens that the thread of an acquaintance is taken up much farther on than where it parted. Dorothy had known Nellie's brother as a semi-relative who was always pleasant but with whom she had never come to feel thoroughly familiar, and here was Nellie's brother saying with suppressed jubilation :

"When I fix my eyes on the chandelier in an abstracted way, like this, you are to snub your interlocutor."

"Oh, but I couldn't ! "

"But you must. What is the use of having a code of signals if you don't follow them? Don't you see how easy it will make conversation? You have only to watch me and you will know how to deal with the different new varieties, without wasting time for original research."

"But you may not always be near."

"That won't be so so hard on you as on me. Now note well. When I open a book, or your fan, like this, you may safely agree with your *vis-à-vis*. When

I shut it firmly, like this, you must deny and defy him."

"Oh, please have more of the other kind."

"When I lean back, close my eyes and snore gently, that means that you are perfectly safe in leaving the burden of the conversation to the other person and that you will have nothing to do but listen."

"That is easiest of all. I was afraid you would leave me no room to exercise my one accomplishment."

"To listen well," said Ralph oracularly, "is a fine art. Any one can talk. The veriest dullard can make a noise that will subjugate his opponents by demoralizing their critical faculties. But to listen, one must have an artistic soul. The perfect listener is as rare as a black diamond, and no less to be prized. She inspires conversation. Rare thoughts can not string themselves into words amid a rattling cross fire of noisy chatter. They require the soft silence of attention, the sunshine of an appreciative smile, to warm them into life. Believe me, the listener is the one who makes a conversation dull or brilliant."

"Are you not content with inflicting your dullness on Cousin Dorothy, but you must try to hold her responsible for it as well?" asked Nita, who had come up in time to hear the last few words.

"You speak under the privilege of a school-girl and a niece," retorted her uncle. "You don't know the first principles of listening."

"Oh, yes, I do. Never do it through a key-hole."

"Hark! I hear the ominous sound of the hall door turning on its hinges. The beginning of the end, Dorothy! Are you perfectly calm? Would you mind letting me feel your pulse under cover of fastening your bracelet?"

"Don't be absurd," protested Nita. "It is only Mr. Worden."

"Only! Do you know what Mr. Worden is? A question asked itself once upon a time and didn't find an answer. In the course of ages it became human. Mr. Worden is the representative of the family in this locality."

"Dorothy, let me present my old friend Mr. Worden," said Mr. Ellis with exceptional cheerfulness, bringing up a tall, solemn stranger.

"This is your first visit out West, isn't it, Miss Vanborough? How do you like it? Do we strike you as very rough and unformed?"

Ralph was staring at the chandelier with a far-away look that made it difficult for Dorothy to face the questioner with becoming gravity.

"The West is my old home," she said deprecatingly. "I lived here fifteen years ago, so I can not see it now with new eyes."

"Oh, indeed," murmured the defrauded inquirer, while Ralph nodded delighted approval of her tactics.

"But of course we must be crude. We might as well acknowledge it," said Nita decisively. It was her chief regret that she had not been born a Roman.

"Oh, the West isn't so bad," Ralph put in. "We may have to get our ideas of the old masters from Soule's photographs, and take our Browning and Dante in fortnightly study-class doses, and admire Irving by an act of faith, but we do have human nature out here, and that has a certain degree of interest as far as it goes. The daily papers show that marriage licenses are in demand, and if you merely substitute Romeo and Juliet or some other melodious names for the commonplace ones generally affected by the contracting parties, you have a drama ready-made to your hand. People plot and scheme and succeed and break their hearts here every day in a way that might set a score of novelists up in business. They even die occasionally, though the salubrious climate—"

"Don't run your advertisements in with your reading matter," interrupted Nita.

Mr. Worden was looking so baffled that Mr. Ellis came to his rescue.

"Worden, don't you think truth is keeping too dubious company to be entirely respectable? Come into the next room and let me show you my new atlas."

"I say, Uncle Ralph, why don't you suggest in the *Dial* that people get up something new in the way of 'living stories'? According to you, there is material enough right here."

"And every day could be a new chapter," suggested Dorothy.

"Yes, and they could fill it with incidents or description or metaphysical analysis, as they might like best."

"There might be something in it," admitted Ralph. "People would probably feel more responsibility about arranging matters so as to have things turn out right if they thought they were writing a book instead of merely a life."

Their schemes for the good of humanity were interrupted by the arrival of humanity in person. Dorothy had expected to have her faculties desert her at the critical moment, but she found it was not so dreadful after all, for her efforts were seconded so enthusiastically by Ralph that she was tided over the stage of tribulation before she knew it.   It must have been the Western atmosphere, she thought to herself when she had time to comment mentally on her own animation; it would have been an impossibility in Edward's house. Conscience suggested that she ought to hunt out Mr. Worden and confess to having discovered something new.   If it would only last until the habit might become fixed !   Nita, passing by, murmured *sotto voce:*

"That is Miss Horsford just coming in."

Miss Horsford!   The heroine of Nellie's drama ! It was with the liveliest curiosity she turned to survey the young woman Ralph was bringing down the room to her.   Without being large, Miss Horsford gave the impression of magnificence.   Her languidly regal air made Dorothy think of the scene in Fedora where Bernhardt drifts on the stage with her *"Charmé de vous voir,"* and the atmosphere is made suddenly electric.   And she was to manage events for this personage ?   Oh, yes !

"Delighted, I'm sure," murmured Miss Horsford, taking Dorothy's measure with a comprehensive glance that let no detail of dress, feature, or soul escape. "Nellie has often spoken of you."

"Nellie has written me about you," answered Dorothy, reddening guiltily.   Chancing to glance at Ralph over Miss Horsford's shoulder she was scandalized to see that young man close his eyes for a moment and sigh sleepily.   It passed like a flash, and then he went serenely away to talk to some one else.

"You lived here some time ago, I think Nellie told me," Miss Horsford was saying.

"Yes, for several years. That was before Hawthorne was anything more than a pioneer town."

"Have you found any of your old friends left?"

"No—at least, not many."

"Did you know Mr. Macdonald then? He told me that he was one of the oldest inhabitants." Miss Horsford was toying with her fan, and though her words were addressed negligently to Dorothy her eyes were on a group near the door.

"Yes."

"That was before he was connected with the *Dial*, wasn't it?"

"Oh, yes. He was a student at that time," Dorothy answered with an effort.

"He is strikingly different from Mr. Wendel, yet they are great friends. But of course you know."

"I knew they were in business together," murmured Dorothy faintly.

"Oh, Damon and Pythias were not more devoted. Your cousin is of the faithful kind, I fancy. I am not so sure of Mr. Macdonald. Are you?" She flashed a smile after her words that made them enigmatical.

"Your acquaintance is more recent than mine," said Dorothy evasively.

Miss Horsford honored her with a direct gaze. "More or less than friends; which is it?" she was thinking. The possibility of an excitement brightened her, but she was too wise to attempt to find what she wanted to know by questions. She led Dorothy on to talk of what she would, and in the mean time took note of more than her words. At the end of ten minutes she had a generally correct idea of the character, capacities, and inclinations of her hostess. Then her interest snapped and she leaned back languidly.

"What quantities of fun you will have all to yourself, seeing the outside of so many new people!"

"Fun!" There was frank confession in Dorothy's laugh. "I assure you it has seemed a serious matter to me."

"Oh, people are always amusing at first, while you see their peculiarities. After you get used to them they are rather a bore."

"Then, I suppose I don't get used to them."

"You mean the longer you know people the better you like them?"

"Yes, almost always."

She was not thinking of any particular illustration, but as she raised her eyes she saw Mr. Macdonald at the end of the room, with the intent look that was characteristic of him on his face. She could not tell whether his regard had been for Miss Horsford or herself, for he came forward at once to bow over her hand.

"Is there room for an old face in this new gallery?"

"Oh, yes."

It is to be hoped he had not expected anything more.

"How late you are," exclaimed Miss Horsford with familiar reproach.

"I plead guilty and throw myself on the mercy of the court."

"You are sentenced to the hard labor of taking me to Mrs. Francis, who is somewhere in the rooms."

Mr. Macdonald bowed, but made no attempt at repartee. Miss Horsford took his arm, and turned to give Dorothy an observant look and smile as they moved away.

"What a fellow that cousin of yours is, Miss Vanborough," said a cheery voice beside her. "Won't you take me under your protection? He actually wants to get me into his charades."

"Ralph? Oh, it is one of his theories that everything must give way to art," she answered. "I will need protection, Dr. Blount, if I aid you in deserting."

"But my gray hair frees me from that kind of drafting. I am going to enjoy myself. Perhaps you haven't had time to learn yet, but my gray hair is one of the institutions of the town. Do you suppose it is every Western town that can boast a man old enough to have gray hair through the natural course of time? Boys, I tell you; nothing but boys out here. Why, not long ago a man came around to sell some sort of a hair rejuvenator. I pitied the poor fellow, for I knew that he must have been driven to pretty close quarters to make a living in that way, so I was going to take a bottle just to encourage him a bit. But somehow the city council got wind of it and they sent around a petition, representing the injury I would do the town by withdrawing its one outward claim to respect, and the upshot was that I had to pay the hair-man and empty out the restorer."

"And what became of the poor peddler?" asked Dorothy, smiling at his merry brown eyes.

"Oh, he must have starved by this time. I knew he would, and tried to persuade him to die for the good of the race, since die he must, but he didn't seem ready to do it."

" How could he ? "

"I told him to worry himself to death, if he wanted to benefit his fellow-men," responded the doctor, coolly.

" Why, how barbarous ! "

" But heroic. The world needs a few martyrs. If I were younger I would consider it my duty to worry myself to death in three months. Perhaps by study I could get it down to two. But I am too old to do it effectively. My gray hair would have to bear the responsibility and the lesson would be lost."

" You bewilder me utterly. What lesson do you mean ? "

"Why, the lesson that the world needs more than any other—to stop worrying. I tell you, nothing but a few martyrs, who will carry out the case under test conditions so that there will be no chance for the doctors—who are a humbugging set, Miss Dorothy—to lay it to a fever or a sunstroke, or something of that sort, will do it. You see the way it is, people are killing themselves all the time, and they don't really know it. How many old men are there in a town ? How many ought there to be ? There's a deficit in the account and this spirit of rush is the defaulting cashier."

" I suppose it is because there is so much to be done and they want to get through," said Dorothy, in gentle extenuation of the condemned class.

" But they ought not to get through and they ought not to want to get through," expostulated the doctor. " They ought to keep on going, like everything else in Nature. Why, people get so tired living that they actually fancy their heaven must be a place where they are going to be forever doing nothing and enjoying it. I tell you, there isn't a healthy soul among them that wouldn't petition to be let out of such a heaven before eternity was half over, even if there was nothing for it but to carry coals in that other place the preachers seem to know so much about."

"But if you object to the work and struggle here, I should think you would want to believe in a rest after this is over," she ventured.

"Rest, yes, but not the kind of rest that means stopping. Do you suppose the trees get tired of growing or the stars of shining? It isn't stagnation that is wanted. I tell you, the modern idea of a heaven was invented by a man who was badly in need of a vacation to set him up in good condition."

Dorothy smiled encouragingly, and Dr. Blount thought to himself that Miss Vanborough was a very appreciative listener. He might have been less flattered if he had known that she was using his conversation as a cover for the study of another man.

She had discovered Macdonald and Miss Horsford, who had apparently abandoned the quest for Mrs. Francis, conversing together at a little distance. It was the first opportunity she had had, free from counter-distractions, to look upon her former friend in his own personality. He was greatly changed ; that was her first discovery. And he was much improved, she told herself with judicial impartiality. Always bearing in mind the fact that he had dishonored himself, and was thenceforth and forever unworthy of all regard, one might still say that he had a noble bearing. She was glad for Harry's sake that it was no worse. How

Harry would have triumphed in his success! Ah, if only— He had really been very kind on the cars; kinder, that is, than one would have expected from a forger, or even from this composed personage who was coolly bandying light nothings with Miss Horsford. As for her, she had become many degrees more radiant than when she was struggling through a ten-minutes' duty conversation with her hostess. Really, Nellie's plot did not seem to need much fostering.

"Ah, there is Macdonald," said the doctor, following her eye. "Upon my word, he is doing the frivolous very well. Who is that? Miss Horsford?"

"Yes."

"Macdonald is a fine fellow. Do you know him?"

"Yes," said Dorothy, devoutly wishing she didn't. Was he to be brought up at every turn?

"It always amuses me to see him letting his Stoic principles slip in favor of civilization. He has been doing it more frequently of late, but a few years ago— He tried to get through life with no luggage but a traveling-bag, and when circumstances were sometimes too strong for him it was good fun for the spectators. I must tell you a little story about that."

Dorothy felt that there might have been good fun in the present situation for a spectator who understood it, but she resigned herself.

"He had rented a room in the house of a widow I know about," the doctor said, settling himself down comfortably. "The room was small and inconvenient enough to satisfy even his ascetic ideas. Anything more would have been tribute money to the Cæsar of self-indulgence. But unfortunately the young Stoic had a tender heart, and he discovered his landlady in tears

one day over her monthly accounts. Of course he
felt bound to discover next that two other vacant
rooms were absolutely essential to his mental and
physical well-being, and, moreover, by some abstruse
mathematical calculation through which the poor little widow's accounts would never have come out alive,
he proved conclusively that the rental should vary in
inverse ratio to the furnishing of the rooms. The
meek landlady had a profound reverence for figures,
as women of her class generally have for their tyrants,
so she never thought of questioning the result. Of
course she could meet the first of the month with less
trepidation, which was well, but the poor, baffled
young Stoic! Luxury had carried the day by a flank
movement, and as he couldn't tell how it had come
about he hadn't a word to say when I teased him
about his extravagance. But it was just as well that
he didn't have his own way in everything."

"Don't you want to talk to me for a while?" Nita
was saying to Macdonald, whom she had deftly disen-
tangled from the maze of Miss Horsford's conversation. "You have been devoting yourself to her so
long that I thought you deserved a reward, so I came
over to rescue you."

"Miss Horsford has great composure of manner,"
said the ungrateful object of her solicitude. "Composure of manner is a very desirable thing. Would
you like to have me repeat that slowly, so that you
can engrave it on the tables of your memory?"

"I am not going to hate you this evening, so don't
waste ammunition. Don't you think my Cousin Dorothy is lovely?"

11

" Yes."

" She is so still and sweet. I wish I might look like her when I grow old."

" Do you call her old ? " he asked with such distinct surprise in his tone that she suddenly reflected that he must be Miss Dorothy's senior himself.

" Of course not really old, but like the people who lived long ago and never knew anything about the pressure of modern life."

Alec laughed teasingly in her face.

" Where did you get your wisdom concerning the modern age, mademoiselle ? "

" I belong to it. I am more modern than the rest of you by several years. But, as I shall probably grow older, I would like to know Dorothy's secret."

" It is the secret of the violins—to grow old beautifully."

" Don't you think," she said, meditatively, " that she is the sort of a person one could fall in love with at first sight ? "

" Don't you think," he responded, with the tactics of a general, " that we ought to do something to celebrate her coming? You think of something and tell me, and between us we will cover ourselves with glory."

Dorothy, feeling a little weary of the endless flash and chatter, had stepped into a deep window where the heavy curtains fell behind her and shut her into a momentary solitude. She probably thought she was thinking of the moonlight on the snow and the sharp black shadows of the bare trees, but in truth the chief idea in her head was a wonder how the boy Alec Macdonald had grown into the man she was beginning to realize she did not know. He had somehow found his way into another world, and she dimly felt that her code, from which she had not thought appeal possible (for was it not the code of the Vanboroughs?), might not be recognized there as unquestionable. There were those evidently who did not consider him beyond the pale of interest. Well, she would wash her hands of the whole affair and leave him to Miss Horsford.

"Oh, yes, so you say. But how is it that men with brains invariably prefer women without?" It was Miss Horsford herself who was speaking.

"If they do, it can only be because they don't know how charming a woman with brains may be," answered Macdonald's voice, with an inflection that pointed the compliment plainly for both his listeners.

Dorothy had no relish for the position of eavesdropper, and was about to pull the curtain back when the next words made her hand fall.

"Our little mouse of a hostess, now. I suppose a great many men would admire her soft style."

Dorothy heard the lazy drawl, but she did not see the quick side-glance that went with the words nor the look in Macdonald's face as he answered quietly :

"I think it very probable."

"You are an old friend of hers, are you not?"

"I am not sure that I may claim that honor. Her brother was an old friend of mine."

"You admired him?"

"More than any one else I ever knew."

"Oh! Is she at all like her brother?"

But Dorothy, with both palms crushed against her ears, heard no more.

When the guests came at last to say good-night, Miss Horsford's cloak was on Macdonald's arm, and there was a new stateliness in Dorothy's manner.

CHAPTER XIII.

Mrs. Ellis to Miss Vanborough.

"DOROTHY, Dorothy, you are a provoking wretch. Of course your letter was very interesting, and I am duly grateful for something besides Richard's bare statistics and Ralph's unreliable rhapsodies, but you simply ignore the vital point. Dorothy, are you going to be obstinate about it? I did not think that of you. My dear, I have no time to read novels, and operas are not allowed in the sick-room, and if you don't help me to a bit of romance you are unworthy the name of cousin. Have you seen Blanche yet? What do you think of her? I hope you will like her, because if you don't it will be hard for you to pull the wires with proper enthusiasm. I am not sure myself that she is just the right person for the position, but I couldn't think of any one else. It is hard to get a heroine who fulfills all the requirements—harder even than to get a faultless nursemaid or an irreproachable cook. Don't you think she will do?

"Why didn't you tell me anything about your experiences on the train that was snow-bound? I was wild to think of you all alone and perhaps starving, though Richard insisted you were not cut off from supplies but only delayed. However, that was bad enough and I am sure you must have had a dreadful time, even if you weren't starving.

"Do write me nice, long letters, and don't consider the postage. It is your duty to contribute to the revenue of your country. I tell Richard that is why I want to go to Europe—so that I can help my country on financially by paying the duty on the things I bring back—but Richard hasn't a logical mind and I can't make him see it.

"Does the hero appear in the next chapter?

"Your expectant   Nellie."

Miss Vanborough to Mrs. Ellis.

"Dear Nellie, I can't. I will tell Sophie what to get for dinner and hear Philip say his lessons and give Nita my opinion on her ribbons, but those higher branches of your work which involve tact and diplomacy and courage must wait for your return. I am sorry for you that you must have so unsatisfactory a cousin in the family, but you will save yourself a great deal of disappointment if you do not expect too much of me. I can keep house for you in a commonplace and prosaic way, but as for managing plots, you must remember that I am only   Dorothy."

Mrs. Ellis to Miss Vanborough.

"My dearest Dorothy, you really will make me a great deal of trouble. I can't manage the affair at arm's length. Do you know what you will drive me to? Not suicide; life is too interesting for that. But you will compel me to enlist the sympathies and assistance of some one else, and you know that too many conspirators are dangerous for the conspiracy. Besides, if this ever gets outside of the family I will be called a dreadful match-maker and my reputation as a harmless member of society will be gone. Think of my distracted husband, my stricken children, my triumphant brother! Will you cast me off, Dorothy, or will you save me because after all I am

Your cousin Nellie?"

Miss Vanborough to Mrs. Ellis.

"Dear Nellie, you really are the absurdest woman living. If you must know the whole truth, I don't like Mr. Macdonald. Ralph would probably say 'Then why don't you marry him to Miss Horsford?' But I didn't say I wanted vengeance.

"I don't believe that sentence looks exactly as I intended it. I don't mean that your magnificent friend is to be regarded in the light of a penalty. Any one who can stand magnificence without being dazzled would doubtless find her to his taste. I admire her myself, though with trembling. I think Mr. Macdonald admires her without trembling. But I can't do anything to strengthen his impression. I mean to be civil to him, of course, since I am hostess in your place, but he must understand that it is as your deputy that I receive him. I will not help him to a wife. Please don't be angry. I can't help my limitations.

Dorothy."

Mr. Ralph Wendel to Mrs. Ellis.

"Dear Nell: Why this frantic appeal for information about Dorothy? You ask if she is a Puritan.

Yes, to a certain extent. Has she changed since we knew her in the East? Very little. But I am beginning to think that perhaps we didn't know her in the East as well as we supposed we did. She seemed very transparent, but doesn't Shelley say something about a veil of light? Transparency may be a very good mask in a world where the other thing is always taken for granted. Is she uncomfortably prim? Not at all. She is a very jolly sort of person to have in the family. Is she obstinate? If you had not assured me repeatedly that a woman is never obstinate, I would have said yes to that. She is obstinate enough in refusing to like Alec, in spite of arguments which would have convinced any twelve men. Is she nice? Well, yes; on the whole, I think the evidence is strongly in her favor there.

"Now, madam, may I be permitted to know the reason for this catechism?   Ralph."

CHAPTER XIV.

ONE of the curious revelations of human companionship is the way in which unexpected relations will sometimes spring up with no special leading of circumstances. Two people may know each other for years and fancy they have explored the whole field of possibilities, when suddenly some chance word will reveal an unsuspected region wherein they may become friends or foes for life.

It was so with Ralph and Dorothy. Ralph would have considered himself particularly well qualified to draw a word picture of his cousin-in-law, and it would probably have run somewhat in this fashion :

"Tall, slight, yielding as a willow. Hair that would be black if it dared to be anything decided. Eyes beautiful, calm, unobservant. All her ways as gentle as the falling of the petals of a flower. A temper that does not know the value of a contradiction. The sort of woman you would fall in love with when very tired, but she should be reserved for the wife of some man who could live in peace with no other daughter of Eve."

Who knew better than he? Had he not seen her a hundred times in her brother's house? Had his sister not married her cousin? Had he not all the family traditions to draw upon? But when she had been in Hawthorne a week he began to suspect that he must dip his brush in deeper colors to do her justice The shades should be darker; that impressed him first. Obstinacy, willfulness, bigotry, had not wholly passed her by in the cradle as he had at first supposed. Their manifestations might have appeared faint on the surface of a different character, but they were nevertheless unmistakable, and he took note of their traces with delight. Then, when the first week of home companionship lengthened into two and three, he began to realize that there was more light in the picture than had been before revealed to him. A flash of ivory white half awed him, a gleam of fathomless blue surprised and quickened him, a hint of the rose red of love, like a sudden illumination, lit unexplored realms. He wondered that he had never seen all this before, and modestly laid it to the charge of his own blindness. Scornfully he scoffed at himself that he, who had dared think himself a poet, should have recognized no tint short of a chromo's. But in truth it was less his fault than Dorothy's. She had never let herself be free before. It was necessary that she should feel herself in some manner essential to those about her before she could begin to live her own life. Some women are born charming; some, it is said, have charms thrust upon them, and some must grow old to charm.

It was amusing, and, from the masculine stand-point, flattering, to see the devotion with which she bent the energies of her soul to house-keeping. One morning he came upon her in the breakfast-room, sur-veying the table with the look a painter might give his picture before it left his studio for the last time.

"Morning, ma'am, morning," he cried gayly. "Ah, I have caught you at your witch-work, have I?"

"What witch-work, then?"

"Conjuring oatmeal and toast and eggs to seem that which they are not. Making breakfast a poem, as our æsthetic friends would say. Are you always at it so early?"

"What is early?" retorted Dorothy. "Weren't you trying last night to make me understand that time is an illusion and terms expressive of it merely sym-bols and figures of speech. You called it philosophy then, though I thought it sounded dangerously like nonsense. But I tried to understand it, for your sake—"

"For why?"

"I said I tried to understand it, and now—"

"For whose sake? Please say that again!"

"And now you come and upset me by talking about

early. It isn't early, though. It is scandalously late. Richard had his breakfast and left long ago."

"I know. He is as bad as Alec about getting the day started ahead of other people. I am more modest. But I won't be for long, if you wait to have breakfast with me. That is enough to go to a man's head."

"I am waiting for Nita. She is just finishing her practicing."

"I thought I heard the sound of her warfare with the ivories. Did you ever go through that campaign?"

"Oh, yes. It was one of the things that cast a blight over my childhood."

"Why?"

"I haven't either the soul or the fingers of a musician. I would be ashamed to confess how much woe there was for me in that little instrument."

"Why didn't you give it up at once? I would have."

"Oh, Edward thought I ought to, and I suppose he was right, only I couldn't."

Ralph made some mental reflections on the hard-headedness of Edward, which he did not think it necessary to repeat to Edward's sister.

"At any rate, you don't need the traditional rings on your fingers and bells on your toes to make music wherever you go."

"Where did you learn to make pretty speeches, cousin?"

"I practiced on Nellie when I knew you were coming."

"Why didn't Nellie turn you over to Miss Horsford?" asked Dorothy daringly.

Ralph gave her a quizzical look.

"She is too fond of me to do that—or of Miss Horsford, perhaps. Nellie doesn't always confine her ambition to possibilities, but she was too wise to suggest that I carry my poetic wares to that market. The grand style suits Macdonald better than it does me."

Dorothy thought she had reason to believe that it did.

"Fancy the frozen condition in which I would be discovered after trying to say some sentimental poetry to her. Now, it would seem very natural to say to you, for instance :

> Thy music I had heard
> By wood and stream, meadow and mountain-side,
> And field and marshes wide,
> Such as nor voice nor lute nor wind nor bird
> The heart e'er stirred,
> Unlike to and far sweeter than them all.

But Miss Horsford—"

"Yet, since the owl is the bird of wisdom, and Miss Horsford is very wise, and those lines were inspired by a ' little downy owl '—"

"I say, do you know them all like that ? Some one else has been saying poetry to you ! "

"Oh, I read Shelley a good deal a few years ago."

"And don't you now ? "

"Not often."

"Why not ? "

She shook her head, but with laughing eyes.

"Don't ask me why. Edward says I never know a reason when I see it."

"Edward be forgotten," he answered vigorously. "You are not to account to him now."

"And when I have learned your lesson of rebellion," she said, putting up her chin saucily, "do you think I will be ready to account to you instead?"

"I would never dare even assume any authority. You would see through the pretense at once.

> As dew beneath the wind of morning,
>   As the sea which whirlwinds waken,
> As the bird's at thunder's warning,
>   As aught mute but deeply shaken,
> As one who feels an unseen spirit,
> Is my heart when thine is near it.

"Is breakfast ready? I'm almost starved. I say, Cousin Dorothy, how awfully pretty you look in that dress!" cried Nita all in a breath, bursting into the room.

There came to be a good deal of this pretty trifling. It was Ralph's way to strew the flowers of speech at the feet of all fair dames, and Dorothy had not had enough homage in the past to grow tired of it. It was pleasantly exciting to have her semi-cousin play the admirer and quote soft sentiments with a laughing look which might mean much or little. She could imagine herself some Lady Ernestine or Geraldine of old listening to a wandering minstrel who sang pretty praises and swore to die for her without the embarrassment of having any meaning attached to his words. It was exhilarating to feel that Lady Geraldine's lightest words would not be indifferent to her adorer, even though Geraldine's brother Edward had an unflattering way of disregarding them. There was always the thought of Edward in the background to prune down

any extravagance before it could get into real life and
do damage. The idea that "Cousin" Ralph might
ever really fall in love with her would have seemed
the wildest fancy. Yet here she sat, in her mental
domino and mask of the Lady Geraldine of the ballad,
provoking, teasing, delighting him in a way that would
have been inexcusably coquettish in an experienced
school-girl of seventeen. She laughed secretly in her
enjoyment of the unrehearsed play, but Ralph only
saw that a dimple broke the smooth curve of her
cheek.

"I say, Alec, I wish that you and Miss Vanborough
were friends," he said one day, looking up from a
pile of manuscript which most certainly held not the
remotest reference to Miss Vanborough.

Alec laughed a little oddly.

"She is really very nice," Ralph went on contro-
versially. Already he felt more like championing
Dorothy than his old friend.

"If she be not nice to me—" paraphrased Alec
lightly. But there was something in his voice which
made Ralph, who knew him so well, say no more,
though he pondered. It must have hurt him deeply,
that condemnation out of the past. It wasn't the sort
of thing one could sympathize about, but—Dorothy
must be brought to see reason somehow. He felt
some confidence in his power of persuasion.

The lamps had been lit to lengthen the short
winter day when the two men walked home together.
They parted at the Ellises' door, and as Ralph sprang
up the steps the hall door above him opened and
Dorothy, after her pretty home fashion, leaned out to
welcome the comer. The light streamed out brilliant-

ly about her, making beautiful the warm room within and the snowy porch without in a way no architect had ever planned.   The man in the street stopped short to look until the door closed, and as he walked on again he still saw only that dark, slender figure with the home halo about it.

"You are a very nice cousin to have about the house," said Ralph appreciatively.

"Was that Mr. Macdonald with you?" asked Dorothy, who had dimly seen a lifted hat as the tall stranger turned away.

"Yes, poor fellow."

"Why do you say that?"

"He hasn't any one to open the door for him and make him feel that 'all's right with the world.'"

Dorothy's eyebrows went up a line, as though to say, what her lips held back, "Well, it is his own fault."

"There's his landlady, of course," pursued Ralph. "I might engage her to do it for so much a month, but—I'm afraid it won't have the same effect."

"No, the charm is broken if it is bartered for money," said Dorothy seriously.   "But is he so very much alone, your Mr. Macdonald?   Surely he has friends of his own."

"We are his friends, of course.   I don't know of any other house that he considers open in the same unceremonious way.   He might have them, of course, but he cares more for a few friends than many."

"Then why doesn't he come here at all?"

She was scientifically piling fresh lumps of coal on the crackling fire, and that of course made it impossible for her to look at Ralph as she spoke and may have accounted for the glow on her face.

"Oh—why—I fancy he has been pretty busy," he stammered. Could it be she didn't understand the reason why?

"He used to come here often, and he hasn't any other friends he cares for, and he hasn't been here since I came." She looked up with a doubtful quiver of the lip "You think I have been horrid, don't you?"

"Not at all," he answered promptly. "You have been just right. Your opinions, in this particular case only, may have been horrid, but they have nothing to do with you."

"What ought I to do about it, then?"

"Ah, Dorothy, how nice you are! Have him up to dinner some evening."

"A dinner party?"

"Oh, no. Just Alec. That will be easy, because it will be reviving a family habit."

"He won't think—"

"You have the faculty of making yourself clearly understood," he said blandly. "There is no danger."

Dorothy probably meditated upon her position as a hostess and considered how far personal inclinations should be subordinated to public duties, for when she found Mr. Ellis alone, later in the evening, she asked him incidentally why he didn't bring Mr. Macdonald up to dinner some day, since he had given over coming without an invitation. Dear, stupid Cousin Richard had been married too many years to give much thought to a woman's fancies unless presented in good, intelligible Saxon. There was a great advantage in having him to deal with in certain cases.

"Glad you spoke of it, Dorothy. He has been treating us shabbily of late. I'll make him come to-morrow."

And he did.

Ralph gave Dorothy an unnecessarily approving glance, and she repelled it with so elaborate an air of unconsciousness that to rectify matters he rushed head-long into safe generalities.

"Eh, but it is pleasant to get back among bonny creatures of flesh and blood," he cried, beaming upon the circle about the table.

"Where have you been, then?"

"Listening to a dissertation on metaphysical anat-omy."

"What?"

"The author calls it a novel, but that is evidently a slip of the pen."

Nita made a dive for the book which he had tossed away, and opened at once to the pages which had been intended as the climax to a carefully prepared cres-cendo of suspense.

"'She paused to scrutinize her inner being'—'the subtle, sub-conscious self-gratification of self-denial' —Serves you right—'the chemical stain of the experi-ence upon the nuclei of her soul remained to tell its ineffaceable story'—for not taking me to the base-ball match instead, as I begged you to!"

"He is probably willing now to count that as an 'error,'" suggested Macdonald.

"I didn't say I didn't like the book."

"But do you?"

"I am enough of a modern to think I ought to like it. If I could get down to my 'subtle sub-conscious-

ness ' I suppose I would find that the impression that
I ought to like a certain thing is a chemical stain indicating that there is a liking for it there which may be
let loose by metabolic processes under proper reagents.
Dorothy, I detect a latent potentiality of agreement in
your manifestation of acquiescent passivity. Do give
it expression and help me out ! "

"I am afraid I was congratulating myself behind
that 'acquiescent passivity' that the old books aren't
all out of print."

"So say we all, if the effect on Ralph is a fair cri-
terion of the new," echoed Alec.

"What do you say, papa, dear ? " asked Nita blandly. "A novel, perhaps I ought to explain, is a book
giving a picture of people as they are or might be."

"I know the article by its effects on the rising generation."

"But still there is something to be said for the
metaphysical novelist," said Macdonald. "If we have
inner consciousnesses and things of that sort, the discussion of them comes within the scope of Nita's definition."

"Yes, and we have skeletons as well. I have heard
of conscientious painters who begin by sketching in
the anatomy of their Venus, but the popular practice
is to add a covering of flesh at least before the picture
is hung."

"I agree with you there, Ralph," said Mr. Ellis.
"The novels that I used to read, and would read yet
if I had time, didn't meddle with abstruse puzzles that
are better left alone, but they were alive and they were
healthy."

"Pirates and hidden mines and imprisoned heir-

12

esses?" laughed Macdonald. "That's because when
you and I read novels in our early days, Mr. Ellis, it
was pure dissipation. Adventure has had to make
way for spiritual questionings, because people nowadays read their novels for a moral purpose. Don't
you, Nita?"

Nita scowled and laughed at the same time.

"Do you?" she asked.

"Of course. For everything short of science.
That I confess I prefer to take dry."

"Exactly. Because you want it true," said Mr.
Ellis. "For the same reason you might as well leave
out all the other elements which have been grafted
upon the true novel—the story of adventure."

"O Dick! As though there were any more truth
in those hairbreadth escapes of yours than in the
modern metaphysical turn of the same imaginative faculty," cried Ralph to trim the boat of discussion.

"They were true to the spirit of life if they did
break its letter," said Dorothy serenely.

Macdonald turned toward her with a sudden gleam
of earnestness in his eyes.

"Do you think then that a lie—a literal lie—may
ever be forgiven !"

"How do you mean," she asked, shrinking a
little.

"Might the truth, for instance, be ever sacrificed to
love?"

"Never," cried Nita with fine enthusiasm.

"Of course not," echoed her father with none at
all.

"Love and truth may each be expressed in terms
of the other," said Ralph. "A lower form of either

might be sacrificed to a higher form of the other, I should say."

Dorothy hesitated as Macdonald looked expectantly at her.

"I can think of cases where it would justify itself to my mind," she said slowly. "But that doesn't prove it."

"I wonder if our practice wouldn't run in inverse order to our protestations if we were put to the test," said Mr. Ellis with a quizzical glance.

Macdonald said nothing, but something so like radiance had come into his face that Dorothy feared she had failed in her efforts to adjust nicely the cordiality of a hostess with a proper reserve on her own account. It is doubtful whether the delicate shading was appreciated, for Ralph was jubilant, and with Nita's assistance, kept up such a fusillade of light conversational firing that it distracted his own attention as well as other people's from the retreat he was trying to cover, and Macdonald was absorbed in an idea of his own. Since his fair enemy had declared at last an armed peace, he must use the occasion wisely and promptly, and while his superficial attention was divided between epigrams and salads, he was concocting a deep-laid plot by which he might gain a few minutes' private converse with Miss Vanborough. Fortunately for the success of the plot, the necessity of scheming was taken out of his hands.

"Will you sing something for us if I count time, Nita?" asked Ralph, opening the piano.

Haughty silence.

"I mean, if I turn your music?"

But forgiveness was not to be so easily obtained.

"Oh, by the way, Nita, I had the privilege of seeing that favorite tenor of yours to-day, Don Roderigo
—Valentino—what is his terrestrial name?"

Wrath was gone in an instant.

"Oh, what was he doing? And how did he look?"

"He was lounging at a street-corner, ogling the
pretty girls, I should judge from appearances."

"How dare you! Tell me the truth this instant."

"Oh, well, then, he was wandering alone on the
edge of the snowy hill, gazing with his best far-away
look at a single star that had come out amid the fad·
ing fires of a dying sunset. He carried a jeweled
locket in his hand, and just as I came away he was
preparing to press it to his heart and sigh. Now after
that you ought to sing two songs for me and let me
choose them myself."

And as she was not unwilling that he should hear
her latest song she concluded to postpone settling the
account which she kept of his impertinences, and gra-
ciously took her place at the piano.

Dorothy had not counted upon finding a *tête-à-tête*
upon her hands, and precipitately proposed joining
Richard, though she knew he hated interruptions
when he was studying the fluctuations of the stock
barometer. But Alec stopped her by asking point-
blank:

"Miss Vanborough, shall I ever come again?"

"We shall always be glad to see you," answered
the hostess before the sustainer of the hereditary feud
could put in a word.

"If you use the 'we' in an editorial way, meaning
your own private opinion and no other, I am well con-

tent. Would that be a fair interpretation? I want your own feeling, and not the family's."

She hesitated, unwilling to wound him but unable to welcome him.

"You must have many friends," she murmured at last. "One more or less can make little difference."

"It makes all the difference in the world," he answered promptly, "when that one is Harry Vanborough's sister."

She looked up resentfully. That name had become sacred by the hallowing influence of death and tender thoughts. To hear it from Macdonald's lips seemed like a sacrilege He understood her unspoken thought, and though his face was pale he met her look steadily.

"I do not ask your friendship for Harry's sake," he went on in a low, rapid tone, afraid that the song at the other end of the room was going to end too soon. "That must come freely, if at all, for no reason but because it belongs to me. But for Harry's sake I ask you to give me a chance to try to win it."

"Do you think that you, of all men, have a right to ask anything in his name?" She was too much shaken to consider her words.

"Yes," he answered steadily. "Harry was my friend."

"That was before—"

"Yes, I know," he said quietly. "But he would have been no less my friend afterward and always if he had lived."

"Ah! If he had lived!" The reproach of that early sorrow was in her low cry.

"He died because he loved me. How bitterly I have mourned his generosity, how gladly I would have taken his place, need not be said. He would have understood. But at least you must know that it was because he loved me that he died. Do you think it would have been different if he had lived? I knew him, and I know he would never have changed, come what might."

She was startled, but she could not deny him. She knew and must acknowledge to herself that his boast was no idle one, and that if Harry had lived this friend of his would not have gone alone through the hard years when, by his own fault, he must have been friendless. A feeling of remorse toward Harry, as of a trust betrayed, came swiftly over her. She had shared all her brother's dreams, had been his chosen companion, his second self. She knew that Harry would never have retreated from his friend while an atom of his obstinate nature remained unchanged. Would he not have expected her to take his place as far as possible?

"For Harry's sake," she whispered, impulsively holding out her hand and lifting dim eyes to his.

"For Harry's sake—for the present," was his unspoken answer. But the gleam of triumph that had leaped into his eyes made her withdraw her hand with sudden shyness.

> " My love he stood at my right hand,
>   His eyes were grave and sweet,"

sang Nita at the piano.

———

CHAPTER XV.

"You are improving very much, Uncle Ralph," said Nita bluntly one day. "You haven't been unpleasant for a long time. Have you had a spiritual awakening, or have you fallen in love?"

"It is your benign influence," Ralph murmured with traitorous sweetness, glancing up over the top of his novel.

"So long as it isn't Miss Horsford's I don't care."

"Miss Horsford? Oh, it is Macdonald that her sun shines on."

"Humph!" was the astute but not very intelligible reply.

Ralph looked at her amusedly.

"For a young thing, Nita, you have strong prejudices. You should conquer them, as I do."

"Indeed! As though you did!"

"Did you never watch the process? Then, behold. The haughty beauty is now at the door herself. She doesn't know I saw her coming up the steps, because I studied Emerson's rules of etiquette in my youth, and therefore don't jump when the door-bell rings. But in a moment she will be in the hall and she will then hear what I say if I raise my voice slightly. Now there are people I like better than Her Magnificence, but—now, if you want an example, Nita, why don't you study Miss Horsford? I notice you are binding your hair with a classic fillet this week, and that thing you are wearing is a moderately successful attempt to adapt the classic robe to a northern climate. Now carry the work into essentials. Let Miss Horsford be your mental and moral Venus de Milo. Make a study of her statuesque poses, her lofty calm, her imperial manner—"

Nita was struggling with her laughter and Miss Horsford was hesitating in the doorway with as near an approach to confusion as ever touched her "imperial manner."

"Ah, Miss Horsford," murmured Ralph, at last turning to face her. "Could you possibly have heard? Don't cover me with confusion by telling me that my inadequate and imperfect tribute—"

"If your opinion must be revised before it satisfies you, of course I will consider it unsaid. That is a good way to consider much of what he says, Nita."

"Oh, *I* know it," answered Nita.

"And she was afraid they wouldn't be able to keep the secret in the family if I persisted in talking so much. I suppose I have done for myself now. To save the wrecks it will be wisest for me to take myself off at once."

"Don't trouble yourself to invent any pressing business, Mr. Wendel. I have only stopped to carry your cousin off on a shopping expedition."

"Tradesman, tradesman, beware of the day
When the ladies shall meet thee in battle array.

You make a regularly triumphal procession of it, don't you? Don't you want a bard to sing your victories in the next issue of the *Dial?* And to think you should have drawn our pacific Dorothy into the warfare!"

"It is interesting to hear one's own name and nothing else," said Dorothy herself, coming down the stairs.

Miss Horsford, with evident relief, went to meet her in the hall.

"Mr. Wendel is in a satirical mood and is wasting on a small and unappreciative audience a store of eloquence that ought to be reserved for the readers of the *Dial*. We will leave him to his conscience."

"Oh, I am too busy to take charge of him this morning," said Nita demurely.

"At least you will permit an unworthy slave to see that the start is properly made," said Ralph. He accompanied them to the waiting sleigh and settled the rugs about them. "Do you drive, Miss Horsford?"

"Did you think I could not?"

"I should have known that your driving, like everything else, would be beyond criticism."

During the next few hours Dorothy came to have some idea of the latent possibilities in what she had heretofore considered one of the burdens of existence. Shopping, if properly managed, might then be made to resemble a royal progress. But at the same time she knew very well that she might as well demand canvas and a brush and straightway proceed to paint a Madonna that would make the world forget the name of Raphael as to attempt to match the genius of her new friend in this feminine art. From the time she lay in her cradle it had been decreed that she should say "please" and "if not too much trouble" when she came to the need of buying a spool of thread. To see the way in which her guide manipulated prices, salesmen, and other apparently stable facts, revived the admiring awe of her earliest impression. Miss Horsford had been most persistently civil during the intervening weeks, but Dorothy wondered curiously

how it would seem to be really familiar enough to call
her by her first name and perhaps make suggestions
as to the way she should do her hair.

"I like to see them all waiting and bowing and
submissive, don't you ¿ " said Miss Horsford in the
course of one of their rapid drives from one shop to
another.

"If I could manage it as you do, I probably
would."

" I think if I could have had my choice, I would
have liked to be one of the old-time queens. Before the
days of impertinent newspapers and rights of humanity and such things, of course. I would have liked to
see crowds about me with uncovered heads and to
know that their very life depended on my word. I
would have liked to lead the armies magnificently to
battle, to ride in triumph through the conquered cities,
or to have men guarding my retreat with their lives if
we were defeated. Everything nowadays is petty compared with such possibilities. Don't you wish you had
lived then ? '

"But the magnificent *rôle* would not have been
mine," laughed Dorothy.

Her companion turned to her with a quick smile.

" No, you would have been some sweet maid working tapestry in a high tower with white doves fluttering about you and tall lilies bending to you. And
there would be a fair-haired page who would love you
and sing sweet songs to the mandolin while you
listened, and you would never care to know what
happened in the world outside of your safe tower.
Then you would marry the page and live happy ever
after."

Dorothy thought of Lady Geraldine and smiled.

"No, I would not love the page, I think."

"Then you would be very hard-hearted, for he would love you and sing the most beautiful songs to you."

Oh, it is good for poets to love," said Dorothy lightly. "It is a part of their training. But to be successful in love—that is dangerous. It might make them forget their visions."

"So you would be cruel to him for his good? But no, you couldn't. It wouldn't be like the maiden in the lofty tower."

Dorothy shook her head. For some reason she resented this reading of a character for her with no chance to have a voice in the matter herself.

"I should not love your minstrel," she said composedly.

"Why not?" persisted Miss Horsford.

"The mandolin would be very pleasant for a summer day, and the songs might be sweet, but as for loving the singer—no, my hero should be some brave knight who had been away for years fighting for the true king, and who would come back at last, through dangers and glory and past the praise of others, to me for his guerdon."

Miss Horsford looked at her kindling face with no responding enthusiasm.

"That is too pretty for a fancy sketch. You must have seen your ideal."

Dorothy shook her head.

"No. There are minstrels now, but no knights since—" "Since Harry died," she would have said, but Miss Horsford could not know of him.

"Indeed! Here are two who would not feel flattered by your sweeping denial," said Miss Horsford. She stopped the sleigh by the pavement as the stream of pedestrians carried Alec Macdonald and Ralph Wendel abreast of them.

"I cast my vote for pearl passementerie on black lace," said Ralph by way of greeting. "That was the question at issue, wasn't it?"

"No, we happened to be discussing that other feminine topic—love," said Miss Horsford with a somewhat malicious smile at Dorothy.

"This is exciting," cried Ralph, looking eagerly from one to the other. "You must tell us what the verdict was."

"Oh, it was nonsense," interrupted Dorothy quickly. "It was only a fairy tale."

"Miss Vanborough declared," the traitor went on with a lazy smile, "that her love could only be won by some Sir Galahad, some spotless knight on whose fame there was no shame and no reproach." Her smiling eyes rested on Macdonald as she spoke.

"Oh, no, that is not it at all," cried Dorothy with an indignant blush, and she too looked instinctively at Alec. His gaze met hers without pain or confusion.

"No one else would dare attempt the high emprise," said Ralph, unconscious of this flashing by-play. "If it be necessary to go back to the days of Bayard and Sidney to find one worthy, that is the misfortune of the moderns."

"For my part, I prefer a live modern to a dead ancient," said Miss Horsford easily.

"As one of the moderns, I thank you," replied Macdonald, to whom her look had been addressed.

"Since the choice is not open to us, we must e'en make the best we can of ourselves and try to be content."

"Your sentiments are as correct as usual, Alec, but I confess I am not wholly reconciled to the necessity of wearing serviceable but most unpicturesque garments in place of velvet doublets with silver fringe and caps with plumes and buckles."

"But the doublets weren't all of velvet, and there were caps without plumes even then."

"Oh, I dare say the moderns are more comfortable, if you are going to be prosaic and economic. They are too comfortable ; that's why they aren't more interesting."

"Oh, not all," said Dorothy earnestly, " Dr. Blount has told me—"

Macdonald turned to her with an illuminating smile. "Already? Dr. Blount is a good guide. He knows more halt and lame and blind than any other man in town."

"I didn't suppose there were any to know in this new town," said Miss Horsford languidly.

"We can't pretend to compare with the effete East in that respect, but we have to keep a moderate supply on hand for men like the doctor and Alec to exercise their benevolent proclivities on."

"I have an idea," cried Miss Horsford, with sudden interest. "Listen, liegemen mine. I want to go slumming."

"To hear is to obey. But I am sorry to say I don't know of any fever district in operation at this time. Will you take your slumming plain ? "

"I will take it with good company. You shall all

go with me. Won't it be fun, Miss Vanborough? I
have always wanted to know how such people live."

"But I warn you beforehand the doctor would not
give you a diploma after one visit."

"You are jesting. I am in earnest," she said imperatively.

"Seriously?"

"Of course."

"It will be unpleasant."

"So much the better."

"Oh, if you are bent on real work, I must turn you
over to Macdonald. I only have charge of the æsthetic side of the business."

She shook the ribbons out over her restless horse.

"I have spoken. Let all true knights attend,"
she said, flashing a smile backward. "It is a quest."

Ralph laid his hand on his heart.

"What has put her up to that, do you suppose?"
he asked.

"To what? Oh, slumming? Just a fancy, I imagine," answered Macdonald abstractedly.

"Will you help her carry it out?"

"I don't know. Your cousin didn't seem to like
the idea."

"Didn't she? I didn't notice. But what has that
to do with Miss Horsford's going?"

"Nothing," said Macdonald, rousing himself. "Of
course I will do what I can to arrange a proper display of misery for her. There is a certain luxury in
touching such facts of life with the tips of one's finger's,
and ladies like Miss Horsford have a divine right to
luxury."

Ralph looked at him curiously.

"Is that outburst the result of my bad example? I thought her likes as well as her dislikes were reciprocated."

The gayety of the shopping expedition had vanished. Dorothy had been put out of tune, and sat silent with face turned resolutely away. The interpretation put upon her little speech and its repetition had seemed most unfair. It had been made to sound like a reflection upon Macdonald, and from her. Would he think they had been talking about him as one who might try to win her heart? Would he believe that she could not only say hard words to him but cowardly words about him? Did Miss Horsford know? Was she so secure in her power that it amused her to play with it?

And Miss Horsford, with a bright spot in either cheek for which the keen air was not wholly responsible, sat moodily beside her and made no effort, as she had done before, to be agreeable. There had been no chance playing in her work, and with keener eyes than Dorothy she had detected signs that told her all she cared to know. She was not sure that the certainty that Macdonald was interested in this soft-eyed woman was after all worth the mortification it brought. Was it worth while to try the extent of the interest? Was any game in life worth the candle?

As they turned into the home street she aroused herself.

"Driving is stupid, isn't it? But nearly everything is. Life is rather stupid on the whole."

There was something under the mockery of her voice that made Dorothy straightway forget her vexation.

"Oh, surely never stupid for you! You can do so much, you have so much, you are rich in so many ways."

Miss Horsford lifted her shoulders impatiently.

> " You bid a hungry child be satisfied
> With a heritage of many cornfields ; nay,
> He says he's hungry—he would rather have
> That little barley-cake you keep from him
> While reckoning up his harvests."

One may tell one's heart secrets to children, sure they will not understand. Perhaps she was not risking much in treating Dorothy like a child.

CHAPTER XVI.

DOROTHY had been in Hawthorne nearly two months. She counted it up one day as she stood by the window looking out upon a snow-storm like that other which had met her at the threshold of the winter. The trees along the edge of the street held up their bare arms to receive the white shower that mimicked the shower of petals they had scattered in the spring-time, and out in the country the white mantle must be folding itself softly about the brown shoulders of the hills. She sighed involuntarily, looking out into the deepening silence. It was very quiet and peaceful, but somehow she was not at rest.

It was a very placid life that she had lived all those past years. She had looked at the tumult and turmoil of human affairs, as she caught glimpses of them through other lives, and half repined that her own safe inlet had no room for storms, no place for possible shipwreck. But now there was a ripple on the smooth water, and out beyond the harbor bar she could catch the white flash of breakers that made her half tremble and half thrill with eagerness to meet them. It dated, she was well aware, from her compact of friendship with Macdonald. She had deserted her position and abandoned an idea which had the authority of habit. Her defection might be justifiable on purely humanitarian grounds, but it had introduced a new factor into her life which she had not as yet been able to dispose of in orderly array, and she was unaccustomed to having emotions flying at loose ends about her. She had been a little doubtful at first of the way in which Mr. Macdonald himself would regard her half-hearted concession. Would he realize that it was entirely for Harry's sake and not at all for his own that she had consented to be ordinarily civil?

But on that score at least she had no need for disquiet. There was on his part a quiet acceptance of her friendliness with all its reservations. He came often to the house, sometimes not seeing her at all, sometimes seeing no one else, but he never overstepped the line she had drawn. Only he knew how deeprooted was her distrust of him, and only he knew his silent determination to conquer it.

She was still looking out at the snow-fall, in a mazy dream of past and present, when Macdonald himself came springing up the steps. He saw her at the window and raised his hat with a brightly confident smile to which it would have been impossible not to respond in kind.

Dorothy remembered what Ralph had once said, and went herself to open the door.

"Isn't this fun?" he asked boyishly, shaking the snow from him. The wind, or something else, had blown a glow into his brown face. "Have you been out?"

"No."

"I thought you liked snow-storms." There was reminiscence in his smile.

"I had only been looking at a glazed and framed picture of this one."

"Through the window? Oh, you were the picture. I thought so as I came up. How does it seem to look out on the world from a frame?"

"I wonder if that isn't what I have always been doing, rather," she said slowly.

"And don't you like it?" he asked curiously.

"Do you think St. John there likes it? He would speak if he could come down."

He held out his hand to her jestingly.

"Come down, fair picture!"

"I can't," she said, drawing back, but smiling too. "Don't you remember the starling?"

"Galatea was a statue, you know, and that is worse than being a picture, and yet she came to live when—" He hesitated, not quite daring to name Pygmalion to her, but there was an odd little smile on his lips. "I came to learn whether I may count on you to make one of Miss Horsford's slumming party."

"Thank you, but—I think not."

"Would you mind giving a reason?"

"Because I don't think I could do any good by going," she said, flushing, "and I would feel that I

was impertinent to go peering into the misery of people's lives just for the sensation I might get out of it."

"Then does the motive decide?"

"Yes—I think so."

"Always?"

She drew back as though fearing a snare.

"Not to the extent of relieving one from responsibility for a mistake, I suppose. A general statement
is rather rash, isn't it?"

"You would rather keep to the slumming expedition. So would I—for the present. Can't we give it
another motive, then, to save it from your condemnation? We might make a Santa Claus party of it."

"What does that imply?"

"Candy and nuts and oranges, and a sleigh to take
us four to half a dozen poor families with children on
Christmas Eve. The almanacs predict it will fall on
next Wednesday this year."

"That sounds very enticing. I would like that."

"If you approve we will consider it settled. Miss
Horsford seemed to leave the arrangement to us. Do
you believe in omens?" he asked after a long moment.

"No, I think not. I don't even know about them.
Why?"

"You have granted the first petition I have presented," he said audaciously. "I was wondering
whether I might trust it as a sign. I may want to ask
something else some day."

She laughed softly.

"I don't think it would be safe. You would soon
become a skeptic if you pinned your faith to such
signs. It is my turn to ask something next."

He flashed an eager look at her.

"Anything—"

"May I make an addition to the candy and oranges? Toys or something of that sort?"

"I suppose I ought to ask the children's opinion first, but it might spoil their sleep beforehand. If you are willing to take their consent for granted, I see no obstacles in the way."

"But I ought to know something about the children —age and number and statistics of that sort."

"Perhaps I can help you, if you will give me a bit of paper."

"On my writing desk, just back of you."

He picked up a sheet, and in doing so scattered a number of scraps of folded paper.

"This looks suspiciously like poetry."

"Oh, yes. We were playing crambo last night. I want you to read Ralph's verse — you'll find it there."

He knew Ralph's hand, of course, and picking it out from the others, read these lines:

> Oh, the earth is as wide as wide can be,
> And so fair that the Day
> In its course might stay
> To dwell on the beauty of land and of sea.
> But a smile or a tone,
> Or a word alone,
> These make all the world, Love, to you and to me.

"Isn't it funny?" asked Dorothy from across the room.

"I didn't know Ralph wrote that sort of thing," he answered, going over the lines with increasing surprise. Had they been addressed to her? It was strange she should discuss them so.

"Why, it is exactly like him," said Dorothy. "I guessed it for his at once."

She came over to look at it, wondering why he was so unresponsive.

"Why, that isn't it. Did you find that here?" She took the half-sheet he held out and read it curiously.

"It is Ralph's hand, and it was right on top," he explained.

"I—I never saw this before. Ralph must have left it here afterward," she stammered, blushing rosily. "He meant it for a joke, of course. This is what I wanted you to see."

She searched hastily among the papers, wishing she could conquer that childish trick of blushing, wondering why Ralph had written so foolishly, and conscious through all that Macdonald's eyes were on her face with a surprised questioning. When at last she found the scrap she put it in his hand and promptly retreated out of range of his scrutiny.

> Weary with twelve months' roaming,
>   Earth came to Nature's knee,
> And begged for a bright, new plaything.
>   "These are old as old can be!"
> And gentle Nature answered,
>   In her mild maternal way:
> "A new, round year I give you;
>   There, child, now run away."

He read the lines twice before he knew what they were.

"Yes, that is very like Ralph," he said at last. "I asked him once why he didn't publish his verses, and he replied by asking if I had ever considered offering my photograph for sale."

"But that doesn't imply that his verses are always true to life," she answered gayly. "He said once that poets lived vicariously. They let other people have the experiences while they spent their time talking about them."

"That makes it rather difficult to know how far to credit their protestations," he said, taking up his hat. His eyes rested, unconsciously perhaps, on the paper she still held in her fingers, and following his glance she blushed again.

"You haven't made me that list yet."

"Your poetry put it out of my head," he answered lightly. He made it out, however, and then soon took his leave. As he walked down the street he pondered on the meaning of the little love song he had innocently intercepted. Was that vicarious, dramatic? Was there any hint of earnest in it? What did her tantalizing blushes mean?

He might have been still more disturbed if he could have seen Dorothy, when he left the room, stop to read the penciled verses again, and then, with a shy, conscious pleasure on smiling lips and eyes, slip the paper into her dress. It was very absurd, of course, for Ralph to write it, but—it was pretty, and people had not often sent verses to her. Lady Geraldine probably had reams of them.

CHAPTER XVII.

"WHAT are you going to wear to-night?" demanded Nita, popping her head into Dorothy's room. Wednesday evening and Christmas Eve with it had come around.

" This dress."

" What wrap ? "

" My cloak, I suppose."

" What headgear ? "

Dorothy laughed.

" Have you any suggestions to make ? "

Nita came in and took up her station on the arm of a wide chair.

"I want you to do something artistic," she said seriously. "You could make a perfect picture of yourself, and what is the use of wasting an opportunity ? "

Dorothy regarded her dress as though it struck her in a new light.

"Why, isn't this all right ?"

" I wish you would let me be your maid."

Dorothy laughed and shook her head. "You are too radical a young woman. I dare not trust you."

"Oh, I will not do anything in bad taste. You shall see. I would only make you a vision of delight to inculcate æsthetic ideas in the little slummers. Just let me try. Sit down and let me do your hair." And disregarding Dorothy's laughing protest, she pulled down the smooth coils of hair with the eagerness of an artist.

" Do you remember the Paris hair-dresser who

wanted to curl Joseph the Second's hair in little tight
rings all over his head because he had the contour of a
negro?" she asked in an interval of hairpins. "I am
not going to be as consistent as that, however, so you
need not be frightened."

"What would you do if you were?"

Nita rolled the dull masses of hair over her hand
and tried different effects.

"Your face is Egyptian," she remarked, after a
critical scrutiny with half-shut eyes. "Did you know
it?"

"No, indeed, I didn't."

"Oh, not like a mummy. Nor like the sphinx.
You know the look I mean—elusive and kind of mysterious. I suppose that was what—somebody—meant
when he said you had a lotus face."

"Who said that, Nita?"

"Ah, you are interested, are you?"

"Of course. I don't pretend to be loftily indifferent. Who was it?"

Nita bent around to peep teasingly in her face.

"Never you mind. Perhaps I will tell you some
day. Now— Hark! There are the sleigh-bells!"

She ran to reconnoitre over the banister and returned immediately.

"Yes, it is Mr. Macdonald. Miss Horsford isn't
coming in, so you must go at once. Where is your
wrap? Oh, not your cloak—that lovely white thing I
saw here one day. Ah, that is perfect! Now—no,
wait a moment."

She flew into her own room and came back with a
soft, white scarf which she proceeded to wind artistic-
ally about Dorothy's head and throat.

"It isn't a bit cold, so this will be all right. You look like a snow-queen," she cried rapturously, falling back to get a comprehensive view. "I am going to peep over the banister and see the effect when you go down."

"I am afraid you have made me look rather theatrical," protested Dorothy, looking with some dismay at the white vision that confronted her in the glass.

"Nonsense. You are lovely. The children won't need to be half-asleep to believe that you are an angel right out of their story books. Come, you musn't keep them waiting."

She swept Dorothy on by the force of her own impetuosity. Wendel and Macdonald were lounging at the bottom of the stairs, waiting, and by the sudden start with which they drew themselves up when Dorothy appeared, the wise young woman above knew that her scheming had produced the right effect.

"Miss Horsford couldn't come anywhere near it," she remarked audibly to herself.

If Miss Horsford was conscious of that fact, it did not seem to cast a gloom over her spirits. She was unusually gay, and the distance which generally separated her from her fellow-beings had been reduced several millions of miles.

"Can you find room between me and that bag of oranges? This paper parcel I will give you to hold in your lap when you are settled. Oh, your cousin is bringing more things!"

'Yes, I added some toys," said Dorothy. "I thought it would make it seem more real."

"I think we all had the same inspiration. We will simply be buried. Mr. Wendel, do you think the driver can be trusted with this bag of candy? We haven't room for it."

"Is it good candy?"

"I bought it myself!"

"Then I think Alec and I will take charge of it. Jump in, Alec. What was that you stepped on? The rubber rattles? I think we can swear the driver in to take charge of them."

"Tell him to drive down Rice Street first. We must take the places in order."

"All right. Ready? Go on, driver." They flew away with the sleigh-bells ringing in sympathetic jubilation.

"Is this what you call taking your slumming plain, Mr. Wendel?" asked Miss Horsford.

"No this is slumming with modern improvements."

"I am glad you haven't improved slumming out of existence with all your progress of the age."

"It is to be hoped the people in the slums share your satisfaction."

"Oh!" she said loftily. "Are you a Socialist, Mr. Wendel?"

"I suppose I am, in sections. But there are Socialists and Socialists, you know. I am still on friendly relations with soap and water."

"Who writes the socialistic articles in the *Dial*?"

"That is a secret."

"Very well; then tell it."

"I beg pardon!"

"Secrets were made to be told, just as nuts were made to be cracked."

Ralph gave her a look of profound admiration.

"My dear Miss Horsford, can't we induce you to take charge of a new half-column department in the *Dial* to be called 'The Mystery of the Cosmos unriddled'?"

Dorothy had been leaning back in her corner listening with a smile to the cross-fire and watching the lights flashing past them. If she looked up she encountered Macdonald's eyes opposite, with a look of supreme content in them. Something made her think of the words—

> It is enough
> Only to be in the same room with you.
> I need not speak to you nor hear you speak ;
> If I but see you I am satisfied.

Was that what his look meant? It seemed to fold her about with an unquestioning possession. Did she want to question it? How long had it lasted? Was she alone conscious of the electric message? With the blood beating in her cheeks she leaned forward suddenly to speak to Miss Horsford. The spell was broken.

"This is the first place," said Alec, signaling the driver. "Will you lead the way, Ralph? You can introduce the subject gracefully."

"I will let my chestnuts speak for me," declared Wendel, providing himself with a pouch of that ammunition.

They followed him down some broken steps to the door of a "squatter's" shanty.

"It is quite traditionally desolate," murmured Miss Horsford. "I didn't know people lived in such places."

"May we come in?" Ralph was saying to the

startled little girl who had opened the door. "Santa Claus sent us to wish you a merry Christmas."

In sheer amazement she held the door wide without a word, and they crowded in. The room was small, but not uncheerful. It had evidently been furbished up for the holiday, for a small Christmas tree on the table made the bravest possible display of its cheap brightness ; the wooden chairs and table and bare floor were clean, and the girl's dress was painstakingly tidy. A little boy of five and a man who walked with a crutch had come forward out of the dim corners and were staring with equal astonishment as their visitors piled up on the table the fruit their Christmas tree had given no signs of bearing.

"Here's some candy, with Santa Claus's love, and here are oranges, with Santa Claus's best wishes, and here are nuts, with Santa Claus's warning, and here's a story-book that Santa Claus thinks the little girl will like," said Ralph with voluminous cheerfulness.

"Who told you the way ? " demanded the baby boy, looking up into Dorothy's face.

" Hush, Frankie," whispered his sister, trying to pull him back. But he persisted fearlessly, his distinct baby utterance made more vivid by his wide eyes and earnest face.

" I thought it might be a mis-take, 'cause one day a 'spress man brought a box, a big box, and he tumed and tuckt it away, the 'spress man did, 'cause he made a mis-take. Addie told me. And I *thought* that prob-a-bly it might be a mis-take."

" No, it isn't a mistake this time. It is all right, ' said Dorothy with shining eyes, sitting down and drawing him to her. "Take a peep into my bag and tell me what you like best."

The bag held a conglomeration of toys suited to various ages, but Frankie's eyes were quick and his mind clear. He gave a squeal of delight, and dragging out a train of tin cars he threw himself flat upon the floor in his eagerness to set them to work.

"They go, Addie! Papa, look! They go!" he shouted, and go they certainly did under the guidance of their energetic if reckless engineer.

"Leave lots of things," whispered Dorothy hastily to her coadjutors. "We can't possibly find any one else so delicious."

"Would you like a doll, little girl?" asked Miss Horsford.

"Thank you," faltered the child, too shy to even look at her new acquisition.

"Santa Claus is ringing his bells. That means hurry up! Merry Christmas, all!"

"Merry Christmas! Merry Christmas!" shouted Frankie, running after them to the door; and even when they reached the sleigh they heard his shrill call, "Merry Christmas!" through the frosty air.

"That was very satisfactory," said Miss Horsford. "How grateful the little girl looked! And the father seemed dumbfounded with surprise. I hope you have some more like that on your list."

"But did you notice the æstheticism of the natives?" asked Ralph. "Did you see the geraniums growing in oyster-cans and the newspaper prints on the wall? I am going to send around some real pictures with frames to-morrow."

"I wonder where the mother was," said Dorothy.

"She is dead," answered Macdonald gently. "Addie is the house-keeper, and a very good one, too, considering the fact that she is only nine years old."

"Oh! That little thing!" murmured Dorothy.

"Her father ought to send her away to some boarding-school or home where she would be taken care of," exclaimed Miss Horsford.

"And Frankie?"

"There must be places where children are taken."

Nobody spoke for a moment, and then Ralph said plaintively:

"It seems to me there is prob-ably a mis-take in the world somewhere."

But they had occasion to laugh oftener than to weep in the course of their adventures that evening. They were met so heartily, with so brave and cheery a seconding, that they fell in love with one and all their pensioners, from the baby who clamorously insisted on having the red jumping-jack instead of the blue one to the lonely old negress they stumbled upon by mistake who hadn't any children but who beamed her gratitude for a double portion of the golden oranges that spoke to her of her old home. After a while the astonished parents had to drag sleeping children out of their beds to see the wonderful visitors, and there were occasions when the graceless young mortals resented the irregular proceedings with language more vigorous than appreciative. At one place the house was all dark, but Alec insisted it was a particularly desolate family, so they shouted their errand through the key-hole. After some exposition the door was opened by invisible agents, and they found themselves inside but in stifling darkness. They waited for developments, but none coming, they felt around until they encountered a table. On this they poured out a miscellaneous store and then retreated in smothered silence. It was gratifying to observe that a light immediately appeared in the chinks of the window, showing that the inhabitants had come out of the inner recesses to view the substantial results of the visitation.

"I think we will only have time for one other place," said Alec at last. "It is rather barbarous to wake people out their first sleep, even to load them with gifts. Let us take an account of stock and astonish one more family, and then it will be almost time for us to bid each other a Merry Christmas."

"My things are all gone," said Dorothy.

Miss Horsford made an investigation, and found that she was still the custodian of three dolls.

"I am not sure whether this is chiefly candy-crumbs or nuts," said Ralph, peering dubiously into his stores. "You see, the papers broke. You are in luck, Alec, to have easy things like oranges."

"Never mind. The children will think it is a new kind of puzzle," said Alec serenely.

They were whirled away in a new direction over untraveled roads, with only an occasional street lamp to make a circumscribed glare in the darkness. What light there was came in some soft, mysterious way from the snow itself. But presently the driver stopped and Alec jumped out to investigate.

"He says he can't take us the rest of the way," he reported in a moment. "It is down a pretty steep hill, and the street isn't open to travel. Shall we give it up or try a scramble?"

"Oh, we will walk," decided Miss Horsford, getting out hastily. "Isn't it nearly midnight? This is the nearest approach to an adventure I have had in this prosaic town. Is this the way?"

"Take care. It is steep and slippery," said Alec, hurrying after her. "Better wait till Ralph comes with the lantern."

She threw back a mocking laugh.

"I served my apprenticeship on the Alps!"

"They seem very gay," remarked Ralph, lingering to relight the lantern. "Are you waiting for me, Dorothy? What a good girl you are!"

"No, only prudent. You have the light. How did you come to know about all these people?"

"Oh, Alec knew. He made up the list."

She walked by his side without speaking.

"Do you remember that first talk we had about Alec?" he went on. "Something came up the other day that reminded me of it, and as it is a sort of sequel to that old story of his, I think I have a right to tell you. Alec is always doing something for people that need help—practical charity, you know, that nobody knows much of anything about except the fellows he puts on their feet. There was one man he got interested in who was a pretty tough character. Knew more about the inside of a jail than any other home. The last time he was discharged Alec was looking out for him, to get him started in some honest work before he had time to go adrift. But the man held off in that sort of water-proof way you can imagine, shivering at anything that bore the stamp of goodness, even Alec's unostentatious kind. Suddenly one day he turned square around, met Alec's advances frankly, took his assistance and suggestions willingly, got the position he had kept for him, and is now putting the same dogged force into living an honest life that he had spent before in holding it at arm's length. Alec told me about the case as a curious example of the inexplicability of human nature, and as I am interested in curiosities I took an opportunity to look the man up and get him to talk about himself."

"Well?" said Dorothy as he stopped.

"Well, the secret was simply that he had somehow learned that story of Alec's boyhood that you and I know, Dorothy. 'I hadn't known before that he was one of us,' the man said. I tell you, it seemed to me there was consecration in such a wrong lived down. It made me wish that I were a reformed burglar, if that would make it possible for me to get at the poor devils."

She did not answer in words, but he was satisfied.

Macdonald and Miss Horsford were waiting at the foot of the hill, and as the cousins came slowly down to them Alec turned to meet them. Perhaps it was the dim light, making Dorothy's face look pale and her loose hair dark under the edge of her white scarf, or perhaps it was her strange white garb, from which her face gleamed whitely, that made Alec think of some descending saint. His heart stood still for a moment, as though a hand had been laid upon it. As long as he lived he could recall at will that white vision coming slowly toward him down the snowy hill, with a light in her eyes that held all the old-time friendliness and something more. Unconsciously he moved toward her.

"Is this the place?" she asked.

14

"Yes," he answered. He was still looking at her as though all his senses were absorbed in that smiling gaze.

"But this is a tin-shop, Alec," exclaimed Ralph.

"Go around to the back door. There is a family living there with two children—little cash girls. Harding is the name."

The mean door was opened at once to Alec's knock, and a dark, handsome woman confronted him with a look of defiance that seemed to have become habitual.

"We have brought some Christmas things for the children," said Ralph with his confident smile.

"They haven't come from the store yet."

"Not home yet! Think of it, Miss Horsford! But we can leave our Christmas greetings with you till they do come."

The woman gave no sign of invitation.

"Aren't you going to let us in, my good woman?" said Miss Horsford impatiently. "Your children may be grateful, if you are not."

The woman made some angry exclamation and walked back into the room, leaving the door open. At this moment Alec came up.

"She's huffy," said Ralph, shrugging his shoulders.

Alec went in and the others followed.

"Mrs. Falkland? You here? This is more of a Christmas party than we expected. Is Mrs. Harding at home?"

"Yes, and likely to be," she answered over her shoulder.

"Do you mean she is not well?"

"A trifle indisposed," she answered mockingly. "The weather has been trying for delicate nerves. Or perhaps the flavor of the last lot of hot-house fruits didn't agree with her. When one's arm has been broken by a drunken husband with a stove poker one may perhaps be fanciful. One may wish to slink out of sight, like a sick dog, and not be troubled, but of course if your fine ladies want to come and see the show it is not for a 'good woman' to presume to object."

Miss Horsford stared, laughed, and moved toward the door, but Dorothy, with a swift comprehension, turned to Alec.

"Will you not introduce me, Mr. Macdonald?"

In some bewilderment he pronounced their names.

"We didn't mean to intrude, Mrs. Falkland," said Dorothy in her unruffled way. "We came on much the same errand that brought you—to try to make Christmas brighter for the little children. Do you think it will be best for us to just leave some little things here on the table?"

The appeal was successful. Mrs. Falkland was not the woman to show herself ignorant of the ways of gentle life.

"They will be right pleased, poor little things. It isn't much Christmas they would have in this house if somebody didn't see to it. If you mean to leave anything, better put it here, where they will see it when they come home."

"Yes, that will be best."

They hastened to arrange the remnants of their stores in as presentable a form as possible, but without much gayety. When it was done and they were ready to say good night, Mrs. Falkland turned to Dorothy.

"Aren't you Mr. Vanborough's sister—Harry Vanborough?"

"Yes," said Dorothy, much surprised.

"My husband knew him well. They were great friends," she remarked loftily, but with a side glance to see how this fact would affect the impassive Miss Horsford.

"Oh, I remember now. I knew your name was familiar," said Dorothy quickly. "Mr. Falkland was in my brother's office, was he not? I would so much like to see him."

Macdonald opened the door for Miss Horsford.

"I can not stop now," said Dorothy hastily, "but you must let me come and see you. Where do you live?"

Mrs. Falkland told her, but with some embarassment. The little string she had pulled seemed to be bringing more about her ears than she had counted on. When the door closed behind her guests she laughed hardly, and then stood silent in frowning thought. But for all that she had a kindly word for the sleepy little cash-girls when they appeared.

"What can we make out of it all?" asked Ralph, as the sleigh flew homeward through more familiar streets. "What is the meaning of that suffering and want? We forget about it in our own busy lives, but whenever we look up there the question is facing us. Why should such evil be?"

"I don't know. I don't know," said Dorothy drearily.

"It must be their own fault, chiefly," exclaimed Miss Horsford. "Of course they don't feel it as we would, but still they could live better if they were not so stupid."

"But they did not choose to be stupid. That is a part of it," answered Ralph.

Instinctively they all looked to Macdonald. He was one of the people. He had known what it was to lie hard and dress meanly and to feel with a boy's keenness the lack of a breakfast. Had he found an answer to the riddle in the heart of the riddle itself? He met their unspoken inquiry with his own serene smile.

"Do you remember how Epictetus compares the circumstances of life to the trials which a gymnastic trainer sets his pupil in order to develop those certain muscles where strength is needed? I believe that, not as a figure of speech but as a living truth."

"But it is rather rough on the poor fellows who have to take the training against their will."

"Then it follows that as soon as they put their will in harmony with the training it ceases to be rough."

"At any rate you can't deny that the training seems to be unfairly distributed."

"But I do deny it. You are looking into the gymnasium during one lesson only. At the end of the term the results will show that the tasks have been equal."

"Then do you believe in other lessons—that is, other lives?"

"A thousand, if necessary. Why not? Granting one, why not others? If one life leaves the work unfinished, there must be others of logical necessity."

"Oh, but that sounds like an impossibility," exclaimed Miss Horsford, breaking silence.

"I can sooner believe the universe founded on an

impossibility than on an injustice," said Macdonald quietly.

"Oh, what is the use of thinking about such things?" she answered restlessly. "Life is pleasant enough if we don't stir it up from the bottom."

"And if we can forget that there are people living down there in the ooze," suggested Ralph.

"Why should we remember? Remembering such things makes one tired. Forget them, and cry with me, *Vive la bagatelle!*" She leaned forward with a gesture of challenge ; there was a glow in her face as though she knew her imperious beauty was trying its strength against some intangible opponent, and she must stand or fall with it. For a moment she carried the mood of the two men with her, then—

"Ah, Eve, Eve!" murmured Ralph lightly, and Alec's eyes went back to the stillness of Dorothy's face and rested there.

Then came the good-nights, quietly and quickly said. Dorothy ran at once up to her room. It was warm and dark, and greeted her like a friend. "'The dear, dark dead of night,'" she said to herself, and then the other words followed :

"You groped your way across my room i' the dear, dark dead of
    night ;
At each fresh step a stumble was ; but once your lamp alight,
Easy and plain you walked again ; so soon all wrong grew right !
Be love your light and trust your guide ; with these explore my
    heart ;
No obstacle to trip you there, strike hands and souls apart !
Since rooms and hearts are furnished so—light shows you—need
    love start?"

She pushed up the window and leaned out into the night, waiting for the midnight chime. Under her lay the city, all wrapped in "the dear, dark dead of night" out of which she had just come. She was smiling softly to herself. "Be love your light—" How wide the world was, and how beautiful! And how true hearts might be—were! "Be love your light, be trust your guide—" Ah, rash to try to read hearts without that light. She held out her arms into the night with a welcoming gesture.

Suddenly the bells rang out over her, tossing a greeting upon the darkness that was caught up and sent back and re-echoed again until it widened into a woven swell of sound. "Peace on earth," was the message, "peace on earth that comes of good will to men." It was a widening of the other song in her heart, "Be love your light, be trust your guide"; yea, for all the world. That is the blossoming of love. Rising and falling and lifting, the waves of sound carried her out and away into a world where discord was not, nor fear, which is discord, nor aught save the great sweep of unity. Then the bells fell away one by one into silence, as pearls are dropped into a waveless sea. Where had the message of peace gone? Out into space, or into the hearts of men? She shivered a little and turned from the chill of the night to the warm, June-scented room.

There *were* roses in the room. She found them now, and forgot the song of the darkness as she hung in still delight over the perfect flowers, drooping with the weight of their own perfume. "Be love your light—" Some thought brought a reflection of the roses into her cheeks.

CHAPTER XVIII.

NITA aroused the household the next morning by
an exquisite rendition of old Christmas carols especially arranged by herself for a dressing-comb orchestra.
Ralph considered it a part of his duty to go down
promptly and congratulate her, and after that there
was no more sleep for the household than for Duncan.

"And what next ? " Nita was asking when Dorothy came down half an hour later.

" I'm relating our adventures, Dorothy.   Set me
right if my memory fails me.   When we left the place
I told you about where nine small children were fighting with tomahawks over a box of caramels, we came
upon a package-delivery man who was scattering cir-
culars warning people against us as a rival establish-
ment which was trying to run him out of business.
We immediately challenged him to mortal combat."

" Wait a minute.   I want to know something first.
Did Miss Horsford wear roses ? "

" No."

" Didn't she, Dorothy ? "

" I didn't see any.   Why ? "

" Oh, for a reason.   This child sees what is going on."

" And she dearly loves to tell and hopes some one
will ask her what it is all about," said Ralph teasingly.

Nita frowned, but the joys of being dignified had
to give way to the joys of retailing her news.

" Oh, perhaps you wouldn't haven't been interested
in seeing your severe, your formal, your unromantic,

and practical Mr. Macdonald buying out the whole stock of June and Co.'s cut flowers yesterday! And perhaps you wouldn't have listened with both ears if you had heard Miss Horsford putting him up to it!"

"Look out, Nita, or you'll be a reporter one of these days."

"But she did all the same. She said how she loved roses, and how much more she loved them in winter than in summer, and how she always breakfasted on rose-leaves at home, or something of that sort. We all happened to be in at June's at the same time. She didn't mind talking before me, because of course I wouldn't understand. I'm only an innocent schoolgirl, even if I have read Romeo and Juliet and classical manuals of courtship like that. Then she considerately went away so as to give him a chance to work on her hint, and, as I told you in the first place, he bought almost all the cut roses in the place. Extravgant? Well, that is a matter of opinion."

" Yes, and he probably sent them down to the Bohemian Flats or to his pet hospital, you frivolous young person," retorted Ralph.

Dorothy had been curiously silent. The explanation must come sooner or later, however, so with a rather elaborate carelessness she asked :

" By the way, whom am I to thank for my roses ? "

" What roses ? "

" I found a basket in my room last night. Don't you know, Nita ? Truly ? "

" Not a word. Some one must have sent them while we were all out. May I bring them down ? "

Dorothy nodded and she darted away. In a moment she was back.

"Oh, you sly Cousin Dorothy ! So the roses were for you, after all ! "

" But there was no card. I do not know at all who sent them."

"Well, I do. I know every bud. Didn't I watch the clerk wrap them up in that very blue paper, and didn't I wish they were for me ? "

" So they are, whoever may have sent them. Let me divide."

"No, not yet. Leave them just as they are for a while. I want Miss Horsford to see them."

The amiable wish was speedily gratified, for Miss Horsford came early in the day.

"We have just been to the different churches hearing the music, papa and I," she said radiantly. "I only came in to make sure that you were not tired to death. It was so good of you to go."

"I am very glad I went," said Dorothy, smilingly accepting the position of chaperon assigned her. " I mean to do the same thing next year."

"Oh, it would be stupid to repeat it. I hate things when they become monotonous."

"I don't believe the children would call twice monotony."

"Oh, it is your *rôle* to be good," said Miss Horsford with a laugh which the loyal Nita promptly resented. " I would always turn instinctively to you for the virtues and beneficences. I haven't any of them myself—but you would make the sweetest possible St. Elizabeth."

"So she would, roses and all," cried Nita, who was rapidly learning how to use her foils. " You haven't seen Dorothy's roses. Aren't they exquisite? The very same we were admiring at June's yesterday, when Mr. Macdonald came in. Don't you think that roses are much more delicious in winter than in summer?"

"Yes, they are very pretty," said Miss Horsford, steadily looking her young antagonist down. "But the perfume is too heavy in such market-like masses."

"But the mass is divisible," said Dorothy, untwining a spray of the sweetest. "Let me fasten these in your cloak."

"Thank you," said the recipient negligently. "Papa is waiting outside and I promised to only look in. Isn't it stupid to have Nellie gone? Good-by, my dear."

She drew up the black furs that had slipped about her arms and nodded her farewells with a brighter eye and a more brilliant smile than ever. But when her sleigh turned the corner there was a flash of color for a moment as a gloved hand dropped a spray of crimson roses into the soft grave of the snow.

When Macdonald came around the corner half an hour later his foot struck against some broken and bedraggled flowers, staining the snow with their crimson petals, but he did not read the message they might have told him. He only wondered whether Dorothy had guessed from whom her roses came, and whether, if she had guessed, she would be displeased or no. His doubt vanished when she greeted him with the same look that had thrilled him the night before.

"I have brought you something, since it is the season of gifts," he said, looking down at her with smiling eyes. "Will you promise to like it?"

"Before I see it? That would be flattering your taste too much," she answered demurely.

He put in her hands a little brown book, worn and shabby.

"Oh!" she cried softly, turning to the title-page. There, in a round, school-girl hand, was the inscription in faded ink, "Harry, from Dorothy." Her eyes grew dim as she turned the pages and saw Harry's marks and notes along the margins. She had forgotten Alec, forgotten everything but the birthday morning when Harry had been so pleased over her present of Keats. And as Macdonald watched, a different picture of what might be arose before his mind—a picture of the same face stricken with knowledge, the sister putting the book away with a bitter pain because it bore the name of Harry Vanborough. Was that what lay within the temptation to clear his name at last which had come to him of late? Dorothy, looking up gratefully, saw the sadness in his face, and, fancying it must be because he too was thinking of the dead friend, she became so sweet and earnest and friendly that it would have been impossible for him to remember Harry or anything else in that insignificant portion of the universe which lay outside the room illuminated by her presence.

But before he left he was brought back to the actual.

"Don't you think it possible," Dorothy asked, "that Mr. Falkland might have some letters of Harry's in his possession?"

"Do you know Falkland?" he asked with a look of dismay.

"No, but that was his wife we met last night.

Don't you remember? When she spoke of her husband being so much with Harry, I thought at once that
perhaps he might have some letters, or something of
that sort—something that had once been Harry's, you
know, and that wouldn't be of any value to him, as
it would to me. I have hardly anything of his."
Her voice was so low and tremulous that Alec was
divided between a wild desire to send the whole
Falkland family off hunting the northwest passage
and a longing tö comfort Dorothy of the tender
eyes.

"Falkland is out of town," he answered, keeping
to the strict line of truth. He did not consider it
necessary to explain that Falkland would stay out of
town just as long as he could keep him away.

"But he will be back, won't he?"

"In any event he couldn't possibly have anything
but business letters," he added hastily. "There would
be nothing that could be of the slightest interest to
you."

"Anything that Harry wrote—*anything*—would be
of interest to me."

"But—I must warn you that Falkland is not altogether reliable," he stammered, wishing that he could
throttle the man instead of being obliged to defame him.
"He is not the sort of a man that Harry would care to
have as a mediator between you two. Less now than
then, even, though Harry overlooked a good deal because of his playing. You know he can play like a
child of Pan."

"I know?"

"Don't you remember the violinist on the train
when you came out to Hawthorne?"

"Oh!" She considered thoughtfully for a moment, and then asked: "What is his business?"

"Studying the science of chance, he would say. In other words, gambling."

"Oh, what a pity! If Harry had lived that could not have been."

Macdonald had some doubts on that subject, but he had no doubt whatsoever that Harry was a lucky fellow to have so much faith poured out on his memory. It was worth while becoming a memory for, and he wondered somewhat ruefully if that was the only way to Dorothy's heart.

No, there was one other way. The thought took his breath away when it struck him sharply upon his recalling Dorothy's words. Falkland was entirely untrustworthy. It was only by a constant pressure that Macdonald had been able to insist upon his keeping his knowledge of Harry's story to himself. Let that pressure be simply withdrawn, and in its place let Dorothy come with her pretty interest and flattering confidence, and the chances were a hundred to one that Falkland would tell all he knew and more. Well, suppose he did? Alec breathed hard for a moment. His name would be cleared, and before Dorothy, and without any action of his own. Did he not have a right to let matters drift? Who could say he had not already paid his debt in full measure? The impulse that had led the boy to shoulder another's guilt had been a mistaken if generous one. And again the boy had not realized what he was doing. He had made his offering recklessly, without counting the cost. He had not even begun to realize what the cost was until Dorothy came again into his life. Now the man must face the fact that the boy had probably tossed away his chances of winning that which made all other values in life seem cheap.

Probably—but not surely. That was the point that stayed him. His temper was of the kind that is fired by difficulties. He recognized that he was handicapped in the race, and that in Dorothy's sight as with no one else he was dragged down by the weight of the past, and yet— He lifted his head with an obstinate smile. If her love could be won from her over her distrust, and faith inspired where it had seemed dead, would not the triumph have a grace unknown to easy victories?

If Alec had been less in Harry's debt, there might have been a morbid self-consciousness about his sacrifice that would have reacted upon himself. But at first his love for his friend, and afterward his clear judgment saved him from any demoralizing self-pity. He had not the satisfaction of playing a heroic part even in the privacy of his own thought. He was simply paying a debt, and that not in full. Harry Vanborough had died in saving his life. According to the popular code, his own life would be only a fair return. But the claims of his friend were even greater than for mere existence. It was Vanborough who had made his life worth living. He had opened the magic portals of knowledge and beckoned the uncouth country boy to enter. He had not created, but he had at least developed those finer qualities of Macdonald's nature which made this very shame so galling. And Alec had too true a perception ever to forget that the clear apprehension of honor was of more importance than the reputation before the world of bearing his honor unstained.

And the experience had done him no harm. Looking back he could not but admit that it had put iron
into every fiber of his nature. The strain, the discipline, the self-mastery had made him a man, able to
stand on his own feet, instead of clinging to even a
good standard because it had received popular sanc-
tion.

No, Falkland must be kept away. The battle
must be fought out with the forces now on the field.
Rightly or wrongly, he had taken his position in his
rash boyhood. He had dared to meddle with the
course of events, and he must have courage to stand
by the results. It would be the act of a child to play
fast and loose with Fate. He would stand fast—
and win against odds.

<hr />

CHAPTER XIX.

DOROTHY had thought much of Harry during these
last weeks ; why, it would be difficult to say. Perhaps
in the truce with Alec Macdonald, which might so
easily become more than a truce, she feared she was
slipping away from her old moorings. A new current
had come into her life, and, without analyzing it or even
fully acknowledging its presence, she felt instinctively
that she was drifting from her old anchorage of thought
and feeling. She hardly dared to question herself as
to what it meant, but with a sense of something like
disloyalty to the past and something like fear for the
future she clung to Harry's memory as to a safeguard.
He had stood for the established order of things in

her safe past. She tried to recall him as a living power
into her life, refusing to see that he had gone into the
realm of the outgrown. It was under the influence of
this sentiment that she caught at the possibility of
finding some tangible link of which she might make a
relic to carry her back to him.

She found the address Mrs. Falkland had given
her without difficulty. There was an inconspicuous
sign, "Dressmaking and Plain Sewing," on the door,
and the dingy house itself and its surroundings were
so eminently undramatic that Dorothy was struck with
a sense of incongruity when Mrs. Falkland appeared
with her erst-time tragic look. An angry fire seemed
constantly smoldering in her great black eyes, and
her petulant mouth was hard. Yet she was a pretty
woman. Her round, childish prettiness showed through
her unhappiness as through a veil. She looked like
some stage outcast, come to hurl curses instead of
tears at her fate.

"How are our friends the Hardings?" asked Dorothy after the first greeting.

"As much alive as ever. I suppose you would call
that well."

"Are they suffering?"

Mrs. Falkland shrugged her shoulders.

"Not more than most people, I suppose."

Dorothy hastened to strike out for shore.

"You spoke of my brother the other night, Mrs.
Falkland. I know that Mr. Falkland was with him a
great deal during the last year or two, and though that
is a long time ago now, I thought there might be a
chance of his having kept some of Harry's letters, or
something else that had been Harry's. Our home was

15

broken up so suddenly that everything was scattered, and I have almost no mementos of my brother. Do you think your husband might have something—something that he would not care to keep himself, of course?"

"I don't know. He might. If he has it is likely to be something he ought not to have, and if there is anything he ought to have you may be sure he won't know anything about it."

"But you will ask him, won't you?" persisted Dorothy.

"Oh yes, if I happen to see him."

"When will he be back, do you think?"

"Probably when he gets out of money."

"Do you think he would call on me when in town? You understand how anxious I am about the matter. I would like to talk with him, at any rate."

"Better not," said his wife curtly. Dorothy probably looked astonished, for she added, with a bitter laugh: "You don't understand these things. It is just as well you don't. I only meant that I never knew him to do anybody any good."

"Then he will have a chance to begin with me," said Dorothy, impotently trying to check the tragic muse with a smile. She rose, but still lingered, wondering if there was not some way in which she could lessen the tension of the unhappy woman's life.

"Oh, this is the new book everybody is talking about," she said, picking up an opportune volume from the table. "That reminds me, my brother has just sent me a package of books, which I shall be a long time going through. If you would care to look at some of them, I should be very glad to bring them

around to you.   I like to have my books in circula-
tion."

"Thank you, but—I haven't much time for reading, and Mr. Macdonald sends me a good many books
as it is."

"Mr. Macdonald?"

"Yes.   My boy Louis is in his office," she answered with a quick softening of manner which showed
that as a mother at least she was not invulnerable.
"He's great for reading, Louis is, and Mr. Macdonald
is always lending him books, and often there is one for
me with them.   Novels, mostly.

Perhaps she judged rightly from Dorothy's face
where the chief interest of the story lay, for she went
on without prompting : "I couldn't tell you if I talked
from now to midsummer what Mr. Macdonald has
done for Louis and me.   I tell you, there have been
times when I have been near mad.   I used to plan
how I might make away with myself.   I couldn't see
any way out, and there was no one that cared a rap
what became of me.   Then Mr. Macdonald found us
out.   I don't know how he does it, but he made me
feel strong enough to keep on living, and I'm glad I
have now, for Louis's sake."

Dorothy listened with shining eyes.

"Let me be your friend too, if you need one," she
said impulsively.   "Come and see me.   Don't feel
that you are alone in the world."

"If you mean it, I will, some time," said Mrs.
Falkland after a searching look.

"I mean it most certainly.   Why should you doubt
it?"

"I have not met with kindness enough from the

world to take it as a matter of course. You think me bad tempered, I dare say. So I am. They say trouble makes saints—but not unless there is saint material to work on. It has made me a hard woman."

" I will not believe it," said Dorothy softly. " You were not hard to the Hardings."

" They need such help as even I can give," she said, a milder look coming into her face. " Mr. Macdonald made me see that."

When Dorothy left the house some strong old words were running in her head which make it the mission of manhood to be a covert from the tempest and a shelter from the storm. Had not Alec Macdonald proved the words in himself? She forgot to tell herself she was glad for Harry's sake. She was glad—tenderly, triumphantly glad—for his own sake. Her old harsh judgment were crumbling before her eyes, and in the light of a clearer knowledge she recognized them as crude and untrue.

Some impulse, which she did not stop to explain to herself, made her turn her steps toward the business part of town. Perhaps it was only the ambition of an explorer that sent her on past the last shops that might have formed a reasonable excuse, down to the block where were to be seen the offices of the *Hawthorne Dial*. But when she got there she went by on the other side ; rather hastily, too. The only rewarding sight was a telegraph messenger with a bunch of yellow envelopes in his hand flinging himself off the steps.

But at that moment Macdonald was reading the telegraphic dispatch with a frowning face.

"I suppose I must go," he said, tossing the yellow missive over to Ralph.

"The Morgan matter? You were expecting it, weren't you?"

"I hoped it might be arranged without my going on."

"Well, it couldn't have come at a better time," said Ralph cheerfully. "You can be spared without anything being the worse for it just now, and the run will do you good. When will you start?"

"At once, it says. There is a train going out this evening." He was still staring at the telegram with unphilosophic rebellion.

"And you will be back—?"

"In two weeks at the outside, unless there are complications."

"All right, old man. What is your last will and testament?"

"About the business? Oh, you must act for both of us, of course."

"I'll try to steer clear of shoals, and when there happens to be any change in the cash drawer I will send you an occasional telegram."

Alec had begun sorting out the papers on his desk.

"You might write me occasionally, as well, if you wanted to be particularly agreeable" he said without looking up.

"You will turn my head with your flattery."

"There is always a lot of time wasted in gathering up the threads when one has been away," Alec explained.

"And you think it would conduce to the greatest good of the greatest number for me to give my time

to keeping you posted, rather than for you to spend
yours in looking into matters when you come back?
I have a dark suspicion, Alec, that the flattering
appearance which your request bore on the surface
won't stand a close scrutiny."

"Oh, but I meant it. You needn't write altogether
about business. Mrs. Ellis once said you wrote letters
as well as a woman. You might give me a few pages
of general news, details about the family, and so
forth."

"Not forgetting to mention casually if I happen to
meet Miss Horsford."

"Confound you, Ralph, why do you try to make
me hate Miss Horsford by dragging her name in?"

Ralph laughed lazily.

"I didn't know I had found a way to do it. What
are you shutting up now for?"

"I must—there are some matters I must see to before I go. I will be in again."

The said matters seemed to lead him in Dorothy's
footsteps, for he went directly to Mrs. Falkland's
house.

"Have you heard from your husband lately, Mrs.
Falkland?"

"Not since he made us that unexpected visit two
months ago."

"Have you any idea where he is?"

"No. I seldom have, you know."

"Nor when he may be back?"

"No."

"I am going to be out of town myself for a few
weeks. Do you think there is any chance of his coming before that time?"

"Not unless what he calls his luck is worse than usual."

Macdonald calculated the chances rapidly.

"I will leave a letter with you for him," he said at last. "You need not mail it. Give it to him if he comes here, or hold it for me if he doesn't."

He sat down to write the message, but the wording of it cost him as much thought as though it had been a valentine. His impulse was to say: "Don't see Miss Vanborough or hold any conversation with her, as you value your life." But he knew that the imperative style was not the wisest one to adopt toward Falkland, and forcibly subduing his instincts to accord with the requirements of prudence, he wrote and sealed the following note:

"Dear Falkland: You probably remember the subject of our last conversation. If you want any further light on it, come to me and speak to no one else about it. You understand. It will be to my interest to have you follow this hint strictly, and you know that what is to my interest in this matter is to yours as well. Yours,   Macdonald."

This he left with Mrs. Falkland, trusting to fortune that in the event of Falkland's return the hint might serve to keep the ex-agent out of mischief, until he had an opportunity to bring him under his personal influence.

Next he went to Miss Vanborough's. It was an unusual hour for his appearance, and she met him with an inquiring look under her welcome.

"Can you give me half an hour?" he asked.

"Has anything happened?" she asked with a startled face.

"Nothing. I am suing for a gift, that is all—the gift of one of your half-hours. You have plenty all to yourself. May I have one?"

She laughed wonderingly.

"Your precision is appalling. Are you so busy?"

"I shall be—after half an hour. For the present I am not on speaking terms with hurry." He composedly establishing himself in the chair that commanded the best view of his hostess. "Some business matters have called me out of town. I must leave to-night, so this is a P. P. C. call."

If he had any lingering, half-hidden hope that she might manifest some sign of dismay at this announcement it must have died speedily. She did not faint nor put her hand to her heart nor even change color and tremble, nor give any other evidence that she was holding despair down by main force.

"How long will you be gone?" she asked placidly.

"About a fortnight. Have you any message for Mrs. Ellis? I shall probably see her on my way."

"Thank you, but I could not think of troubling a business man with frivolous feminine messages."

"Why is the frivolous kind the only one that suggests itself in connection with me? Couldn't you trust me with a serious feminine message?"

"Then you may tell her— Let me think. If I am to make use of an envoy extraordinary instead of a postage stamp, the message must be worthy the occasion. Tell her—" She laughed softly—"tell her the work she left me is not finished, but I submit what has been done to her inspection."

He looked puzzled.

"Is that a cabalistic saying? What will happen if I say it backward?"

"Nothing, except that I will trust to postage stamps next time."

"I feel a great sympathy at this moment with our staid old forefathers who condemned traveling as a tempting of providence," he said after a pause. "So many things may happen while one is away."

"But two weeks is not a long time."

"'It is not so deep as a well nor so wide as a church-door, but it is enough,'" he quoted. "It may be long enough for you to forget me."

"If I do," she answered, flushing, "I stipulate beforehand that you are to be announced in your proper character when you re-enter."

"My proper character!" He laughed oddly. "If it does not announce itself I don't think it can be taken into consideration."

He was restless and unlike himself. Leaning his head on his hand, he watched her, as she talked, with an unconsciously intent gaze that melted into something more like an illumination than a smile whenever her eyes were lifted to his. It made her shy, though she did not understand the reason, and to protect herself she talked more rapidly than usual.

"Have you anything to read on the train? Can't I lend you something?"

"I will be most grateful."

"Have you read this?" she asked, picking up a book from the table.

"No. What is it?"

"Oh, just a novel. See if you think it looks interesting."

But he made no motion to take the book.

"Tell me, please," he smiled insistently.

"Do you like stories to end happily?"

"Most certainly. In books as well as out."

"This does, but the author leads you through devious ways to get to the sunshine on the last page. I think as a rule your heroes and heroines don't deserve much sympathy in their scrapes. They could generally get themselves out if they would only explain like reasonable beings."

"But consider the authors, O tyrant! A novel without a misunderstanding! Bricks without straw are not to be mentioned in the same breath."

"But you must be in sympathy with your beset hero."

"What would put him beyond the pale of your sympathy? Something wicked?"

She gave him a startled look.

"Do you insist on perfection?" he asked again.

"Oh, no," she answered, and she tried to keep her voice careless "Perfect heroes are apt to be prigs."

"If books are to hold the mirror up to nature there won't be many of that kind, for human nature is still symbolized by the golden statue with feet of clay. The people in real life have to work their way out of complications sometimes the result of their own mistakes and sometimes of others, and a book with any truth in it must take its hint from life."

"But their reasons are so far-fetched," she protested. "Of course you feel bound to accept it as all right, because it is the author's business not yours to look up the hero's credentials, but at the same time it is often painfully evident that he could save himself many pages of misery by being just simple and honest."

"But the poor fellow caught in the snare must go through all the tribulations before he learns the lesson that you seize instinctively. There was probably a time also when you could have tripped him up on the table of sevens."

He was talking lightly but with a significant undertone that had set her heart to beating tumultuously. She felt that he was thinking, as she was, of the time when she had said, "I can not forget." She had been hard! With drooping eyes she answered:

"If the wrong-doing is through ignorance—"

"Isn't it always? Ignorance, in the truest sense, of the laws that are broken?"

"Then the hero may be a hero still, in spite of his blunder."

"Then you could forgive—say a lie, for instance— in the course of thirteen chapters? How if the chapters were years?"

There was a moment of absolute silence before she answered almost inaudibly:

"A living hero would have a right to claim more than a hero in a book."

And then with reckless volubility she plunged into miscellaneous topics, and gave no opening for anything like personal views or their particular application.

But Alec was well content. He would not hurry her, he said to himself. He would let the thought grow. Had he not been taught in the school of patience? And then before he knew it he had himself shattered his fine resolution to bits.

He had made his farewells and was standing at the door, hat in hand, when some impulse on which he had not counted prompted him to turn again and say:

"You have given me new courage."

"Oh, you know my opinion doesn't count," she said, rather breathlessly.

An odd smile curled his lips and his eyes fell before hers.

"Yes, it counts."

"Will you see Nellie when you go or when you return?" she asked, clutching at the first conversational straw within reach.

"It counts more than anything else," he proceeded unheedingly, "because—I love you."

And before she could grasp what the words meant he had left her.

CHAPTER XX.

I.

Miss Horsford to Mrs. Ellis.

"My dear Nell: This is a valedictory. Papa finds it necessary to return home, and I shall go with him. To tell the truth, Nell, Hawthorne is a stupid place when deprived of your presence. For that matter, most places are stupid when you know more than a little about them—and most people, too. Even the promise of an impending winter carnival with a street masquerade sounds forlorn when I picture it with a setting of Hawthorne citizens. If you won't be dreadfully shocked I will confess that I found even your Mr. Macdonald a trifle dull. Why must one take life so seriously? With his standards and his theories keeping one always a-tiptoe, he would wear me to a shadow in six months—if I saw him more than twice a week. I don't think I like people very much. They always are tiresome as soon as you have explored their boundaries. That is why it is such a strain to me to know and unknow new people. And at home—oh, I know just how it will be when I get back. There will be half a dozen young men about who will try to be agreeable and who will bore me dreadfully, and I shall go to all the affairs in our set and be bored worse, and then out of sheer *ennui* I shall marry some one of them, it doesn't matter much which, and settle down to be bored for the rest of my days. It doesn't sound very exhilarating, but at any rate it is better than being on the stretch all the time from taking things seriously.

"I hope this same mail may bring you a letter from a more cheerful correspondent—your cousin Dorothy, for example. I imagine she would write comfortable, contented, purring little letters, which would be as soothing after my restless caviling as a nursery song after a serenade of Chinese gongs. I don't think she was ever troubled by the hollowness of things in general. Ah, Nellie, why couldn't you have stayed here this winter? Well, the winter is gone—and I am going. As ever, yours,

"Blanche Horsford."

II.

Miss Vanborough to Mrs. Ellis.

"My dear Nellie: It is on my mind that I have been neglecting you lately, but this engrossing family of yours must bear the blame. What have I been doing? Oh, I don't know. Just listening to Ralph when he takes his station on the hearth-rug and discourses of sublimities by the hour at the time, or trying, generally without success, to trap Richard into expressing a preference for fish, flesh, or fowl, or standing by to support Nita with my sympathy, in lack of better help, when she gets into one of her struggles with something—algebra, or fate, or a new hat. As for Philip, we are lovers. I tell him stories and he tells me truths, and I dare say you will find that all proper branches of his education have been neglected when you come back. But you will like him. Then your friends have been very friendly, and altogether I have been whirled through the weeks I hardly know how. And I do think Hawthorne is the prettiest place in the winter that I ever saw. Why haven't you been more enthusiastic about it? But perhaps you have lived here too long to see it. I didn't see it when this was my home. But the white rim of hills around the town, and the crisp sparkle of the sunlight against the snow and the moonlight—do you remember how the hills look under a full moon, with the white ridges clear and luminous, and the shades so black between? You are probably asking indignantly if I don't remember that you have lived here for some years. Yes, but you haven't seen it under snow for twelve months, and twelve months is a very long time.

When I look back to my last winter it seems half a lifetime away. There has been so much living between, and that—not days—is what separates us from the past. Everything has widened for me. I can't explain it, but it seems to me I am more alive than I ever was before. I suppose it is just because I had a chance here to be of some use in a little corner of the world.

"I have talked about nothing but myself, and rather incoherently, too, I am afraid. I must send the letter, such as it is, or you will miss a mail ; but to-morrow I will write a sensible, lucid letter, and tell you all the family news. With love,   Dorothy."

III.

Mr. Ellis to Mrs. Ellis.

"My dear Wife : Yours received, and I inclose check for amount requested. The canceled check will be a sufficient acknowledgment.

"Glad to know the mother is mending, and hope you will soon be able to come back. We are all well and Dorothy is a good housekeeper and a nice cousin, but of course the house doesn't seem the same without you.

"I can't put my hand on your last letter at this moment, but I remember you asked something about Macdonald—whether he was devoting himself to Miss Horsford. My dear, I'm sure I don't know. You wouldn't want me to ask, and I don't see how else I could tell. I rather thought Ralph was her cavalier. I don't believe that Macdonald cares much for ladies' society. He seems better pleased to spend a quiet evening here, talking to Ralph. They have a good many interests in common, though I am not in with them altogether. The truth is, Nellie, I miss you dreadfully. You suit me, somehow. I always thought so, but having you away this winter has made me as desolate as I was when your family carried you off—do you remember ?—just after we were engaged. These young people about us are planning their lives, and enjoying it, I suppose, but ours is all planned. When are you coming back, dear ?

"Phil has just brought me the inclosed scrap which he says is a letter for you. You may know the cipher in which it is written, but I confess I had to ask him to translate it. He says it is to tell mamma to come home quick—a request which I indorse, waiving protest. Faithfully yours,   R. Ellis."

IV.

Anita Ellis to Mrs. Ellis.

"Dear Mamma ·

"Yes, I am wearing the flannels you sent.

"No, I haven't had a cold this winter.

"Yes, I take a walk every day—with my new hat.

"Now, *you* won't think that sounds silly, will you, mamma ? because you know a really beautiful hat is a work of art. Uncle Ralph acknowledged that, even though he teased me about it and said he knew I would write you about it the first thing. But I told him I wasn't taking dares and I would write you just what I pleased. All the same, HE likes pretty things, if he does think it necessary to pretend to be lofty and transcendental. He admired Dorothy's dress when I

fixed her up for the Santa Claus party. (Did I tell
you she looked like a perfect dream? Yes'm, it was
your daughter's æsthetic idea that achieved that triumph.) But when I examined him afterward on the
subject he was too absurd. Said he didn't want to
know the secret. When he looked at a picture he
didn't want to have to think about the names of the
color-tubes and the make of the brush. He left that
to the manufacturers of pictures. And he didn't know
whether Dorothy wore cloud-web, cut bias, edged with
a border of moonlight, or something that came out of
a shop, and, what was more, he didn't care. But I
think that Mr. Macdonald sent her those roses (just
stacks of them, only she says she isn't sure it was he,
but I am), just because she looked so bewitching in
that white ringamajig that I made her wear.

"Papa had just come in, and he will ask what I am
writing about, and as I couldn't show him *this* letter, I
will seal it up in a hurry. Good-by.　　Nita."

v.

Mr. Wendel to Mrs. Ellis.

"Dear Madam: This will serve to introduce to
you a deserving young man by the name of Alexander
Macdonald, who will reach your town about the time
this missive does. It gives me pleasure to state that I
have always found him invaluable in correcting a co-
editor's lapses of memory, useful in making up a party
of four, persevering, diligent, and successful in having
his own way. I feel confident that he will, without
the slightest betrayal of his real feelings, declare himself delighted to do anything you may require in the

16

way of chaperoning bandboxes or translating time-tables.

"I have the honor to be, Madam, with great re-spect, your obedient younger brother,

"Ralph Wendel."

VI.

Card, presented to Mrs. Ellis by the maid.

MR. ALEXANDER MACDONALD.

VII.

Mrs. Ellis, writing in her diary an hour later.

"I would not confess it to any one in the world but myself, but I am completely demoralized. To think that, after all my scheming, Fate should quietly come in and take my pawns to play a little game of her own with on my board. Why in the world didn't that combination strike me? Then the game would have been mine and I could have congratulated myself for the rest of my days. Now the only forlorn little feather in my cap is the fact that at least I have dis-covered how things are going without any of them suspecting that they have told me anything. But why couldn't I have managed it? Desolation!"

CHAPTER XXI.

THERE are various ways of making the fateful dec-
laration which comes into most lives and all novels,
but probably the lover's heart beats with the same
trepidation whether, in the stately manner of Lord
Fitz-Edward Roncival, he drops gracefully on one knee
and murmurs : " I adore thee, Ethelda Violetta ; wilt
thou be mine?" or whether he takes the opportunity
when driving home from singing-school to adjure
Hannah to "name the day, and let's quit foolin'."
But in the worst case he does not bear a fair share of
the burden of that rapid question and answer. He
speaks from deliberate purpose. He has had a chance
to ponder the question, to weigh the outcome, to
scrutinize himself, and when at last he makes the
avowal it is his own fault if his words do not represent
his calm and well-considered conclusion. But Ethelda,
Violetta, and Hannah, though they may not give their
hearts unsought—all maidenly traditions forbid !—are
yet expected to decide on the spur of the moment the
question which settles their destiny beyond recall.
When society is reorganized, proposals will be submit-
ted only in writing, and any lover who demands a
reply in less than thirty days will find his claim barred
by the Statute of Precipitancy.

But it is doubtful whether Alec Macdonald was in
the proper state of mind when he left Miss Vanborough
to derive any moral comfort from the reflection that he
was a pioneer in a reform. He was simply filled with
dismay at the thought of what he had done. That he,
of all men, trained as he had thought himself in self-

restraint, should peril everything by his boyish rash-
ness! Would he ever be able to restore the friendly
confidence which he knew had begun to spring up
toward him? He recognized the extent of that confidence truly enough to know that he must not try it
too far if he would not give up all his daring hopes.
As it was, he could risk no attempt at an explanation. Dorothy would feel the necessity of leaving no
doubts as to her position, and as her position was
one which he was bent on changing, he objected to
having it strengthened by a verbal definition. During all the busy days that followed, filled with traveling and business and superficial claims of all sorts
upon his attention, he was really living on one thought.
Everything real would be suspended until he could
look into Dorothy's face again and learn, without the
danger of words, how much he might have lost—or
gained.

It would have been impossible for him to guess the
bewildered state of Dorothy's mind during those days.
Had he meant what he said? Then why had he said
nothing more? It was not in that way those words
were usually spoken. And then the words themselves
would come back to her, making her laugh and blush
and drop her face upon her arm. His dispassionate
tone had perplexed her, his lack of curiosity as to her
sentiments was irregular, but his words haunted her.
Over and over they repeated themselves like a charm
that she could not break.

"What makes your eyes so bright?" asked Philip,
stationing himself before her that he might study the
phenomenon favorably. "Have you got a surprise
for me somewhere?"

She put her arms around him and hid her face in his soft hair.

"Oh, Philip, Philip!" he heard her murmur. Why, he knew as little as she.

Ah, the waiting that comes to women teaches many a tender truth.

Then one morning she awoke with the thought that the fortnight was ended. What would come next? The question made her heart tremble for a moment, and then a sense of quiet restfulness came to her. She could trust him. He was too true a man not to be a true friend if he might not be a lover. But she went through the day in a dream, silent even for her silent way. Even Philip's beloved prattle was not in tune to-day, and when the afternoon began to wane she slipped out for a little hour alone. Yet she couldn't think. There was nothing to define. She could only wait. Trying to think made her restless, and she fell back into her hushed mood, watching the sky and the hills and the brown trees along the way.

The children smiled up at her as she passed, and Dr. Blount, hurrying by with even more than his customary briskness, stopped, lured by her look.

"Ah, Miss Dorothy, good-day to you. Not that you look as though you had waited for my recommendation to find it good."

"It is all the better for your greeting, Doctor."

"I have just come from the hospital—I have told you about our new separate hospital for dangerous cases, haven't I? It is to be opened to-morrow. Everything is ready, and I assure you it is as perfect as a poem—a whole volume of poems, in fact. Won't you come in and look it over?"

"But you have just been there—"

"Oh, I'll be glad to go again. It is only a step. In fact, I really have to go back anyhow."

This was too transparent a fiction to deceive even Dorothy; but she saw that he would indeed be better pleased to return with her than to proceed on his proper way, so she let him lead her back to the street where the new hospital was waiting for active service.

"It really is a passably fine-looking building," he continued, with so evident an effort to be judicially impartial that Dorothy laughed secretly. "It was designed by Holden, you know. For a building of its size I don't think it could be very much improved. I really don't think it could be improved at all."

He beamed at her so cheerily that she laughed outright, and he laughed too; not because he had any idea why, but because he was so pleased that he was ready to take any flimsy pretext for laughing aloud.

"I hope you won't be tempted to waylay and assault some inoffensive citizen in order to get a patient into your wards," she said with meek malice.

"Fortunately there is a family down with small-pox in the lower town, so it won't be necessary to adopt your suggestion," he retorted coolly. "There, do you see the entrance? Fine effect, eh?"

He led her through the entire building, stopping on every possible occasion to call her attention to some detail in construction or architecture, with all of the enthusiasm of a connoisseur showing a picture.

"There is only one thing I find lacking," she said, when the tour was finished.

"Lacking! What is it?" he asked, with quick alarm.

"The picture of the founder," she answered smilingly.

"Oh, I am glad it is nothing else. That would have to be a composite photograph, I think."

"I think I know who could be taken as a representative."

"You mean Macdonald?" he asked genially.

"Why no. I meant you, of course."

"Oh, the hospital owes a great deal more to Macdonald than to me or any one else. Not simply in the way of money, but for energy, clear-headedness, and those business virtues that we professional men are very apt to despise until they pull us out of a tight place. Of course he took it out in making us live up to his views; but we are used to that. That's the advantage these abominably obstinate men have. You may have all the arguments and fun on your side, but they have their way."

Dorothy let him run on in the fullness of his heart without much assistance. She was looking into the clean white wards and down the airy halls with new interest. She let her hand linger caressingly on the carved post at the head of the stairs.

"His work," she murmured to herself, and then, with deepening color in her cheeks, she hurried away, leaving the doctor with a half-finished explanation on his lips.

She smiled happily to herself as she walked rapidly homeward, and then her eyes widened with something like remorse. And under everything else was a little wonder, which she did not put into words even in her thoughts, whether it could really be true that he loved her as he had said. What would he say when she saw him? How could they meet?

Then suddenly she did see him, coming down a cross-street toward her at a rapid pace. It was only half a glance she gave, but she knew surprisingly well the poise of that head over the square shoulders. Her heart leaped into her throat, and the only thing in the world she was sure of was that it was utterly impossible for her to go on and meet him. By means of the frivolous excuse of bestowing a silver dime on a small boy of her acquaintance who was zealously endeavoring to improvise a rink from the frozen gutter, she managed to turn her back to all the rest of the world. If the boy's conscience had been properly developed, he would have straightway declared that he deserved a lecture rather than a dime for stealing off surreptitiously with his sister's skates, but probably he thought she got her money's worth by her embarrassing questions as to whether he was fonder of arithmetic or geography. But when a tall gentleman came up to her quickly, she smiled so prettily that even a victim must forgive her lack of tact in choosing a subject for conversation.

In truth, the smile was as unexpected a gift to the man as the silver was to the boy. All that long fortnight he had been tormenting himself with the thought of her anger, and her brown eyes had come constantly before him with a rare look of dignity in their startled depths. Yet here the same eyes were smiling at him in the serenest possible way, with no hint of remembrance in them.

"Back so soon?" she exclaimed with a vivacity that was a little overdone. "How does Hawthorne seem after an excursion into the great world?"

"Like the haven of all my thoughts."

" Did you see Nellie ? "

" Yes, and I gave her your message."

" Forward or backward ? "

" I didn't dare meddle with it.   She commissioned me to say in return that she would never again presume to compete with so consummate a mistress of the art. "

"Oh ! "

" At least that is what I think she said.   The messages were so obscure that I felt inclined to believe they were intended to make game of the unsuspecting messenger."

" Did Nellie say when she is coming home ? "

" Very soon, I think.   She did not give any date."

" That will end my winter here.   Edward is anxious to have me home as soon as possible, and even talks of coming for me at once."

He gave her a quick, inquiring glance, and then looked away without speaking.

" Of course I must wait for your carnival.   I am looking forward to that street masquerade as the crown of the winter.   I would feel tempted to mask myself, if it were not for the necessity of setting an example of propriety to Nita."

It was all bravado, her assumption of ease.   Inwardly she was quaking with fear lest this transient composure, which she had snatched from the very intensity of her trepidation, should desert her as suddenly as it had come, and leave her at the mercy of events. But Macdonald, looking at her in a baffled, masculine way, was ready to believe that he had dreamed that swift scene in the hall.

"Has the date been fixed for the masquerade?" he asked, when the pause aroused him.

"Yes, for Thursday—the day after to-morrow. To think you should not know!"

"That isn't the only thing I don't know."

"I am glad to have been the humble instrument in saving you from betraying your ignorance. What might not have happened if you had chanced to meet some one else first!" She spoke, and laughed lightly, but she was profoundly conscious herself of the unnatural strain of her gayety.

"Has Ralph secured a place for you to see the pageant? There will be a crowd in the streets."

"But we are going into the crowd. That is the chief fun. Won't you join us?"

"Thanks; with much pleasure."

Then there came one of those pauses that are so dangerous when a forbidden subject trembles just beyond the lips. Dorothy felt her forced composure rapidly deserting her as she perceived that in the silence Alec was regarding her intently.

"Were you offended?" he asked in a different tone.

The quick color flashed into her face and her eyes fell hesitatingly. Her lips trembled so that she could not answer, but he must have guessed her perplexity, for he looked away with a patient air.

"I do not want to trouble you—ever," he said in a low tone. "I did not mean to tell you—yet, but the thought is with me so constantly that it is hard sometimes not to speak of it. But you must never be sorry that I love you. Think of it only when it will be pleasant for you to remember that another life has been brightened by yours. That is what you have done for me, ever since those old days when we were only children. The sweetest thing that ever came into my life—the dearest thing that ever can come into it—is just to have known you. Does it make you unhappy to have me tell you this, when I ask for nothing?"

She dared not speak or raise her face, lest he should see the tears under her lashes. She shook her head slightly in answer to his last words.

"I am glad of that," he said with his rare gentleness, "because I do not want you to send me away. I want to stay here and see you, if you will let me, just as I always have, as a friend. I will be content with that—at least until—" He did not finish except by a hard breath.

"I am so sorry," murmured Dorothy tremulously.

"You must never say that. There is no reason. Do you remember," he added hesitatingly, "when I asked you to be my friend for Harry's sake?"

She bent her head silently.

"If you could tell me now that you would think of me as your friend for my own sake, I would be more grateful than I could tell you. Am I too impatient?"

"I do, indeed," she answered earnestly. "I am glad to have you for my friend."

She lifted her eyes trustingly to his, but something in his steady gaze made her falter suddenly. Her varying color warned him that he must guard his eyes as well as his voice.

"Then you will please ask me to come in and have tea with you," he said lightly.

She laughed a little unsteadily, but he was content

that the tension of their mood should pass off so.   He knew—who better?—how easily he might startle her out of this new, sweet confidence, which for the present he was most anxious to maintain.   So, without much assistance from Dorothy it must be confessed, he carried the conversation back to safe channels, and talked simply and naturally about his journeying and what he had seen and heard.   It was enough that Dorothy was walking by his side through the twilight, and that from time to time he could win from her a smile or a direct look.

When they reached her door he stopped and looked at her with an expectant smile.

"Won't you come in and have tea with us?" she murmured shyly, following the programme.

"With all the pleasure in the world," he answered gayly.   In his secret heart he felt that he would have accepted a cup of hemlock juice without a tremor, if proffered by her hand.   As they went in he turned back for an instant to look again down the white, wind-blown street and fix it in his memory forever.

Nita, in the middle of the room, was twirling a pair of Indian clubs about her head, with an occasional eye to the furniture, and Ralph, lazily stretched out on the sofa with his arms behind his head, was criticising.   Philip, with his fingers in his ears, was abstractedly turning the pages of a picture-book with his chin.

"Here she is," cried Ralph eagerly, springing up from the sofa as Dorothy appeared in the doorway.

"And Mr. Macdonald too," echoed Nita, applauding with her clubs until Philip looked up reproachfully.

"Alec, old man, is it you for a fact? Welcome home, oh, wanderer, to these desolate arms!"

"Ralph, stand off! At your peril! Nita, I demand your protection! I will not be publicly embraced!"

"Oh, that's always the way," said Ralph. "The tendrils of my heart are snipped off faster than they can grow. No wonder I am a hardened young cynic before my time."

"You shall have a cup of tea, and then the world will look brighter," said Dorothy, who had been smilingly silent. "Has your father come, Nita?"

"He came in a moment ago and went up to his room."

"Because Nita cracked her clubs and made his head ache," explained Philip conscientiously.

"Uncle Ralph was teaching me a new figure, only he was too lazy to stand up and show me properly," supplemented Nita.

Dorothy went out into the dining-room, where the tea-table was already spread, and while Ralph and Alec conversed in low tones, Nita softly played broken bits of melody at the piano. It was a simple and homelike scene, and to the man who had had little home-help in his life, it was as blessed as is a vision of his native valley to a wanderer in a far land. Under the shadow of his hand his eyes followed the queen of his heart flitting about the rooms, with a conscious shyness in her tell-tale face and a soft color that came and went at a word. He could be patient, very patient. But— In the shadow he passionately pressed his cheek against the fur of the cloak she had thrown upon the chair.

"Just listen to the expression with which she renders that *barcarolle*," Ralph was saying with an air of discriminating admiration.   "Don't you hear the very sound of the waves rippling against the side of the boat, and the grating of the rusty oar-locks in the key of C sharp?   Now he is calculating how many fish he will have to buy in the market on his way home—hear the sharp, decisive tone of his imaginary bargaining. Now he falls to dreaming of the days of his first flirtation—that sentimental minor chord may always be safely translated as 'never more.'"

"Is it true, Nita?" asked Philip, looking at the piano wonderingly.

"Nonsense.   He doesn't know a Christmas carol from the Dead March in Saul."

"Did you think it meant all that story, Uncle Ralph?"

"Oh, he was just trying to develop his imagination so as to be ready for his next editorial on the single-tax question," explained Nita, with a patronizing nod at her uncle.

Mr. Ellis came in presently, with his customary air of having lost too much sleep, and after a brief but kindly greeting to Macdonald they all gathered around the waiting tea-table.

When a man is in love there are few attitudes of his beloved that lack charm to his eyes, but at the head of his table she has a peculiar grace.   While he is still very young and romantic, his soul may perhaps be more deeply stirred when she floats on his arm through a ball-room, or sings tender ditties that mean what no one can understand but he.   But when the season of sentiment and serenade is past, he loves bet-

ter to dream of a gentle wife who will be the presiding
genius of his home, and then the housewifely apron is
more bewitching than tulle draperies, and fragrant
puffs of steam from a singing kettle are more becoming
to her than the tenderest moonlight on a terrace. Macdonald watched the white hands filling the dainty cups,
and while he tried to listen just enough to make his answers coherent, he was daring to fancy how it would
seem if they two were at breakfast together, and he might
kiss the gracious fingers that handed him his coffee.

What they talked about he never knew. He heard,
as in the distance, the sound of Nita's warfare with
Ralph, and he listened to Mr. Ellis's opinions with unusual deference. But the events of the evening were
the words that Dorothy added now and then, and the
occasional glances, shy and yet frank, which he sometimes caught from behind the urn.

There is only one objection to perfect things—they
are subject to the law of change. The sonnet will
stop after fourteen lines, and the sonata consents to its
limits, and the sunset has too pressing an engagement
on the next hill-top ever to respond to an encore.
Macdonald was obliged at last to recognize that the
evening had gone. When he had made his farewells,
"as a friend might do, or just a trifle longer," Ralph
remarked carelessly:

"Oh, by the way, do you know that your musical
attaché, Falkland, is in town again?"

"Is he?" asked Macdonald, with a quick glance
at Dorothy, who had come forward eagerly.

"Yes, I saw him on the street yesterday, as *debonair*
as ever. Don't try to reform him, Alec. I like him
better as he is."

"I am glad you spoke," said Dorothy. "I want to see him myself. I will go down to Mrs. Falkland's to-morrow morning."

"That is not the likeliest place to find him," said Macdonald dissuasively.

"Oh! Do you think, then, you will see him?"

"I? Yes, I think it probable."

"Then, couldn't you ask him for me about Harry's papers, you know? Or ask him to come and see me. That will be better."

Macdonald bit his lip.

"I think I can assure you beforehand that his visit to Hawthorne will be brief," was all he said.

CHAPTER XXII.

An uninitiated outsider might have supposed that his business would have the first claim upon Macdonald's attention after a two-weeks' absence, but instead he spent the best part of the next morning in an ineffectual hunt for Falkland. The result was such as to justify the deduction that when Fate comes to call, she will look for us at home. His zeal defeated its own object, for during those fruitless hours Falkland was lounging at the entrance to the *Dial* office, restively waiting for the senior editor, and inwardly anathematizing this same waiting as a nuisance. He whistled a fragment of an opera air, then stopped short and scowled at the doves fluttering tamely at his feet. He had always found it necessary to take his courage in both hands for an interview with Macdonald, and he had some open doubts as to whether he would be able to maintain his hold upon it if the meeting was long delayed. The spirit of daring was a familiar of his, and on ordinary occasions it could masquerade for courage passably well. But it was a tricksy sprite, and apt to take to its heels at the prospect of a long strain, and that was what might be expected if he was to have his own way in dealing with Macdonald. But since the world is constituted as it is, one must have money to get along in it. It is an unmitigated bore to have to bother about it, and it is a ridiculous arrangement at the best that one should be required to produce certain ugly and intrinsically valueless coins in exchange for the joys of living. How the standard of comparative values was determined, Falkland for one could not guess. Who could say that so many ounces of earth were a fair exchange for so many bubbles of bottled sunlight? How did the door-keeper know what the price should be for a ticket to fairyland, *via foyer* and foot-lights? It was manifestly absurd on the face of it.

But since it was the way of the world, one must even comply with it, and his pockets had an exasperating way of proving empty just when nothing could be more embarrassing.

Macdonald had plenty of money, of course; business men always had. It was another instance of the irony of fate. In the name of the everlasting fitness of things, why couldn't they grub, since that was what they found their delight in, and leave the money to him and his fellows? Money was a mystic talisman whose formula they did not know, while in his hands— presto, change!—it was no longer a mass of yellow dirt, but a pass-key to the Realm of Delight.

17

If Macdonald would only see things from the same point of view! He pulled his hat over his eyes and tried to think out the best way of presenting the subject. If he could be sure that he had not worn out the old Harry Vanborough vein, that would suit him best. There was something dramatic in the situation that appealed to his sympathies. He liked to play the *rôle* of the masterly villain holding the tame and prudent business man in his power. It had worked very well for several years, while the young Macdonald was still strongly imbued with the idea of devoting his life to shielding his friend's memory. But somehow of late the thread seemed to have grown less secure. It would be like his luck if those old letters which he had carried about so many years should prove to be only so much waste paper in the end. Fate always used loaded dice in playing with him.

He viciously threw a snowball at the busy pigeons, and wondered if it wouldn't be better after all to postpone his visit till the next day That would give him twenty-four hours to decide on the plan of operations.

At that moment his quick eye caught sight of a gray-cloaked figure on the opposite side of the street which at once drove away his half-uttered curse on his star and showed him in a flash a new expedient. Harry's sister was surely as profitable a field for him to work as Harry's friend. Moreover, she was a woman, and of course that would lessen the friction immensely. She would not be calmly and uncomfortably sarcastic as Macdonald might. Macdonald wouldn't like it, to be sure, but, dispassionately considered, what had that to do with the matter? It rather added a zest to it. Besides, she had never been called on before, and she really owed him some arrears. By the time he reached the corner he had come to feel that his claim had the indorsement of the strictest justice, and when he got across the street he wasn't sure but that she had treated him rather shabbily in never giving him this opportunity before.

His spirits rose rapidly, and as he slouched after the lady up the street he pulled his hat low over his eyes and glanced darkly about and behind him after the accepted code of dramatic villains. When she reached her door he quickened his pace and stood beside her.

" Madam ! "

She turned, a little startled.

" Will you give me five minutes ? I have that to say to you which must be said in your ear alone."

She had drawn back in astonishment with her hand on the door, but now as he lifted his hat she recognized him.

" Mr. Falkland ! Forgive me, I did not know you at first. Will you come in ? "

She beamed such kindliness upon him that he at once felt himself promoted to the circle of her intimate friends. Not that that would hinder the execution of his plot. It only made things easier.

" I hope that you have come to tell me that you have found some of my brother Harry's possessions for me," she added eagerly, leading the way into the empty parlor.

" Are we alone here, Miss Vanborough ? "

" Certainly."

" By your leave I will make sure." He gravely looked into the adjoining rooms, drew the *portières,* and then pulled up a chair opposite Miss Vanborough, who had watched his actions with silent astonishment. He really had no great fear of being overheard, but it was his pleasure to dramatize the situation whenever possible, and throw the calcium light of effect over the prosaic details of common affairs.

"Do you remember the Panesco Mine affair, Miss Vanborough, and the check that Alec Macdonald forged?"

Dorothy half rose.

"Is it necessary to refer to that?" she asked with unusual severity on her gentle features.

"Absolutely necessary. That is the very pith of the matter. The letters of your brother are on that subject. Control your emotions, madam, till you have heard me out."

With any one else he would have curbed his genius, but like all actors he quickly caught the tone of his audience.

"I remember," Dorothy answered. Had she been able to remember anything else for the last few months?

"A youthful pecadillo, madam," he continued airily. "You and I know that. Nothing but a boyish scrape—a trifle not worth mentioning, a bubble running over the brim of—of genius. In fact, rather to his credit than otherwise. His was never a nature to be measured by a two-inch rule."

Dorothy listened with a chilling unresponsiveness. In truth she felt like crying out against this man's defending Alec Macdonald. Was it for him to try to explain that hateful thing in Macdonald's life which she had come to feel not even her thought could reach? The idea that he could mean any one else no more occurred to her than it occurred to him that Miss Vanborough might not know the truth of that page in her family history.

"I speak with feeling, Miss Vanborough. I knew him well. I may say that I was the chosen friend of his young soul. Alas, where are now the friends of the past?"

He gazed into the ceiling, where it is well known answers to such questions are usually found.

"You were saying—" suggested Dorothy.

"I was saying—thank you, Miss Vanborough. I must not let my feelings carry me away. I was about to say that a lot of old letters giving the true, inside history of that whole affair—you understand me—have turned up. They are now in the hands of a man I know. The thing was kept out of the papers at the time, you know. It now rests with you whether it shall remain forgotten or be dragged out to the garish light of day."

"With me?"

"Yes, madam. To be plain, the man that holds those letters proposes to give the whole thing to the press. The *Key-Hole* wouldn't object to paying something for a couple of spicy columns bringing in the names of prominent citizens and extracts from private letters. It would double the sale of the Sunday morning edition."

Dorothy, with hands clasped, had been leaning forward to listen intently.

"That would be shameful," she cried vehemently, a crimson spot glowing in either cheek.

"That's what I said. In fact, those were my very

words. 'Jim,' said I—the man's name is James, Miss
Vanborough; I called him Jim because I knew him
pretty well, in a fashion—'Jim, it would be a shame
to go tearing in among people's feelings in that unexpected sort of way.' I felt sure you would not
allow it."

"No, it must not be," said Dorothy earnestly.
"It would be too cruel after all these years. You
were very kind to think of coming to me. Tell the
man, please, that those old papers must be de-
stroyed."

She rose as she spoke. Her voice had not lost its
customary softness, but any one who knew her well
would have seen that she was thrilling with a strange
excitement. Falkland also rose, looking very much
nonplussed at this turn of affairs.

"But—" he faltered.

"There must not be any question. Say it as
strongly and clearly as you can."

"But I'm afraid my saying so won't prevent him
if he has made up his mind," he said with unusual
embarrassment.

Dorothy opened her eyes.

"Why, what can it matter to him?"

"Well—you see—I say, Miss Vanborough, how
would it suit you to buy those letters?"

"That would be best, of course. I did not think
of that. What will he take for them?"

Falkland thought he was nerved to meet the point,
but he stammered as he named the sum. A new light
came into Dorothy's eyes.

"Is he a bad man?" she asked simply.

"Far from it. His is a lofty soul, though it has

been the foot-ball of Fate," he answered with unconscious warmth.

"Then you must have misunderstood him," she
said gravely.

Falkland's zeal as an advocate instantly abated.

"He is a very set man. Fire and tongs wouldn't
turn him when he gets the bit in his teeth. I tried to
get him to reduce his price. Said I, 'Jim, don't be
hard on a lady,' and says he, 'If it wasn't a lady, sir,
my figure would be double that.' After that of course
I couldn't say anything, except to offer to see you myself, as of course you would rather have to do with a
friend you know than with a no-account sneak like
that."

Dorothy sat down with a sudden feeling of helplessness. The blackmailing character of the demand
was apparent, and as she remembered what Macdonald had said about Falkland she divined that
he was probably not altogether the outside party to
the transaction that he represented himself to be.
But what could she do? She had not been accustomed to deciding matters of moment. Her home
life had been such as to keep her, even more than
most women, apart from the graver questions of life.
Yet here she must act for herself, and at once. It
was impossible to call on Edward, or even on Richard, for advice. She knew instinctively that their way
would not be the way on which she had decided, even
while she was trying to make herself believe she was
deliberating about it. If she paid the money, no
one need even know her folly. And if she refused,
and that old story should be brought up now to
shame Alec Macdonald— Her pulses were throb-

bing dizzily, but she made an effort to keep her voice calm.

"How am I to know that the man will deal in good faith—give me all the papers and keep nothing back for another claim?"

"The amount you pay will be your surest guarantee, Miss Vanborough."

She looked mystified.

"He wouldn't dare let—anybody see him again, that's all," he added with a short laugh. "I'm not sure that he has made a good bargain, though I suppose he thinks the ready money is worth some chances."

"Chances of what?"

"Of getting more in the long run. But of course it is nothing to me. As I said, I am acting in this as your friend, for the sake of old times, but if you want my advice I would say close with him and get those old papers and burn them up. If that had been done thirteen years ago, it might, perhaps, have been better for the poor—fellow."

"I will pay what he asks."

Falkland stooped to pick up his hat from the floor, though he should have known that Miss Dorothy was not given to reading facial confessions.

"When and where can I see him?"

"I will see him and let you know," he answered, reflecting that it was not prudent for him to be too well posted as to " Jim's " movements. "When would it be convenient for you to have the money? I think I could make him wait a few days, if you like."

"No, the sooner the better," she answered feverishly.

"And — could you make it bank notes? Less trouble, you know, and no names."

"Yes, yes."

Falkland longed to get away at once, but he feared to leave without some assurance that no one else would be drawn into consultation. While he wavered, Dorothy unconsciously came to his aid.

"Of course he must never know anything of this," she said with a little catch in her voice.

Falkland was quick, but her thought went beyond him.

"Who?"

"Mr. Macdonald."

"Of course not," he said with undisguised relief. "Neither he nor any one else. You may depend on me." He fervently hoped that he might depend on her.

As Falkland left the house he ran against Louis.

"Hello, father!" cried the boy cheerily. "Mr. Macdonald has got home. You wanted to see him, didn't you?"

"Yes, but I won't have time. You can mention to Mr. Macdonald, though, that I have left town. I am going at once."

"Are you, father?" Louis walked silently beside him a few minutes, and then asked timidly, "When are you going to get through with that business and come home to stay?"

"Oh, don't ask questions about things you can't understand. And don't forget to tell Mr. Macdonald what I said."

He nodded carelessly and struck off into another street.

Left to herself, Dorothy went slowly up to her own room and locked the door. The long habit of a lifetime had kept her outward calm unbroken, but her pulses were beating so wildly that she heard none of the sounds of the outward world. What had she done? Nothing less than indentify herself with Alec Macdonald against the ghost of his old sin. It was no use for her to tell herself that she would have done as much for the veriest stranger. Why did she feel that to save Alec Macdonald from shame she would go to the ends of the earth if need be? Why did the thought that she could serve him without his knowledge thrill her with such keen joy that she trembled under it? She felt that all her old reproaches, her old scorn, had simply vanished like a cloud that melts into film under a tense gaze. Incoherently she was protesting to herself that she did not care what he had done, what he had been.

She walked up and down the room with uneven steps, stopping now and again, but with no consciousness of her action. All her life was absorbed in the struggle as her old faith and the new met in a deadly conflict. It stood for all that she had thought fixed and stable, that old habit of thought of hers. Yet from the day when Macdonald's eyes looked into hers as he snatched her out of death's way, something had been growing up within her that was now able to shake all her old forms of judgment into ruins.

Suddenly she stood still.

" I love him," she said aloud. Then in a moment she had dropped down, tremblingly hiding her face. With the fateful words came an awed recognition of what they implied of burden sharing, of indentity.

He might never know the changed relation in which she must forever stand to him, but it had already become one of the facts of her existence, as immutable as the coming of spring. She held her breath to recall his every look, his every tone, with a new sense of sharing that made her eyes luminous and gave a shy, conscious curve to her lips. Then—

"Oh, if it were not for that shame of your past, Alec!"

Then, in the silence that followed the cry of her soul, the knowledge came to her like a sudden revelation that, after all, to lead a virtuous life is not the end of one's being, but rather to train that attitude of self which will make anything but a virtuous life impossible. A soul must struggle if it would grow, must know the depths if it would measure the heights. Not the station one has reached, but the direction in which his face is set is of supreme moment.

The flashing vividness with which the truth forced conviction upon her left her pale and trembling. Intellectually she would have before assented to such a proposition as a commonplace. Now for the first time, vivified by the intuition of love, it was real to her. She had pushed open the door into one of Truth's chambers, and its light fell directly upon her without being refracted by some other mind. Her old standards stood convicted. Old habits of thought must be recast. But in the mean time one thing was clear, and her whole being bent in tender and grateful acknowledgment of its blessing; she might dare to love Alexander Macdonald without shame and without fear.

CHAPTER XXIII.

AND all this time Ralph had been unconsciously pressing forward upon the way of destiny with a softened light in eyes that were always dreamy, and a deep joy in life that grew daily more tender. He was listening to a harmony that held no discords.

He had never dallied with love. As a boy he had thought slightingly of the tender passion. He had ordered his life and left no place for the wayward . god, and now it had come for its revenge. He would have none of Love, would he? Oh, he was so brave and proud, this fine gentleman, that nothing should have power over him? Then let him look to his foils, for Love is a foe that is not pleased with defiance. Love should whistle the air to which his thoughts must dance and lead the procession of all his waking dreams.

How could he note what might be happening about him, when all his soul was bent to understand the revelation that had come to himself? Of Dorothy he was certainly conscious. Underneath all the course of his daily life the thought of her ran like an undercurrent, coloring all his thoughts and all his actions. But it was a dream-Dorothy, rather than the real woman, that he knew. He had woven a halo about her that hid her from himself.

How had it come about? He looked at the calendar with a happy amusement to think that it was only what men would call a few months ago that he had known nothing of this reality which was now more than all the rest of life together. A rosy mist had fallen softly about him. He could easily have pushed his way clear of it at the first, but he had seen too well that it was an illusion to fear it and it had been too beautiful to be banished. So it had deepened about him, until now—he tried his strength against it, and laughed to know how powerless he was. He did not want freedom. This was truth—this knowledge which translated all the philosophy and mystery of life into the language of the heart. Without this master-key, life was a hopeless jangle; with it, a grand harmonious chant.

He scarce could feel that aught lay beyond. He thought he had explored the waters that encompassed the earth because favoring gales had blown his hope-winged bark far out on the bosom of a smiling sea. He told himself that at last he knew; he felt that his rim of sky, where he saw the stars dip into the everlasting waters, was the uttermost horizon of his soul.

And if he was too romantic, Dorothy was too simple for anything like ordinary love-making between them. At first it had pleased her to have him play the gallant, and she had amused herself by listening to his pretty speeches and trying to fancy herself some grand lady to whom fine flattery was offered as a matter of etiquette and accepted without obligation. But for some time now she had instinctively dropped the pretty pretense. She might not be ready for the true king, but at least there should be no masquerader on the throne. So in one feminine way and another she had managed to evade the old confidential chats, and to merge the romantic into the cousinly. Alec would probably have taken the direction of matters more into his own hands, but Ralph would no more have dreamed of trying to manage events than of lending aid to a rose-bud which he was waiting to see blow. He was well content as things were He was even ready, with Montaigne, to forsake the presence of his mistress that he might have the more subtile pleasure of holding her in his thought.

One evening—it was the evening after Falkland's visit to Dorothy, but of that he knew nothing—Ralph had been busy with some writing in his room for an hour, and when he came down-stairs he found Dorothy sitting alone, gazing into the fire in the idlest possible manner.

"Where are the others?" he asked.

"Richard has gone to some meeting and Nita to a school exhibition," she answered. He was struck by the vibrant ring in her voice and something like subdued radiance in her look.

"And you? What are you going to do?"

"Oh, I have some sewing here."

"A sop to your Cerberus of a conscience, so to speak. I never could understand why you women feel that you are morally accountable for every moment that you spend in quiet. If you are determined to be industrious, may I read to you?"

"That will be the best of everything." she said, lifting her light-filled eyes for a moment.

"I shall make my own selection, mademoiselle."

"What is it," she asked with a smile, as he threw himself down on the sofa opposite with a book in his hand.

"An old love story," he answered with a curious glow in his face. "A book that every true lover must read reverently—the book that holds the heart story of one of the truest lovers that ever lived. Dante called it the history of his New Life."

And then, with a voice that trembled sometimes under the weight of the love-fraught words, he read of " that most gentle Beatrice," and of the young poet who felt that there no longer remained to him an enemy in all the world when blessed by his lady's marvelous salutation.

> "When she passeth by
> Love casts a frost upon all caitiff hearts,
> So that their every thought doth freeze and perish.
> And what can bear to stay on her to look
> Will noble thing become, or else will die."

Was it indeed in an old Tuscan city six centuries ago that the Lord of Love had imposed it upon his liegeman to speak these words in praise of a fair lady, who " was not as other ladies are, whose hearts are lightly moved " ? Ralph almost felt them to be his own, they expressed so truly his own reverent homage to her who in his sight was always " clothed on with gentleness and peace and love."

Then he read the patient, restrained words in which the lover records, with pathetic lack of the flowery phrases which he had loved to fling at the feet of Lady Bicë living, how this most gentle one was called to glory and the city left solitary, as a widow. But to his sorrow-dimmed eyes there came a vision, and then he wrote no more in the book of his youth, for he held the hope of being one day worthy to write of her what had never yet been written of any woman.

Dorothy's work had fallen from her hands as she listened. To her also the words had been more than the rhyming of a dead poet. She too was reading her own heart by their help. The new unrest that had possessed her, and that made her tremble even while she thrilled with strange joy, fell from her under the spell of that clear harmony. This must be what love was—a steadfast recognition of the best, which should shield her evermore, for love's sake, from all that was low and mean. A great calm, a sense of consecration, came upon her, and when Ralph closed the book and turned to her there was a look of exaltation on her face that made his heart stir with something like awe. For a moment he dared not speak.

"Was he not a true lover?" he said at last. "Who could guess from his pages that Florence was full of riot and bloodshed and deadly quarrels? All these had faded from what he calls the book of his memory, when he turned back to read the sonnets and *cansoni* of its early pages, and we see only the Courts of Love, and misty figures of fair dames surrounded by a rosy atmosphere of reverential devotion. It is not Florence, but an enchanted city where Love is lord and only poetry is understood."

"Do you think there are such lovers now?" asked Dorothy. The firelight threw a swift red glow over her face.

"I believe it. But how he shames the thoughtless men and women who take the word on their lips without understanding its glory! If they knew how they hold a magic talisman that can open the gates of paradise itself, would they be content to use it only as a key to a cottage?"

"If they don't know, it isn't for lack of schooling. You poets have done your best," she said with demure sauciness.

He came and stood before her. In the glow of the fire his face had an almost feminine delicacy, heightened to-night by a fleeting tremulousness that showed itself in the wavering color of his fair face and the fitful smile that half parted his lips.

"It is a secret that can't be told. No one understands the poet's rhymes until he doesn't need them to teach him. And no true love song was intended for publication. It was meant for eyes that could read between the lines."

"Why don't you write, Ralph?" she asked gayly.

He bent down smilingly to look into her eyes.

"Because I am too busy living."

"Poetry is a part of your life."

He put his hand caressingly on the book that lay near him.

"Here is poetry After that I do not dare."

She shook her head seriously.

"That is Dante's, not yours. You need not make poetry for the world, but for yourself—oh, for yourself your own would be truer than ever his could be."

"The modern harp has forgotten the stately chants of old, and only tinkles an accompaniment to gay villanelles and jesting rondeaux."

"What is a villanelle?" she asked idly.

He threw himself down on the rug at her feet, so that he could see her face, and repeated :

> "When my love doth smile on me
> Winter wears the grace of May;
> All the earth is fair to see.

> "Doubts that came to vex me, flee;
> Skies grow blue that erst were gray,
> When my love doth smile on me.

18

"Grief, they sigh, is mortals' fee.
  Who will boldly dare to say
  All the earth is fair to see ?

" That may be as it may be,
  But upon the golden day
  When my love doth smile on me

"There's a spell of witchery
  Over all no power can stay.
  All the earth *is* fair to see.

" What care I though storms blow free ?
  What though Fortune say me nay ?
  When my love doth smile on me
  All the earth is fair to see."

Would she divine that he had written the words for her?

She had been listening dreamily, hearing less of the words than of her own pulsing thoughts. The pause roused her to the needs of conversation.

"What is going to become of Poetry, if all her servants take to light trifling like that?" she asked.

Ralph's laugh was a little constrained, and after a brief conference between his vanity and his honesty he decided that there was no absolute necessity for him to confess his authorship just then.

"I suppose, though," pursued Dorothy, "that if those verses were intended originally as a love gift, according to your theory, they had a value the cold public would not see. Do you suppose any one else ever saw in Dante's sonnets what Beatrice found there?"

"Probably not." After a moment he added with a certain timidity : "Do you think, then, that a love gift, be it a verse or a heart, has a right to a lenient judgment?"

"Surely," said Dorothy. But her eyes fell in a remorseful rush of feeling. There had been little leniency in her long condemnation of Alec.

But Ralph saw nothing of this, and there was an eager look in his eyes as he answered:

> "Gifts? Nay, I bring all my life to my love,
> Graceless the while,
> Lacking her smile.
> Cares else untold I will lay at her feet,
> Hopes that her sharing alone makes complete;
> All of my soul,
> Joyance and dole,
> This is the gift I will bring to my love."

Was he waiting for an acknowledging glow? She smiled at him frankly and with a sympathetic pleasure, but her face was as serene and untouched as a child's. The half-purpose he had cherished to pour out his heart to her to-night faded away under her calm gaze.

"Not yet," he whispered to himself, and for a few moments he spoke no word, but only gazed unseeingly into the fire. Then he spoke seriously and frankly, as he could have spoken to no one else.

"To be Love's liegeman may not be at the first demand. The soul must have wrought and learned, before that crowning privilege may be claimed. I wonder what work there is for me to do."

"Wait and see," she answered gently.

"I am afraid I shall grow impatient and want to claim the reward before my work is done," he said, looking up with a gleam in his eyes. "And I would have to wait long to make up for the easy time I have

had so far. Do you know, I feel like a boy beside
Alec Macdonald, for instance. He has lived so deeply, so genuinely. Do you remember what he once
said about the needed opportunity coming to every
one? He has lived out that theory. He has made
mistakes, but I believe that he has always tried to
stand ready to do what might be required. That tells
in the long run. You can't be with him, as I have
been, without being inspired by the high reach of such
living."

He looked up at her as he spoke, and then, for
blank amaze, he could not look away. A veil of light
seemed to have fallen upon her face, and beneath it
she was transfigured. There was no need for words.
In that one moment of time Ralph learned by a flashing recognition how hopelessly long must be his trial,
how the heart which he had dreamed might one day,
after patient waiting, be his own, was already another's.

His fixed look recalled Dorothy to consciousness
of her own self-betrayal. A blinding blush swept the
illumination from her face, but for a moment she tried,
by a brave effort, to meet him fairly and give denial
to the unspoken inquiry in his startled eyes. Once,
and again, she tried and failed. Then slowly, as a
flower bends at night, her head sank low until it rested
on her hands in confession that could never more be
recalled.

There was silence in the room. Ralph had risen
and was looking into the fire with wide eyes that saw
nothing. Then he came to where she sat, her head
still bowed under the weight of her maiden shame.

"Cousin," he said (and it was long since he had

used the word), "do not be sorry that I should know. Let me know at least that you trust me. I can not bear to think that I should have troubled you."

Still she did not raise her head, but she put out one trembling hand. He held it for a moment, then bent to kiss it gravely, and, murmuring under his breath "Bless you, Dorothy," he left her alone.

He went steadily up to his room and shut himself in.

"It is at an end," he said to himself, and quietly he tried to gather up his broken life. All must be changed. He had been drifting with only his heart to guide him ; now the current must set in another direction. He must be needed somewhere. There must be work waiting for him in the world, and one check like this must never make him useless. He would not stop to think of his hurt. He must keep his eyes ahead.

Then suddenly he broke down altogether. What was left? What was the use of going on, with all the courage gone from life? He hid his face and groaned aloud. He knew now how all the forces of his being had been, unconsciously to himself, drawing toward this one center. The routine of life which he had followed had been but a mask to shield his heart, as Dante had masked his love for Beatrice by a poet's licensed devotion to another fair dame. The words of the Tuscan's lamentation came back to him :

"How doth the city sit solitary that was full of people !"

But even in that hour he never quite lost faith in himself or in his power to come through the trial. He could not conquer the despair of the hour, but he knew that beyond was the clear light of the stars, waiting to shine for his guidance.

"I must be patient with this heart of mine," he murmured as he walked his room with blinded eyes. "I must wait and be patient."   •

At last he slept, for the struggle had exhausted him. In his sleep something came to him which was neither a vision nor a dream, but rather a clearness of apprehension before which mists of emotion vanished and nothing but peace remained. When he awoke it was with the feeling that he had left something behind him forever, but in the clear light of the morning despair could not dwell. A patient sadness had come in its place, but the peace was in it and would grow.

If words could touch that inner thought they might shadow it forth as this :

"To the pilgrim soul, journeying from the unknown to the dim and far, love is a fair garden by the way-side. Here the weary one may rest and haply think his journey done, yet wiser he who pauses not as one whose task is past, but only to win strength for wider quests. The unrest of love—what is it but the impatience of the soul rebelling at its narrow bounds? The heart is content with the white flowers that grow in the meadow, but the soul, with eyes fixed ever on the blue fields where bloom the eternal stars, seeks what lies beyond and will not be stayed. And then the heart is grieved, for what is beyond seems barren and cold and vast, and it pleads with the soul to be content, murmuring, 'There is nothing more.' But the soul whispers, 'What we hold can never grow less. Let us onward.' And the timid one, fearing that all it has loved is to die, goes on with tear-dimmed eyes, seeing only the white flowers it has gathered in the meadow. And as it gazes suddenly it knows that they are the stars, grown near and dear and eternal."

CHAPTER XXIV.

"IT is to-day at last, sure enough, and carnival's begun," ejaculated Louis Falkland, springing out of bed that Thursday morning at an hour when it may be safely declared not even the executive committee had begun to struggle back into the world of badges and clubs. In extenuation it must be remembered that none of the executive committee, with all their honors on their heads, had the glory of being President of the Wild Cat Toboggan Club.

"Won't it be a jolly go, though? Grand procession at two, with the Wild Cats leading the second division "—he interrupted himself to rehearse some semi-military movements—"then the review by the Governor, then the illumination and street parade in the evening. Jiminy! There's enough in one such half-holiday to last a week, if spread out thin."

He restrained himself with difficulty from practicing the peculiar call of the Wild Cats, and gave his attention instead to his masquerade toggery. This was a complicated affair, which, for the sake of secrecy, had been chiefly evolved by the inventive brain and undaunted fingers of the owner. As a work of art he was justly proud of it, and he found the common difficulty of authors in putting himself mentally at a sufficient distance from his creation to judge it dispassionately. It seemed complete, and yet— He looked at it critically. The shield was all right, and the sword was immense, and the visor of the helmet was what actors call " practicable," but his heart longed for some distinctive adornment. Henry of Navarre himself would hardly have lived on the page of history without his snow-white plume. Even a bunch of cock's feathers would be better than nothing, and by the same token he had some in the attic. They didn't sound heroic, but they would serve as a modern substitute. Having no desire to be reminded that his first duty on rising was to make the fires, he slipped off his shoes, possessed himself of some matches, and stole softly up to the attic, with a prudent heed to the boards that creaked. But when his ascending head reached the level of the upper floor he stopped sharply. Some one was ahead of him. There was a glimmer of light in the darkness that revealed the movements of a dusky form—whether a ghost or a burglar or a Frankenstein monster, it would have taken a steadier eye than his to tell. The next moment he had recognized his father. Mr. Falkland was rolling a faded toboggan suit into a bundle, and at his feet lay a clown's mask. The boy took it all in deliberately, and then he stole softly down again with a triumphant grin on his face. So! That was why his father had stayed over instead of leaving Hawthorne yesterday as he had said he would do. He was going to mask in the carnival ! And that was why he had so sharply shut up Louis's questions last evening as to his change of plan. Well, Louis would be among the maskers, too, and it would be hard lines if he didn't get some fun out of his knowledge of the clown mask. The pros-

pect filled him with such joy that he deemed it a
proper caution to simulate great drowsiness when he
answered his father's call half an hour later.

"Louis, you know where Miss Vanborough
lives?"

"Yes, sir."

"Here is a letter I want delivered to her to-day.
It must be given to her, and no one else. You've got
a head on your shoulders and will know how to manage it without blundering."

"All right," said Louis, highly flattered. "I can
take it around when I leave the office at twelve. I
have a half-holiday to-day."

"That will do very well. Oh, did you happen to
mention yesterday to Mr. Macdonald that I was leaving town?"

"Yes, he asked if you were here. I think he
wanted to see you. I can tell him this morning that
you stayed over."

"No, don't say anything about it. I won't have
time to see him anyhow, and I am going off to-day, so
it amounts to the same thing."

Louis thought of the mask and with difficulty re-
frained from winking.

It was a long forenoon to the office-boy, but twelve
o'clock sounded at last. Then in his haste to reach
the headquarters of the Wild Cat Club he came near
forgetting the letter, and must race back with it under
horses' heads and through blockades of sleighs. This
speed brought about a catastrophe, for the letter
slipped out of his mittened fingers, as he dodged
across a street, and when he recovered it, it was so be-
spattered that he gazed at it in dismay. It was impos-

sible to think of placing such an object in the hands of the daintiest of ladies.

But Louis was a youth of resources, and hastily seeking the nearest stationer's shop he proceeded to invest a penny in a clean envelope, rejecting, on mature second thought, the one with embossed Cupids around the edge which he had at first demanded. He tore off the soiled envelope, and the half-sheet lay open in his hand. The first words caught his eye, and they were of so exciting a nature that it would have taken a sterner fiber than Louis was made of to resist reading the half-dozen written lines.

" A masker in the carnival to-night will give you the letters. Be under the Sheaf of Wheat Arch between 8.30 and 8.45, and have the money with you in a sealed envelope. Don't fail, unless you are willing to have him dispose of them elsewhere."

Louis was much puzzled, but he sealed the letter in the new envelope, and ten minutes later he had placed it in Miss Vanborough's hands. But as he proceeded again on his way to the rendezvous, still turning the strange words over in his mind, a light broke suddenly upon him which made him stop short and whistle. After a few moments of perplexed rumination, he turned and walked rapidly back to the office of the *Dial*. Mr. Macdonald was still there.

" Mr. Macdonald, may I speak to you a minute ?"

" All right, Louis ; what is it ?"

But the boy found unusual difficulty in beginning.

" Father didn't go yesterday," he said at last. " He stayed over."

" Oh, I am glad to know that. I want to see him. Will I find him at home now ?"

"Yes, I think so," said the boy quickly. That was what he wanted. "Will you go there?"

"Yes, at once."

"And—Mr. Macdonald—"

"Well, anything else, my boy?"

"I wish you would—do you think you could—get father not to take any money from Miss Vanborough?"

"What do you mean, Louis?" asked Macdonald quickly. He was looking serious enough now in all conscience.

"I don't know as I ought to tell. He's my father," said Louis with a little choke.

Macdonald thought to himself that might be a better reason for keeping faith with him in some other case than Louis's, and aloud he answered: "I think this is something I ought to know. You can trust me to forget it if it isn't."

"It was a few days ago I heard him tell mother you would have to give him some money. He didn't know I heard. I listened because mother cried and I thought— But he wasn't angry with her, only laughed and said she would be glad enough when he got it. He said it was a business arrangement, that you owed him the money, and you would miss him if he didn't come."

"Yes, yes. Go on."

"Yesterday morning he came here and asked for you, but you weren't in and he didn't wait. But at noon I saw him coming out of Miss Vanborough's."

Macdonald smothered an exclamation.

"He told me he was going away at once, but when I got home last night he was there, hunting for some old letters that had been in a trunk in the attic for a long time. They were letters that Miss Vanborough's brother that died, you know, wrote long ago, and he said that he had promised to look them up for her for keepsakes."

"Yes," said Macdonald as quietly as though it were a matter of course. "Did he find them?"

"Yes, sir, after a while. But—I think he means to sell them to her, instead of giving them." Louis had presence of mind enough to remember that it might be as well not to give his reasons for this conclusion. "And I thought—if you owed him some money— wouldn't you just as soon pay him now, and then he wouldn't have to sell the letters? Miss Vanborough has been so nice to us, mother and me, I wish he would just give her the old things for keepsakes if she wants them."

"Yes, I must see your father about it at once. You are going home? I will go with you. You were quite right to come to me."

In spite of this assurance Louis had some nervous tremors at the thought of his father's discovering that he had talked about the matter, and he could not repress a sense of relief when they found that Mr. Falkland was not at home, and that the hour of his return was entirely problemetical. They continued their course down the street again together.

"Louis," said Macdonald after a period of silence, "there are other reasons beside the money why Miss Vanborough should not have those letters. They belong to me, if to any one, because they relate to business matters between myself and Mr. Vanborough, when we were partners long ago. Your father would understand this if I could see him, but if I can't see him I want you to tell him that I will pay more than Miss Vanborough. Get the letters themselves, if you can, for me. Do you think you can find him before he sees Miss Vanborough again ? "

A brilliant idea flashed into Louis's head and made his eyes fairly dance.

"Yes, sir, I think—I am *sure* I can. He won't try to see her to-day, I know. And before he does I will get the letters from him."

The boy's face kindled with a delight that seemed to border on the reprehensible, but Macdonald was too perplexed and preoccupied to give it much heed.

" I hope you can," he answered, and leaving Louis he turned toward the Ellis habitation. He felt it absolutely necessary that he should see Dorothy on one pretext or another, and discover if possible what Falkland had told her. He had wanted money, of course. To get it he must have presented some claim. Dorothy was tender-hearted, and any pitiful tale would have served the purpose as well as the story of Harry's fault. Still, Falkland was quite reckless enough to play his trump card first. And if she knew it, would her heart be broken ? Would she hate him for hiding it for so long or for not hiding it better ? He had not dreamed thirteen years ago, when he took what seemed so simple a matter into his hands, what complications lay within it.

But when Dorothy came into the room to greet him with a soft, shy look in her face that he had never seen there before, he knew all that he cared without any words. Women were proverbially incomprehensible, but he knew Dorothy Vanborough well enough to be sure it was not in that way she would have met him if she had just learned that for years she had been doing him an injustice. She gave him her hand for the briefest moment, without raising her eyes. He gave some reason—he hardly knew what—for his call, and stayed but a moment. The old secret was still safe. Now to find Falkland.

That, however, was not so easily done, for the very evident reason that Falkland had no intention of being found. That gentleman might not be very far-sighted, but he was perfectly well aware that he had practically cut himself off from further supplies from Macdonald by opening negotiations direct with Miss Vanborough. In one way, of course, his claim was as good as ever, but he remembered one or two passages with Macdonald, and involuntarily shivered. No, thank you. If he once got that neat little sum from Harry Vanborough's sister, he would give up that lead as exhausted and keep out of the way of unexploded bombs. Till then, if Macdonald wanted him, Macdonald might whistle. There were too many risks involved in an interview.

It was chiefly for the sake of secrecy that he had conceived the idea of giving Miss Vanborough the papers during the masquerade. It was the simplest way of transacting the business without making his own instrumentality known or facing the danger of engaging a confederate. Then, too, it was more effective. The gay carnival—the secret appointment—the veiled lady—the masked villain—" Madam, 'tis I " —the very satisfactory transfer of papers for—paper— why waste such an opportunity by doing the thing in a stupidly prosaic way? It was melancholy to think how many people had no just appreciation of the strong points of even an ordinary life.

But the little drama was to have more actors than Falkland had cast for the parts.

When Macdonald called for his friends that evening it was not Dorothy but Nita, in a brilliant toboggan suit, who came to meet him.

"Cousin Dorothy isn't going. Isn't it provoking? But, of course, you will come with Uncle Ralph and me. I am perfectly wild to see it. Do you suppose we will be late?"

"I hope Miss Vanborough is well," he exclaimed.

"Oh, yes, but she begs to be excused. Are you ready, Uncle Ralph?"

Macdonald conjectured anxiously what this might mean, and longed, but did not dare, to ask whether Falkland had been at the house since noon. It might be safe to say to Dorothy, "I have two apples in my right hand and two in my left, but don't add them together, please, because I would rather you should not know how many I have altogether," but Nita was a young woman of a different sort.

Ralph now appeared and the three left the house together. Nita had to bear the burden of the conversation, for both the men were unusually distrait and silent, but she was equal to the emergency.

Dorothy, feeling very much like a conspirator or a novice taking his first lesson in burglary, sat with her watch in her hand for ten minutes after she heard the hall door shut. Then she went in search of the housemaid.

"Sophie, will you go down town with me? I have

an errand to do, and I don't like to go alone.   We will
see the illumination, too."

Sophie lifted a swollen and tear-stained face.

"O Miss Dorothy, I've got the neuralgia so bad
I don't know what to do."

Dorothy looked so distressed that Sophie probably
gave her more credit for sympathy than she had any
right to on this occasion.

"You must not go out, at any rate," she said.
"Come to my room a minute.   I think I have something that will help your face."

But after Sophie was doctored and dismissed, the
vital question remained.   Should she venture alone
into the carnival crowd?   Well, why not?   She was
not a school-girl to be frightened by imaginary dangers.   There was no real danger in the well-lighted
streets.   The only thing she feared was not getting
those papers into her possession.   She was willing to
bargain with Fate that it might arrange the means as it
chose, only so that the object should be gained.

It must be confessed, however that her heart beat
a little faster as she shrouded herself in an unfamiliar
cloak and hood and went out into the night.   The
streets were already fast filling with people gayly and
fantastically dressed.   Bright eyes are never brighter
than under the coquettish tassel of a crimson toque,
but Dorothy gave them little heed.   She had the feeling that her dark garb and her errand, so different
from the rest of the world's that night, must remove
her so far from the gay throng as to make her in a
manner invisible.   Yet she noted incidentally the
strangeness of the unusual scene.   She was even
amused to mark staid women of years and responsi-

bilities dashing fleetly by in jaunty carnival costumes. The air echoed with songs and merry shoutings, and occasionally a brass band broke in and drowned the jolly discords. The man who held aloof from the fun lost caste, rather than the neighbor who joined with his children in the sport. The spirit of boyhood had broken loose, and dignity was at a discount.

Whether the way was long or short, or how many times she escaped with her life in the gay stampede, she had no idea. She had no distinct impression of much beside a great deal of glare and noise and an electrical feeling in the air that gave her a strange sort of courage. But when she reached the main street, where the maskers were leading the revels, the illumination was so brilliant that she trembled with a sudden apprehension of discovery.

Here, under arches and festoons of gas-lights, ice-kings and fire-kings, demons and monsters, courtiers and peasants, and polar bears mingled in a jolly fellowship, chaffing each other and the crowd of spectators. It was bewilderingly brilliant, but though she longed to stop, she pressed on hurriedly. Nita and Ralph and Alec were in the crowd somewhere. If she should suddenly come face to face with them! Her heart was in her mouth. She pulled her hood lower over her face, and falling in with the current which set toward the central square, she managed to keep near the inner edge of the pavement, where the pressure of the human tide was the least. She could already see in perspective the illuminated arch from which was suspended a sheaf of wheat in electric lights. The sight made her breath come fast. If anything should happen at the last moment! If she should miss the

man! How the people pressed and jostled! The
great city clock chimed out the half-hour. She started
nervously. Suppose she were too late! The current
of advance was so slow that it hindered rather than
helped her, and she pressed in between the people
with a feverish haste that made more than one turn to
look at her. At last the drooping stalks of yellow
light were over her head. Now she must struggle
against the pressure to keep from being carried past
the place. She worked her way to the edge and
found an eddy on the leeside of the electric-light
mast. Here for a moment she rested. What next?
No one came. The shifting sea of faces before her
made her dizzy. She waited a minute—two—five—it
seemed an hour. Would she fail now at last? Then
in desperation she pushed back her concealing hood
and let the light fall full upon her face. In a moment
one of the masqueraders who wore the grinning mask
of a clown stopped before her.

"Did you bring the money?" he asked in a rapid
undertone.

Macdonald had made the circuit with Nita and
Ralph and then had taken the first opportunity to part
company with them. He felt all the impatience of a
strong-willed man compelled to drift at the mercy of
events instead of directing them. As he stood alone
for a moment, seeing less of the gay crowd he was
watching than of what was passing in his restless mind,
a fantastic masquerader with a crest of cock's plumes
nodding over his barred helmet glided up to him.

"I'm piping the main," he whispered gleefully, and
then took himself off as swiftly as he had come.

Macdonald laughed in spite of his annoyance when it dawned upon him that the mysterious apparition was none other than Louis. The boy was getting all the fun there was out of the situation. But did he mean anything?—for instance, that Falkland was in this crowd? To look for him would at least be doing something. Alec gave himself up again to the stream, scrutinizing every face he met. There were many lithe, slight figures that startled him with a chance resemblance, but Falkland was not among them. Then it struck him that by looking down upon the crowd instead of facing it on a level he would be able to get a more comprehensive view. He had reached the Sheaf of Wheat Arch by this time, and his eye was caught by a platform erected on one side for a band of musicians. That would give him the vantage he wanted. He ran up the half-dozen steps and looked down on the sea of humanity. The first face that grew distinct out of the maze was—not Falkland's, but Dorothy's. He stared and stared again in unbelieving astonishment. Then, while he might have counted ten, the little drama was played out before him. This is what he saw :

A clown detached himself from the shifting mass of revelers and stopped before Dorothy, whose uplifted face looked pale and startled in the glare of the gas. She gave him something which he at once thrust inside his blouse, handing her in exchange a small white packet. Even at that distance the brilliant light verified Macdonald's swift guess that it was a package of letters fastened with a rubber band. But the next instant the papers had been snatched from Dorothy's very hand by a third actor, who immediately darted

off and lost himself in the crowd. The man in a
clown's mask made a gesture of astonishment and
promptly gave chase. The robber was masked, but
Alec had had time to note that he wore a knight's
helmet with a crest of nodding cock's plumes.

He flung himself to the ground and pushed his
way across to the place where Dorothy, left alone,
was shrinking into the shadow.

CHAPTER XXV.

The robber was light of foot, and he slipped
through the crowd with the quickness and ingenuity
of an animal, but there was something of the animal as
well in the man who followed. Together they doubled
and turned and twisted, the one ahead vainly endeavoring to elude the steady pursuer on his track. The
crowd, before, had seemed dense and impenetrable as
a forest; now, it was transparent, and as the pursued
glanced back from time to time he saw always that
lithe, sinuous clown bearing directly down upon him.
He worked his way to the edge of the hindering press,
then suddenly slipped into the shadow of a side street
and broke into a run. Half-way up the block the
friendly darkness of a wide entrance-way opened upon
his left, and he dodged into its shelter. He was just a
second too late. Falkland had seen the vanishing
flash. It was the entrance to a business block, and
half a dozen stone steps led up to the doorway.
Falkland stopped before it, breathing quickly, and
then, after a backward glance into the street, he

leaped lightly up the steps. A crouching figure at the top darted out suddenly and tried to slip past him, but he was too quick. They clinched, and for a moment they swayed and strained in a silent wrestle; then the slighter fell, striking the stones sharply and slipping from one step to another till he lay motionless at the bottom.

Falkland stood still in startled suspense. His first impulse was flight. He thought the whole street must have heard that terrible fall. But after a moment, when no one came, with the assurance of personal safety his old bravado returned.

"A pity. But his obstinacy made it necessary," he murmured coolly.

He softly descended and bent over the prostrate figure. Was the man dead? He was not sure. He lifted the arm, and it fell back heavily. The movement revealed the fatal packet of letters in the blouse pocket, and at the sight of them Falkland's lips curled in a faint smile of triumph. So! Fortune favors the dauntless ever. He drew the papers out softly, though there was no great need of care, and then with the smile still on his lips he turned to go. But an impulse of curiosity made him turn back. He would see who it was that had tried to outwit him. He raised the gay carnival mask, and a ray from the street lamp fell full upon the pale face lying against the snow. It was Louis.

How long Falkland knelt there, dazed, he could never know. Conscious life was suspended. But at last thought came slowly back to his numbed brain. He put out his hand to touch the boy lying silent before him, but drew it back with a shiver. For years he had been building a wall between himself and all that is good, but there was still one door that had never been closed, and it was his tenderness for Louis that had kept it open. He had grown shy of the boy of late, feeling that the eyes of even this son might grow too much like the rest of the world's not to look on him with the world's distrust, but all the love of his nature had been given here. And now he had killed him. The one fate on earth that could have uunerved him had overtaken him.

With a gasping shudder he struggled to his feet. The white packet of letters for which he had striven lay on the ground. Mechanically, and with no feeling even of resentment, he picked it up and quietly thrust it back into the boy's blouse. Then without a backward glance he turned and walked rapidly away. The streets were as gay, the people as merry, the music as intoxicatingly sweet as before, but he walked in a soundless solitude. A passing friend tossed him a greeting, but he did not hear it. Rapidly and aimlessly he threaded his way through the streets, and ever as he went he was saying over and over to himself, " This is the end. This is the end."

It had been his habit to meet events coolly. He had thought he would always be able to laugh his way ·through life. Yet this was the end of it all. He had evaded trouble, he had denied all share in the world's burden of care. Disasters were for other people. He did not know how they met them. He had meant never to know. He had thought himself invulnerable. And now this was the end of his gay defiance, this was the end of his wily scheming, this was the end of life. He had thought his years might be blown away as lightly as bubbles from his wine-glass. Now they came back upon him with their empty hands. He might have put strength into them for his hour of need, but through his fault they were as helpless ghosts.

Impatiently he tried to shake these thoughts from him, but they came back with a dull persistency, like the haunting refrain of a chant. He heard himself saying aloud, with a dreary iteration, " This is the end."

Some one jostled him roughly, and he became aware that people were running past him. Walking rapidly yet aimlessly and without heed to his way he had left the scene of the masquerade far behind. This part of the city was strange to him. He glanced mechanically at the name of the street and immediately forgot it. A fire-engine dashed by, scattering a trail of red cinders across his path. He turned indifferently and followed the stream of boys running to the fire.

A crowd had gathered before a small frame house wreathed with curling tongues of flame. The hot breath of the burning made the air tingle against Falkland's cheek. He pushed his way through till he stood in the inner ring of spectators.

" That's the end," said a man in the crowd.

Falkland turned to look at him.

" The end ? " he repeated in a surprised way.

" They can't save it now. Too much headway, you see. They will have to give it up."

Then a shout arose. The roof of the next house was smoking.

" Bring a ladder ! "

"Break in the door!"

"Quick, there!   Room for the hose!"

But the ladders were on the other side of the burning house.   The sparks on the roof were leaping up in little tongues of flame.   Suddenly Falkland sprang forward with a strange look.

"Give me that rope!   Lend me a shoulder, you! I can get there!"

A waterspout ran down the side of the house near an angle in the wall.   Bracing himself between the two he lifted himself easily above the crowd.   He was light and strong and could climb like an animal, and he had the cheering of the men below to urge him on. Higher and higher he drew himself up, and the lines about his mouth grew tense.   He glanced back once and wondered what those men below would say when they saw him die.   For he meant to die.   That was the only way that was left to him, and in his stunned state it struck him for the first time that death would be easy. Just a misstep—they would think he had grown dizzy —and then the whole thing would be over and done with.   He climbed on till the cornice was within reach of his hand.   It must be now.   He swung one foot free—and then a sudden physical horror came over him, and with a convulsive clutch he pulled himself up safely on the roof.   He was shaking with fear and the cold drops stood on his face.   He did not dare.

Some hours later Falkland was standing on the rear platform of an out-going train, watching the lights of Hawthorne fading out in the darkness.   The gray skies hung low and starless overhead and the white earth was forever slipping away from under his feet.   While he watched, a strange fancy came to him that he was

one who had no share or part in either the heavens or
earth, and that for all time he must go rushing on between the two—swaying, clinging. shaken—rejected of
the universe. He smothered a groan and went drearily in.

CHAPTER XXVI.

By the time Alec reached Dorothy's side he had
come to a pretty clear understanding of the situation,
and in his satisfaction with the outcome he felt that
he could afford to be generous to the vanquished.

"Have you seen all the *putz und ceremonie* you
care to?" he asked with radiant cheerfulness. "I
am entirely at your service if you care to complete
the giddy round."

She looked up, fear, relief, and defiance struggling
in her face.

"How did you find me?"

"Would you believe me if I said by accident? I
wouldn't myself."

"Were you surprised?" she asked with a little
quiver in her voice.

"For a moment, yes."

She looked at him askance.

"Didn't you think it strange to find me here, after
—after—"

"Yes, but I haven't asked any explanation, have I?
You shall tell me as much or as little as you like."

"Then—I will not tell you anything."

Her words were brave, but her tone rather depre-
cating. He only smiled.

"Then shall we go on like all the rest of these people, and see what is to be seen?"

"No, take me out of this, please. Take me home."

Her voice shook a little. She wanted to be alone to cry over her failure, but she couldn't tell him so.

He cleared the way for her with a promptness and ease that made her remember her own efforts with lofty commiseration. In a few minutes they had reached a side street, and were free to guide their own course.

"I love my brother man," said Alec gayly, "but too much of him in one place is apt to be oppressive. This isn't much like your first winter day in this 'section,' is it? Do you remember that first snow-storm? Which do you prefer on the whole—winter plain or mixed with humanity?"

"I can't judge," said Dorothy demurely. "Even that picture on Memory's wall has a specimen of 'brother man' in the foreground."

"Yes, that is another of the many sins that unfortunate specimen must answer for. But you can wash him out if you want to."

"I'm afraid not."

"Do you want to?"

Dorothy was saved the embarassing necessity of a reply to this query, for at that moment they came upon a dark entrance-way, within which a policeman was helping a boy to his feet. Macdonald looked twice before he realized that it was Louis, and then he dropped Dorothy's arm and stepped back alone.

"What has happened?"

"I'm all right," Louis said quickly at sight of him. He tried unsteadily to stand. "I—knocked my head on the stones and fainted, I suppose. But I guess I can get home."

"He'll need some help, I'm thinking, sir," said the policeman.

"Call a cab for him, will you? This will pay you. You're sure it is all right, Louis?"

"Yes, sir," said Louis. He was beginning to look more like himself. "I got the papers, too."

"Never mind," said Macdonald, with a warning look. But the boy was still somewhat confused and had not noticed the lady in the shadow.

"They're here, sir," he said, pulling out the packet after some fumbling.

Alec took it perforce, with a hasty glance at Dorothy. It was enough to show him the flash of recognition and the look of profound astonishment that crossed her face. He gave a few hasty directions to the policeman, and then joined her. The papers were still in his hands.

"Appearances would indicate that I instigated that robbery," he said at once, "but I knew nothing whatsoever about it. I wanted the papers—I have been trying all day to find Falkland and prevent their coming into your hands—but Louis worked out the plan of recovering them after his own dramatic ideas. I was as much amazed as you could have been when I saw the exploit a moment before I joined you."

Dorothy had been so bewildered by the sequence of events that she hardly knew whether she would have reason to be more glad or sorry when she came to think things over, but for the present at least she was greatly relieved to know that the fatal letters were where they belonged, however they got there.

"I do not want them," she said with a little gesture of rejection. "I would have given them to you—if I had dared."

"I said you should tell me only what you wished to, but may I confess that I am desperately curious?"

She laughed shyly.

"You know so much that it will probably be prudent to tell you all. Yesterday morning Mr. Falkland came to tell me that some one—he did not say who—had come into possession of some old letters of—of Harry's, which he was going to publish. I did not want them published, so I agreed to buy them. I came out to-night to get them, because I didn't know of any other way."

"Why didn't you want them published?"

She hesitated, wondering how much he knew or guessed.

"Do you know what they are about?" she asked.

"Yes. Do you?"

"Yes," she answered with drooping eyes.

He gave her a keen look. She probably thought she knew, but he doubted it.

"Then why didn't you send Falkland to me?"

She looked up at that, with a sudden courage.

"Because I was glad to think I could get them myself and destroy them without your knowing it. Perhaps you won't understand, it is a woman's feeling, but it seemed like a reparation for my—injustice and hardness. No, you must let me say it. I know now that your fault, atoned for by so many years of true living, was no worse than my severity in condemning you. I am glad to say it and have it off my mind."

For all that, her voice was so low and tremulous

that as he bent to catch her last words he saw the glimmer of tears on her eyelashes. And he saw something else, too, which was enough to make him instantly forget all about old letters and plots and secrets— all secrets but one, at least, and that wasn't much of a secret any longer.

"Do you mean that at last I have won a right to have that old score forgotten?" he asked eagerly.

But she turned her face away like any schoolgirl and would say neither yea nor nay. If they had not been in the public street he might have pressed for an answer, but he knew now he could afford to wait.

"What shall we do with these letters?" he asked instead.

"What you will."

"You do not care to read them?"

"Oh, no!"

"Then suppose we burn them? They will make a better bonfire than anything else I know."

"Now? We are at home, you see."

"I didn't know where we were. Yes, the sooner the better. And when they are all in ashes there is something else I shall say to you—Dorothy," he added under his breath.

There was no light in the parlor but the flickering light from the open fire in the grate. It wavered over Dorothy's downcast face and made so fair a picture of her as she stood before it, with her cloak slipping down over her shoulders, that Alec had hard work to keep from taking her in his arms then and there. But he had made up his obstinate mind that a certain ceremony must be first performed, and he turned his eyes away. When the papers were all irretrievably de-stroyed, then, indeed, he would turn to her and speak the words that crowded to his lips, but while it was still within his power, if nothing else would serve, to blacken the name she bore in order to prove that the one he offered was unblemished, he would not put his strength to the test.

"Now for the bonfire," he said quickly.

She offered him the packet of letters.

"No, not I—you must throw them in one by one, and we will see them burn away before our eyes."

She smiled and obediently drew one out from the packet and dropped it upon the bed of coals. A tongue of flame leaped to meet it, curling the edges with a glowing line that grew black and faded into a delicate film which fluttered in the breath of the fire. They both watched it with fascinated eyes.

"Put in another. See how it melts away at last after guarding its story all these years! So the story itself shall be wiped out and be as though it had not been. Another! Did you see the writing blaze out? A name. A name that belongs to the past. Put them all in and let the secret they held go out in the smoke that is climbing up to the sky."

He was strangely excited. Dorothy looked at him in wonder, but under his smiling eyes her own fell.

"All gone? Every last one? So, buried forever."

He thrust the poker into the mass of coals and scattered the shreds of white film. Then he turned in the firelight and took her hands in his.

"Dorothy!"

A voice in the open hallway echoed the name.

"Is Dorothy here?"

Dorothy, trembling and blushing, sprang to the door.

"Edward! You here? When did you come?"

"An hour ago. There was no one at home, so I had the maid show me a room. Hearing voices, I came down. Why don't you have the gas lit?"

"Edward, don't you see Mr. Macdonald?" The name clung to her lips.

Whatever Alec might have been thinking in those swift moments he had recovered his composure by this time, and he came forward now with outstretched hand. It was deliberately ignored.

"Macdonald?" Edward was saying in slow surprise. "Mr. Alexander Macdonald?"

Alec bowed, with flushed cheek.

"Pardon me, I did not expect to meet you in my cousin's house or with my sister. It will be pleasanter for both of us if this first interview is the last as well."

"Brother!" cried Dorothy with such dismay and shame in her tone that he stopped suddenly and looked from Alec to her in amazed questioning.

"What do you mean, Dorothy?"

But she was clinging to him, shaken with a burst of sudden tears. He drew his arm about her.

"I may be mistaken," he said slowly, "but your presence here, Mr. Macdonald, and my sister's agitation make it necessary that we should understand each other now and clearly. Are you here as a friend of Mr. Ellis's?"

"I am here now as a suitor to your sister," said Macdonald steadily.

"Then, as Dorothy's only living brother, I must remind you that such an alliance is impossible. I am sure that I speak for her in saying this."

"I will receive my answer from Miss Vanborough," said Alec quietly. He was pale to the lips and his eyes were gleaming.

"I repeat that I speak for Dorothy," Edward said coldly. "The name my sister bears is an old one, and has never known a stain. You force me to speak of this. What have you to offer?"

Alec had drawn back and stood with one arm resting on the mantel, looking down into the fire where white films, like ghosts of letters, were quivering and dancing over the coals. Now, without raising his eyes, he answered in even tones:

"I have nothing to offer."

"Then I say that the past can not be forgotten. In that past lies sorrow for our house and shame for you. We can not forget our brother's death, our mother's broken heart, the dreary end of our father's life. We can not forget that the agent of this was one whom Harry trusted—mistakenly. The world is wide enough for us both, Mr. Macdonald, but our paths can not run together. It would be as impossible for us as it would be fruitless for you to attempt to ignore the wall between us."

If Macdonald had been conscious of the guilt laid at his door, he would have hated Vanborough at that moment, but the words that recalled the old struggle brought back as well the reasons that had made him enter it. Now for Dorothy's sake, as then for Harry's, he must bear the burden he had assumed. But even in that swift moment he had time to wonder scornfully at himself that he should have deemed any sacrifice he had made worth counting since this remained possible.

Then in the pause he lifted his head to answer. His resolution had brought a clear, passionless light into his face that made even Edward yield an unwilling admiration.

"What you have said I neither meet nor deny. You have called upon the past, and I do not question your right to adopt your own standard. If by that I am condemned, I do not ask you to change it. So far it rests with you." Then suddenly the fire leaped into his words. "But the standard is wrong! Who bears an unsullied name, if you go into the past? Not you—not I, even though I were cleared of all shadow of the particular charge you have made. For that reason I neither meet nor deny it. It is dead and twice dead. Judge me fairly, by the living present which is born of the past."

It was to Dorothy he was pleading, but Dorothy, shaken with sobs which she tried to stifle on her brother's shoulder, scarcely heard the proud humility of his restrained tones. Edward's arm was about her, Edward's voice had said it was impossible, and all her life long Edward had represented the tribunal beyond which lay no appeal. Instinctively, in her shaken state, she fell into the old habit of acquiescence, as a startled deserter will respond involuntarily to the old word of command.

"This is needless and useless," said Edward with as near to a touch of impatience as his stately manner would admit. "You must see that further discussion would be unpleasant to my sister."

"I do not wish discussion. I want an answer—one word—from her."

20

Dorothy shivered, but speech had left her. She could not even lift her face until after a long, long moment of silence she heard the sharp closing of the door. Then she sprang from Edward's arm and threw back the hair that had fallen over her flushed cheeks.

Alec was gone.

CHAPTER XXVII.

THE long day that followed was drawing to a close, and Dorothy, with the shield of a book which she was not reading, stood by the window looking out into the white street as she had stood and looked many times during the day. Her face was paler than usual, but a calm had come upon it which showed her sleepless night had at last brought her to a clear decision. It was a new look, and it had puzzled and annoyed Edward, as anything unfamiliar was apt to do. He had watched her askance all day, wondering what the intangible something was that made this silent woman, whose eyes seemed to be resting on unseen horizons, so different from the sister who had always lived out his ideas and never made one thought more than usual necessary on his part. Dorothy of old had been wont to watch his very moods; this Dorothy was so far away that he felt words could not span the distance between them. It couldn't be possible—pshaw! of course not. But he wished he had never come to Hawthorne. Yet who could possibly have foreseen— He must take her away without a day's unnecessary delay. It may not have been wise, but it was eminently characteristic of him that he decided on this step first and announced it afterward.

"Dorothy, how soon will you be ready to go home?"

She looked surprised.

"Why, not till Nellie comes back."

"Yes, I know that is what we originally planned, but it will be better for you to return with me, and I can't wait more than a day or two."

"But I certainly could not go away while Nellie thinks I am here."

"Nellie would understand the advisability of your returning with me. Nita is quite old enough to take charge of the house when it will only be for a week or two. I will explain to Richard."

"No, I shall not go, Edward. I shall stay here until Nellie comes back. Please consider that settled."

Edward looked astonished, but he bowed stiffly. When had she ever before said she would or would not do what he opposed? To cover his discomposure he took up the book she had been reading. It was a little copy of Undine, and he laid it down again suddenly, looking as though a new and disagreeable idea had struck him hard. Undine! That was the story of the woman who found her soul by loving. Was it the habit of women who found their souls in that way to defy their brothers and take it upon themselves to direct their own affairs? He went in search of his cousin and succeeded so well in presenting and pinning down certain ideas that when the family gathered around the tea-table a little later, Richard Ellis immediately cast a cheerful bombshell into their midst by remarking:

"Well, Dorothy, Edward tells me he is going to carry you off."

"Who gave him leave?" demanded Nita with prompt resentment.

"Nita, don't be rude," said her father severely.

"It would be ruder if I let Dorothy go without a word," protested Nita.

"Are you going home, Cousin Dorothy?" asked Philip calmly. "Then is my mamma coming to our house too?"

"Pretty soon, Phil, but not just yet," said Dorothy with lowered eyes. "I shall not go until your mamma does come, dear," she added sweetly and clearly.

Edward looked disagreeable. It was contrary to his instincts to make open use of coercive measures, but it was equally repugnant to him to yield one iota of his determination. Richard unwittingly came to his assistance.

"That is very good of you, Dorothy," he said innocently, "but you must not let us stand in the way of what is best for you. As Edward says, you are looking tired, and I dare say we have worn you out with these noisy children and everything."

"Papa, you are really too bad," expostulated Nita with quivering vehemence.

"I am not the least tired," said Dorothy hastily. "I have had a delightful winter here. You surely know that."

"But you are looking a little pale," persisted Richard with a kindly scrutiny. "Edward saw it at once. I am afraid we have been imposing on you, Dorothy, as everybody does, only you won't confess it. I hadn't noticed it before, but you are looking tired and worn. Don't you think so, Ralph?"

"No, not in the least," said Ralph coolly. He had been listening and drawing his own conclusions.

"But Edward does. You must not think we want you to go, Dorothy. If I thought you would listen I would try to persuade you to stay and finish out the year with us. We will miss you dreadfully. Ralph will say so, too."

"No, I won't say anything about it, having nothing at command but just plain, ordinary English," answered Ralph with a grim gayety.

Dorothy gave him a swift smile. She felt that he at least was not in this conspiracy to send her off before—before—

"But since we can't keep you and you must go, we must not make your departure inconvenient for you as well as melancholy for us," continued Richard with blind self-denial. "Edward tells me you greatly dislike traveling alone, so of course it will be better for you to go on with him."

"But I don't dislike traveling alone," said Dorothy in a low voice. She had a feeling of being hunted. "I came out here alone."

"You forget," Edward interposed. "I put you in Mr. McConnell's care."

"I never saw anything of him. Nothing at all."

"That is strange. Did you come through alone, then?"

Dorothy certainly could not be accused of any alarming pallor as she answered:

"Mr. Macdonald was on the train."

There was an awkward pause, and then Ralph came to the rescue.

"You may think this is a safe plot, Dick, but I want it understood I am not in it. I am not Nellie's husband, but only her brother, and when she comes to require an explanation I want to be able to prove an alibi."

Nita, who had been entirely neglecting her bread and butter in the discussion, caught at the idea.

"Of course she can't go before mamma comes. The very idea! Why, we have planned ever so many jubilations and celebrations."

"I certainly would like to stay over to see Nellie," said Dorothy with outward meekness and inward joy. "I haven't seen her for several years now ; just missed her when I came out. I really think I must stay over, Edward, long enough to have at least one day with Nellie."

It sounded so reasonable that Edward foresaw surrender inevitable, and he was mentally arraigning all the powers of circumstance which were treacherously aiding the insurgent, when Sophie came in with a telegraphic dispatch for Mr. Ellis.

"Why, this is timely," he cried, after hastily reading it to himself amid a general suspense. "From Nellie. 'Shall start for home to-morrow. No time to write.'"

"Is mamma coming now, right off?" asked Philip.

"Yes, my boy." Mr. Ellis's eyes were smiling.

"Hip, hip, hurrah," said Nita in a solemn whisper.

"That is just like Nellie," murmured Ralph languidly. "She is always shedding a shower of exclamation points about her."

"She will be here the day after to-morrow, then," said Edward to Dorothy. "I can wait over for that. You will have your day together, after all, and then we will start Monday morning. That will suit us all."

And Dorothy bowed her head to fate and swallowed her tea cold.

Nita dared not break into open rebellion, but her wrath grew through the hours, and when she found her uncle alone late the next afternoon she gave it vent.

"Are you busy, Uncle Ralph?" she asked.

"No, not very," he answered with a start. Unless one may be busy with dreams he certainly was not.

"I want to free my mind. I can't talk to Dorothy, because after all he is her brother, and papa of course will uphold him because he is a man, but don't you think that Cousin Edward is perfectly horrid?"

"Thank you, my dear girl. I wanted to say that myself, but traditions of good manners restrained me."

"They wouldn't restrain him. I know Dorothy just hates to go back. We are much nicer than Cousin Edward's people, don't you think? Honestly now!"

"Well, if you put me in the confessional, I suppose it is—a matter of taste!"

"Dorothy's taste, then. Couldn't you see she wanted to stay? What sort of a woman is Cousin Gertrude? I don't remember her well."

"Just the sort of a woman to be Edward's wife."

"Oh, poor Dorothy! No wonder she looked so kind of meek and fluttered when she first came. It is a shame to send her back when she has been so much happier here. It is wicked. Why can't she stay with us instead?"

"Because you and I can't have our way, Nita. Her brother's home is naturally hers."

"I shall talk to mamma about it. Oh, do you think mamma might possibly come to-day instead of to-morrow?"

"No. Impossible."

"Oh, dear, there will be so many things to talk about to-morrow, if Dorothy is going the day after! I hoped she might come to-day. Dorothy thinks so, too."

"Why, Dorothy must know the time-tables won't allow it. Did she speak of it?"

"No, but I know. She wouldn't go down the street with me, and she goes to the door herself whenever the bell rings, and she keeps watching. Of course it can't be for any one but mamma."

Ralph was staring at her with so absent an expression that she shook his sleeve.

"Don't look like that when I am speaking. It isn't polite for you to go off to the Himalayas and leave me talking to your empty ears."

"I beg your pardon. I was trying to hint delicately that your conversation, charming as it is, is keeping me away from the office."

But Nita was too much broken up to resent this fling. She clung to his arm and conducted him to the hall door.

"Do you know, Uncle Ralph," she said meditatively, "as I get older I am finding out that there are not so very many very nice people in the world, after all, but you are nicer than most.

"Then I must try to live up to your opinion," he said with a queer smile as he left her.

The business that demanded his presence at the office could not have been very pressing in its nature, for he loitered on the way in a very unbusiness-like manner, and when he finally got there he went to Alec's office instead of his own, and talked for some time of various trifles. When at last he was about to go he turned back at the door.

"Will you come around to the house, to-night, Alec?"

"No, I am afraid I can't," said Macdonald with a start.

"To-morrow, then?"

"Thank you, old man, but I am not sure that I sha'n't be out of town to-morrow."

"But Dorothy is going Monday. Edward has come for her, much to our disgust. Of course you must come up before she goes."

"So soon? I didn't know. I will try to be at the depot to make my adieus."

Ralph looked at him searchingly.

"Don't you *want* to see her?"

"There are some things I can't talk about even to you, Ralph," said Alec defiantly, turning away.

Ralph followed and put his hand on the other's shoulder.

"Then let me talk."

"I can't give you the right."

"I think I have the right," Ralph answered winningly, "because it might have been possible for me to love her myself."

Alec looked profoundly astonished and moved.

"It was only a possibility, and of course I had no chance. I only told you to buy your frankness in return. Is there any misunderstanding between you and Dorothy?"

Alec sat down suddenly by his desk, shielding his face with his hand.

"Not much misunderstanding. She sent me away, that is all."

"When was that?"

"Thursday night. I saw her after I left you."

"Thursday? That was when Edward came. Did you see him?"

"Yes, he was there. Of course that wasn't my choice. He rather forced matters, perhaps—but there was no misunderstanding."

"I think I begin to see. That is why Edward is so bent on carrying her away at once. Are you going to let him do it?"

"It isn't for me to say."

"Will you see Dorothy again?"

"No. I can't."

"Are you firm about that?"

"Yes. It would be needless pain."

"But suppose that she wished to see you?"

"But she does not," cried Alec, springing up passionately. "Good heavens, man, once is enough."

"Then she will come to you," said Ralph quietly. "I don't say she loves you—that is for her to say if any one—but when I found out that I would have had no chance I learned that you might. If, in your pride and obstinacy, you will not take the first step to prevent a mistake from bringing unhappiness into your two lives, then she will, when I tell her what I shall, and you will have to go down on your knees to entreat pardon for having forced her to do it." His voice was quivering with something that was not weakness. "You are holding off because you think it would be unpleasant for you to risk a second repulse. But whether it would be pleasant or unpleasant for you has nothing whatsoever to do with it."

"You are right, Ralph. It has nothing to do with it," said Alec with a sudden flush on his face. "I thank you, and I understand what you have done, though I can't say anything about it."

But Ralph held up his hand and shook his head with a faint smile.

Dorothy was standing alone in the early twilight watching the first stars coming out into the sky, and trying to hold down the dreary sense of forsakenness that had been crowding upon her since she knew that her last day was gone and what she had looked for had not happened. She was only thinking that she must not stop yet for a while to look things in the face. She must hold them at arm's length until she was far away. But it was very lonely—lonely as those vast fields above, so far, so deep, so unregardful, which seemed to sink the earth and the lives of all that dwelt thereon into hopeless insignificance. She shivered and turned away, her eyes dim with burning tears. At the door stood Alec Macdonald.

She had no time to think of what her face might tell. She only felt that the tangle which had seemed to involve the whole universe had fallen away. She only saw the long look and the swift, faint smile she knew so well as he came quickly toward her.

"Are you glad, then, to see me?"

"Why did you stay away?"

They were both trembling, and both knew that there was nothing more to be said.

L'ENVOI.

So it was nothing but a love story, after all.   True; but is there so much love in the world that there is no longer any need of telling its story ?   When love stories become the rule of human lives there will be no more need for their syllabled shadow.   Till then, they have a right to their frame of words.   Of all the readers of books, one in a hundred, perhaps, may lay to heart the gospel of the grammarians; the scientist speaks to an audience reduced again by a hundred, while the philosophers count their labors not in vain if one soul arises in a generation that can follow whither their cobweb subtleties lead.   But every heedless child of the human race must try his 'prentice hand at love and friendship and find weal or woe as luck, rather than knowledge, guides his experiments.   To this majority is dedicated this story of a man whose only claim upon memory is that he was a loyal friend and a gentle lover.

THE END.

29. IN THE WIRE-GRASS. By Louis Pendleton.

"An unusually clever novel is 'In the Wire-Grass,' by Louis Pendleton (Appletons). It presents a vivid picture of Southern life by a native of the South, and abounds in incidents and characters racy of the soil. . . . The humor is everywhere bright and genuine, and the action uniformly brisk."—*The Sun.*

30. LACE. A Berlin Romance. By Paul Lindau.

"'Lace,' Lindau's novel, of which the Appletons have just published a thoroughly good translation, gets its name from the fateful *rôle* held in it by a marvelous mantle of Brabant lace. This mantle wanders through the mazes of this story like a specter that will not down, and, rarely beautiful as it is, grows in the end into a veritable robe of Nessus. . . . Altogether, 'Lace' is one of the most effective pieces of work that we have seen for a long time."—*Commercial Advertiser.*

31. AMERICAN COIN. By the author of "Aristocracy."

A satirical picture of impecunious English peers in search of fortunes, and of the daughters of American millionaires in search of titles.

"'American Coin' is a remarkably clever and readable story."—*N. Y. Herald.*

32. WON BY WAITING. By Edna Lyall.

"The sentiment of the story is delicate and uplifting, and the style is uncommonly spirited and active."—*Boston Gazette.*

33. THE STORY OF HELEN DAVENANT. By Violet Fane.

"Neither Miss Braddon nor the author of 'The House on the Marsh' could have contrived a more ingenious story than that of 'Helen Davenant.'"—*The Academy.*

34. THE LIGHT OF HER COUNTENANCE. By H. H. Boyesen, author of "Gunnar," "Idyls of Norway," "A Daughter of the Philistines," etc.

The scenes of this story open in New York, but the action soon shifts to Italy. The characters are mainly American and English. The incidents are picturesque, and the movement animated.

35. MISTRESS BEATRICE COPE; or, Passages in the Life of a Jacobite's Daughter. By M. E. Le Clerc.

"A simple, natural, credible romance, charged with the color of the time and satisfying to the mind of a thoughtful reader."—*The Athenæum.*

36. KNIGHT-ERRANT. By Edna Lyall.

"'Knight-Errant' is marked by the author's best qualities as a writer of fiction, and displays on every page the grace and quiet power of her former works."—*The Athenæum.*

37. IN THE GOLDEN DAYS. By Edna Lyall.

"The central figure of her story is Algernon Sidney, and this figure she invests with singular dignity and power. Some of the scenes are remarkably vivid. The escape is an admirable narrative, which almost makes one hold one's breath to read."—*The Spectator.*

38. GIRALDI; or, The Curse of Love. By Ross George Dering.

"'Giraldi' is undeniably a clever book; satirical, humorous, and amusing; full of consistent sketching of character; . . . an original and readable novel." — *The Saturday Review.*

39. A HARDY NORSEMAN. By Edna Lyall.

"All the quiet power we praised in 'Donovan' is to be found in this new story." — *The Athenæum.*

40. THE ROMANCE OF JENNY HARLOWE, and Sketches of Maritime Life. By W. Clark Russell.

"'The Romance of Jenny Harlowe,' supplemented by other sketches of sea life, offer capital reading. The story is exciting enough to satisfy the most exacting on this score.' — *The Academy.*

41. PASSION'S SLAVE. By Richard Ashe-King.

"Mr. King is a refined and pleasant writer. . . . His tact is generally beyond reproach." — *The Athenæum.*

42. THE AWAKENING OF MARY FENWICK. By Beatrice Whitby.

"We have no hesitation in declaring that 'The Awakening of Mary Fenwick' is the best novel of the kind that we have seen for some years. It is apparently a first effort, and as such is remarkable." — *The Athenæum.*

43. COUNTESS LORELEY. From the German of Rudolf Menger.

"An exciting novel, the scene of which is laid principally in Germany just before and after the Franco-Prussian War. The characters, which embrace besides the two principal ones a Breton duelist, a lion-hearted Englishman, a Russian diplomat, and others, are presented in a spirited manner." — *Boston Gazette.*

44. BLIND LOVE. By Wilkie Collins. With a Preface by Walter Besant.

This posthumous novel was unfinished at the time of Mr. Collins's death, although in course of serial publication. By means of the ample notes left by the author, Mr. Besant was enabled to complete it along the lines laid down by the author. "The plot of the novel," says Mr. Besant, "every scene, every situation, from beginning to end, is the work of Wilkie Collins."

45. THE DEAN'S DAUGHTER. By Sophie F. F. Veitch.

"The passages in it which deal with the morally distorted and tragic passion of Vera Dormer recall to some extent the vanished hand of the author of 'Jane Eyre.'" — *The Academy.*

46. COUNTESS IRENE. A Romance of Austrian Life. By J. Fogerty.

"This is a charming story, interesting and *mouvementé*, with some highly dramatic incidents. . . . The pictures of Viennese life and manners are admirable, and the descriptions of Austrian country-house life amid the magnificent scenery of the Salzkammergut are most attractive." — *Westminster Review.*

12mo, paper cover. Price, 50 cents each.

New York: D. APPLETON & CO., Publishers, 1, 3, & 5 Bond Street.

47. ROBERT BROWNING'S PRINCIPAL SHORTER POEMS.

Browning was so voluminous a writer that his complete works are practically inaccessible to many readers. The present collection includes everything by which he is best known, except the dramas and very long poems.

48. FROZEN HEARTS. A Romance. By G. WEBB APPLETON.

"A well-laid plot, strong characters, and striking situations, give the story an absorbing interest throughout."—*Baltimore American.*

"It is a clever, well-written, interesting story of Paris in the earlier days of the Orleans succession, rich in Waterloo, the Napoleonic and Bourbon reminiscence, and as clean as clever French authors can make the same subjects unclean."—*Brooklyn Eagle.*

49. DJAMBEK THE GEORGIAN. A Tale of Modern Turkey. From the German of Von Suttner, by H. M. JEWETT.

A romance in a new field, affording some novel pictures of life, social and political, interwoven with and subordinated to a stirring and romantic love-story.

"'Djambek the Georgian' strikes us as altogether a spirited and probably faithful presentation of conditions which existed prior to the last Russo-Turkish War, and which have certainly been changed for the better since then, though not through Turkish reforms of any kind."—*New York Tribune.*

50. THE CRAZE OF CHRISTIAN ENGELHART. By HENRY FAULKNER DARNELL.

"A novel of more than ordinary quality and strength is 'The Craze of Christian Engelhart.' It is marked by vigorous action, original types of character, and a mystic atmosphere enveloping some of the most remarkable passages. As an intellectual effort it deserves high praise."—*New York Sun.*

51. LAL. By WILLIAM A. HAMMOND, M. D.

"It possesses the great merit of being interesting from beginning to end. The characters are striking, and several of them have an element of originality; the incidents are abundant and effective."—*New York Tribune.*

52. ALINE. A Novel. By HENRY GRÉVILLE.

53. JOOST AVELINGH. A Dutch Story. By MAARTEN MAARTENS.

"No novel superior to this has appeared in the Town and Country Library, of which it is No 53. . . . The story surprises the fiction readers of the world. . . . The story at times rises into the intense, and descends at last into the 'vale of peace. . . . The story is realistic in a very high degree, and is beautiful as a picture of Holland with its life and politics. . . . To read the story is like passing through all kinds of dangerous roads, with storms, precipices, and raging streams, to come out at last upon a high, central table-land where the sun shines in beauty, the air is full of charm, and the soul dwells in safety and high endeavor for evermore."—*Public Opinion.*

12mo, paper cover. Price, 50 cents each.

New York: D. APPLETON & CO., Publishers, 1, 3, & 5 Bond Street.

54. KATY OF CATOCTIN; or, The Chain-Breakers. By GEORGE ALFRED TOWNSEND.

"I think the historical value of 'Katy of Catoctin' is great and permanent."—The Hon. JAMES G. BLAINE.

"Katy is a beautiful character, and as a heroine preserves her piety, sincerity, and pure and loving nature to the end."—*Brooklyn Eagle.*

"Much that passes for authentic history is not more literally true than this novel, and is certainly not half as readable."—*Journal of Commerce.*

55. THROCKMORTON. By MOLLY ELLIOT SEAWELL.

"The plot of the story is excellent—full of quick turns and surprises. . . . The way in which Judith falls in love with the hero, notwithstanding the uncanny barrier that lies between the two, and the way that barrier disintegrates and fades away, in the end, is well worked out, and in a fashion to charm all who believe that the course of true love ought, at least, to run smooth."—*The Commercial Advertiser.*

"Taken as a whole, it is an entertaining picture of Southern family life, and as such recommends itself to lovers of romance, and is an excellent addition to Appletons' Town and Country Library."—*The Springfield Republican.*

56. EXPATRIATION. A Novel. By the author of "Aristocracy."

"This skit on the bad manners of the titled Briton and his American imitator is animated and biting. . . . The story will have a short life and a merry one; and it deserves commendation in so far as it preaches a sturdy Americanism and ridicules the Anglomaniac's effort to seem other than he is."—*The New York Tribune.*

"'Expatriation' . . . is a bright and clever novel by an author whose former work attracted considerable attention for its biting, sometimes almost violent satire. It is a book which somehow carries on its face testimony that convinces us that its satire is deserved, and so it makes us blush for ourselves."—*The Chicago Times.*

57. GEOFFREY HAMPSTEAD. A Novel. By THOMAS S. JARVIS.

"There are so many vivid pictures in 'Geoffrey Hampstead' . . . that it is hard to pick out a chief one among them in the matter of narrative, emphasis, or of tragic force; and, after all the passages of intenser character have been considered, it is still difficult to determine whether they are not all made secondary by the great interest of the philosophical discussions in which this strong and versatile book abounds."—*The New York Sun.*

"'Geoffrey Hampstead' . . . is a novel of much ingenuity and force. While it is a story of incident, it presents several keen, analytic studies of character also, and the novelist makes the incident illustrate the characters without going into long, tiresome analysis and description."—*The Chicago Times.*

58. DMITRI. By F. W. BAIN, M. A.

"The story of the impostor Dmitri, the wandering monk who learned soldiering from the Cossacks of the Dnieper, and, pretending to be the son of Ivan the Terrible, overthrew Boris and Feodor Godrunoff, and reigned for a while in their stead, is one of the most remarkable chapters in Russian history, and might well be taken as the framework of an historical novel."—*The Saturday Review.*

"He has got a capital subject—the story of the false Czar—and he has treated it with freshness and spirit. 'Dmitri' is a decidedly promising first effort."—*The Athenæum.*

12mo, paper cover. Price, 50 cents each.

New York: D. APPLETON & CO., Publishers, 1, 3, & 5 Bond Street.

www.ingramcontent.com/pod-product-compliance
Lightning Source LLC
Chambersburg PA
CBHW021213270326
41929CB00010B/1106